Cultural-Historical Perspectives on Teacher Education and Development

Teachers, both in and beyond teacher education programmes, are continual learners. As society itself evolves, new settings and the challenges they provide require new learning. Teachers must continually adapt to new developments that affect their work, including alterations to qualification systems, new relationships with welfare professionals, and new technologies that are reconfiguring relationships with pupils.

Cultural-Historical Perspectives on Teacher Education and Development is an international volume that clarifies the purpose of initial (pre-service) teacher education and continuing professional development, and the role of universities and higher education personnel in these processes. An edited collection of chapters by leading researchers from the UK, the US and Europe, it gains coherence from its theoretical orientation and substantive focus on teacher learning. This book:

- demonstrates the contribution of sociocultural and cultural-historical activity theory (CHAT) towards our understandings of teacher learning;
- offers a strong exemplification of a research focus on teachers as learners in specific sociocultural settings;
- shows what teachers learn, how they learn and where they learn, using specific research examples, in the context of broader interests in the development of professional practice and professional education.

As the only volume now available that applies CHAT principles to teacher education and learning, *Cultural-Historical Perspectives on Teacher Education and Development* will be highly useful for teachers and teacher educators undertaking postgraduate and doctoral studies, particularly in the area of professional learning and development. It will also be of relevance to the continuing development of teachers and other school-based professionals.

Viv Ellis is University Lecturer in Educational Studies at the University of Oxford, UK. **Anne Edwards** is Professor of Education in the Department of Education at the University of Oxford, UK, and a Visiting Professor at the University of Oslo, Norway. **Peter Smagorinsky** is Professor of English Education at the University of Georgia, USA.

Cultural-Historical Perspectives on Teacher Education and Development

Learning teaching

Edited by Viv Ellis, Anne Edwards and Peter Smagorinsky

Routledge
Taylor & Francis Group

LONDON AND NEW YORK

First published 2010
by Routledge
2 Park Square, Milton Park, Abingdon, Oxon OX14 4RN

Simultaneously published in the USA and Canada
by Routledge
270 Madison Ave, New York, NY 10016

Routledge is an imprint of the Taylor & Francis Group, an informa business

Typeset in Baskerville by Wearset Ltd
Printed and bound in Great Britain by CPI Antony Rowe,
Chippenham, Wiltshire

British Library Cataloguing in Publication Data
A catalogue record for this book is available from the British
Library

Library of Congress Cataloging-in-Publication Data
Cultural-historical perspectives on teacher education and
development: learning teaching/edited by Viv Ellis, Anne Edwards
and Peter Smagorinsky.
p. cm.
Includes bibliographical references and index.
1. Teachers–In-service training–Cross-cultural studies. 2.
Teaching–Social aspects–Cross-cultural studies. I. Ellis, Viv, 1965–
II. Edwards, Anne, 1946– III. Smagorinsky, Peter.
LB1731.C84 2010
370.71'55–dc22   2009030574

ISBN10: 0-415-49758-2 (hbk)
ISBN10: 0-415-49759-0 (pbk)
ISBN10: 0-203-86010-1 (ebk)

ISBN13: 978-0-415-49758-9 (hbk)
ISBN13: 978-0-415-49759-6 (pbk)
ISBN13: 978-0-203-86010-6 (ebk)

Contents

Figures

Tables

Contributors

Viv Ellis is University Lecturer and Tutor for English Education at the University of Oxford. He is co-convenor of the Oxford Centre for Sociocultural and Activity Theory Research (OSAT) and chaired the 2008 international conference, 'Sociocultural Perspectives on Teacher Education and Development'. He completed his PhD at the London Institute of Education and worked as an English teacher in secondary schools before moving into higher education. In his research, he maintains a focus on learning, subject English and the education of teachers from a CHAT perspective. With Brian Street and Carol Fox, he edited *Rethinking English in Schools* (Continuum 2008).

Anne Edwards is Professor and Director of the Department of Education at the University of Oxford, where she is also co-convenor of the Oxford Centre for Sociocultural and Activity Theory Research. She has written extensively on teacher education, professional learning and cultural-historical analyses of practices and learning. Her current research focuses on developing understandings of the relational aspects of expertise.

Peter Smagorinsky has taught in the English Education programmes at the University of Oklahoma (1990–1998) and University of Georgia (1998–present) since receiving his doctorate from the University of Chicago in 1989, following a career as a high school English teacher in the Chicago area. He has written on a variety of topics, including literacy across the high school curriculum, the teaching and learning of the English curriculum, the dynamics of small group and whole class discussions of literature, the composition of non-verbal texts across the high school curriculum, the discourse of character education, and related topics

Gill Boag-Munroe undertook her PhD at the University of Birmingham, investigating how teacher-mentors constructed identities to assist their work in Initial Teacher Education. The research additionally aimed to find ways to unpick the relationship between language and concepts that would assist sociocultural understandings of activity. Recent work, undertaken in partnership with Jan Georgeson (University of Chichester), has included developing a way to 'read' the buildings and spaces used in Early Years settings to understand how they construct identities for those using and working in them.

Ann Childs is University Lecturer in Science Education at the University of Oxford whose principal teaching responsibilities are in the initial teacher education and in the supervision of master's and doctoral students. Her main research interests are science teachers' professional knowledge and the ways in which this is developed in and by different contexts, and how technology, specifically the Internet, can be used to enhance teaching and learning in secondary science classrooms. Her research draws largely upon sociocultural theoretical perspectives.

Alaster Douglas has worked as a teacher and senior manager in four secondary schools in the UK, becoming a deputy head teacher in London. This position, being responsible for staff development, led him to be particularly interested in the role schools play in developing student teachers. He completed an MA in Education (Publishing) and an MSc in Educational Research Methodology before undertaking doctoral research at the University of Oxford. In September 2009, he took up the position of Senior Lecturer in Education and Professional Practice at Roehampton University.

Corey Drake is Associate Professor of Mathematics Education at Iowa State University. As a researcher and a teacher educator, her primary interest is in supporting teachers in learning to incorporate new resources into their teaching. These resources include family and community funds of knowledge, as well as new curriculum materials, policies and teaching practices. Recent publications span the areas of mathematics education, curriculum studies and teacher education.

Linda Fisher is Lecturer in Education at the Faculty of Education at the University of Cambridge. She co-ordinates the initial teacher training programme for Modern Foreign Languages (MFL) and is involved in extensive work with secondary school teachers of MFL. She jointly plans and delivers faculty-wide mentor training, and teaches and supervises on the MEd, MPhil and PhD programmes. Research interests are primarily in language learner motivation and teacher education. She has experience of qualitative and quantitative research projects and is co-director of the DCSF-sponsored research project 'Language learning at Key Stage 3: the impact of the Key Stage 3 Modern Foreign Languages Framework and changes to the curriculum on provision and practice'.

Eva Hjörne is Associate Professor in Education at the University of Gothenburg, Sweden. Her main interests are in the analysis of learning and social interaction, processes of marginalisation and mediated action with special focus on categorising and identity formation of pupils in school. Her current research project includes meetings between experts in school (so-called 'pupil health team' meetings) when negotiating and identifying who is in need of special services and what pedagogical implications this will have when pupils, for instance, are placed into special teaching groups.

Cecilie Flo Jahreie is completing her PhD at InterMedia, University of Oslo, Norway. Before starting her doctoral studies, she worked as a researcher at InterMedia and Network for IT-Research and Competence in Education (ITU), University of Oslo. Currently, her research focus is on student teachers' learning trajectories between university and schools from an activity theoretical perspective. Her interest is in studying how individuals work discursively, and how talk is regulated in terms of social, cultural and historical relations.

Thurídur Jóhannsdóttir is Lecturer in Educational Studies in the School of Education at the University of Iceland. Her research focus is on information and communication technology and distance education. In 2002–2005 she was project coordinator of the research project LearnICT – using ICT in learning and teaching in Icelandic schools, funded by the Research Council of Iceland under the Information Technology research programme. She is currently finishing her PhD thesis on teacher education through distance learning. She has a background in language and literature and was Iceland's representative in BIN, Nordic Child Cultural Research Network from 2001–2004.

Pernilla Larsson is a teacher and post-graduate student at the University of Gothenburg, Sweden. Her studies include analysis of teaching and learning practices within special classes organised for children diagnosed with ADHD or Aspergers.

Yongcan Liu is Lecturer in Language Education at the School of Education and Lifelong Learning at the University of Exeter. He was trained as a linguist in China and received his PhD in education from the University of Cambridge. His doctoral research is an ethnographic study of teacher learning in the workplace in a university department. His recent research focuses on sociocultural theories of learning and narrative inquiry of intercultural communication. He is particularly interested in using community of practice and activity theories to look at issues related to educational change, teacher development and multi-agency workplace learning.

Jane McNicholl is Lecturer in Science Education at the University of
Oxford; her principal teaching responsibilities are in initial teacher
education. Her main research interest involves science teachers' professional knowledge and the ways in which this is developed in and
by different contexts. Her research draws largely upon sociocultural
theoretical perspectives.

Charles Max is Professor of Learning with Educational Media at the University of Luxembourg. His research interest is concerned with learning
and development from sociocultural and cultural-historical perspectives, both at the organisational and individual levels. He leads the
DICA media research group, which is focusing on digital media technologies, their design and the impact they have on learning, interaction
and community building. He is also the scientific director of the innovative initial teacher education programme, Bachelor in Educational
Sciences.

Lori A. Norton-Meier is Associate Professor in Literacy Education at the
University of Louisville. As a classroom teacher, Lori taught for seven
years in an urban environment, where many of her students lived in
poverty and for whom English was a second language. This experience
generated many questions and she has spent recent years studying students' literate lives in and out of school contexts. Her interests include
early childhood literacy, family literacy and media literacy, particularly
related to gender. She has multiple publications in literacy studies
including a forthcoming book on ethnographic studies of family literacy in and out of school contexts.

Eli Ottesen is Associate Professor in the Department of Teacher Education and School development at the University of Oslo, Norway. Her
doctoral dissertation (2006) was a study of student teachers' learning
during internship periods in schools. Student teachers' and mentors'
discourses were analysed in a sociocultural perspective. Her research
interests are in the areas of workplace learning in schools, educational
administration and leadership, and supervision.

Roger Säljö is Professor of Education and Educational Psychology at the
University of Gothenburg, Sweden. His research interests include learning and interaction in a sociocultural perspective. During recent years
he has worked with issues of integration and marginalisation in Swedish schools, in particular with reference to how teachers and other
school staff interpret and attempt to remedy school difficulties. He is
also director of a Linnaeus centre of excellence for research on learning and media.

Annalisa Sannino is Lecturer in the Center for Research on Activity, Development and Learning (CRADLE) at the University of Helsinki, Finland. She completed her PhD at the University of Nancy, France, and worked as a researcher at the University of Salerno, Italy. Her research is focused on discourse, experiencing, and learning in formative interventions in educational institutions and work organisations. She has published research articles in English, French and Italian. She is the leading editor of a special issue of the *Journal of Educational Change* (2008) on 'activity theory and school innovation' and the book *Learning and Expanding with Activity Theory* (Cambridge University Press 2009).

Willem Wardekker worked until recently as Professor of Education at the Department of Theory and Research in Education at VU University, Amsterdam, and at Windesheim University of Professional Studies, Zwolle, the Netherlands. For most of his professional life, he has carried out research in education from a cultural-historical point of view, specialising in the possible contribution of schools to identity formation, citizenship and moral education. Together with a number of Dutch teacher educators, he has recently co-published a book (in Dutch) on the education of teachers for Vygotsky-inspired primary schools. He is also a board member of the association of teachers in such schools.

Acknowledgements

The editors would like to thank Philip Richards in the Department of Education at the University of Oxford for his help in preparing the manuscript and Emily Laughton at Taylor & Francis for her editorial support.

Viv Ellis would like to thank Tony Burgess for his constructive feedback before, during and after the 2008 Socioted conference at Oxford University. Oh dear, another conference.... .

Figures 7.1, 7.2, 7.3 and 7.4 of this book are reproduced from Viv Ellis', *Subject Knowledge and Teacher Education* (2007) by kind permission of Continuum International Publishing Group.

Figure 7.5 of this book is reproduced, by kind permission of Cambridge University Press, from 'Putting Vygotsky to Work: The Change Laboratory as an Application of Double Stimulation', by Yrjö Engeström in *The Cambridge Companion to Vygotsky*, edited by Harry Daniels, Michael Cole and James V. Wertsch.

Chapter 1

Introduction

Viv Ellis, Anne Edwards and Peter Smagorinsky

Teacher education has been constructed as a problem for almost as long as it has formally existed (Cochran-Smith and Fries 2005; Labaree 2004). The American Educational Research Association (AERA) Panel on Research and Teacher Education noted that, as a mode of professional formation and as a set of institutional practices, teacher education has been shaped in response to fundamental societal questions such as the nature of childhood and adolescence, the challenges of globalization, the rise of a professional class and the role of the state, as well as specifically educational concerns such as school effectiveness and teachers' impact on educational attainment (Cochran-Smith and Zeichner 2005; see also, for example, Furlong *et al.* 2000; Zeichner 2009).

The 'peculiar problem of preparing teachers' (Labaree 2004: 39) has played out rather differently around the world, but it is possible to discern a constellation of concerns that have achieved greater relative importance at different times and places. One of these might be posed as the question of the 'contribution' of higher education to the initial (pre-service) education of teachers. This concern speaks to the status of both teachers and teacher educators as professionals or academics as well as the kind of learning that is privileged. A related concern has been the nature of the association between the universities and the schools in teachers' learning processes. From this concern arise questions of 'partnership' and 'internship' or 'learning on the job'. Another has been an interest in teachers' uniquely 'professional' knowledge and, following on from this, questions about what, where and how teachers learn – and how their expertise and the development of their expertise might be conceptualized. Often, it seems, the capacity of individual teachers for reflection has been pre-eminent in answers to these questions.

Until relatively recently, much of the thinking about teacher education and development has been informed by dualistic understandings of the relationship between thought and action which seeks proof of the transfer of learning through the evident application of knowledge. From this perspective, teachers' minds become storage devices; university curricula and mentor (supervisory) teacher feedback are inputs; classroom teaching and learning is the output. Highly valued outputs can then become codified into competence statements or professional 'Standards' either imposed by the state or developed from inside the profession by researchers. 'Standards' can then be employed to measure both teachers' effectiveness and the quality of the teacher-education programmes they have followed.

We are less confident about the coherence and integrity of this way of thinking about teacher education than many policy-makers, and want to suggest a shift in perspective. The argument of this book is that a cultural-historical perspective on teacher education and development offers a powerful theoretical and methodological lens through which both to analyse the problem of teacher education and to design new curricula and programmes. The chapters come from a range of international authors who have been using cultural-historical theories to understand teacher learning and professional development, analyse relationships between universities and schools, interrogate the nature of teacher knowledge and expertise and seek to understand the potential of formative interventions into teacher education in developing a theory of practice. They do so across a range of different national contexts in Europe, the United States and China. Our book doesn't claim to offer representative coverage of education systems worldwide; rather, the chapters raise interesting questions about teacher education and teacher learning, show how these questions play out in local settings and why a cultural-historical perspective helped each contributor to analyse the issues and act on them.

We next define what we mean by a cultural-historical perspective, outline how this perspective differs from vaguely 'social' theories of learning and suggest what some of the possible distinctions within the perspective might be.

A shift in perspective: Vygotsky and the cultural-historical line

Cultural-historical theory and cultural-historical activity theory (CHAT) provide the perspectives on teacher education and development that inform each of the chapters in this volume. Sometimes, the authors use the term 'sociocultural' and it might be helpful to distinguish between uses at this point. Sociocultural, cultural-historical and CHAT all arise from the work of Vygotsky and his methodological interest in the mediation of human activity by physical or psychological tools. A sociocultural line has been taken up by educationalists, anthropologists, sociolinguists and others, and one of its distinguishing characteristics is the insight that social practices are situated and that people learn by engaging in these practices, working with the resources that are 'stretched over' (Lave 1988) specific settings for practice, settings that are in a dialectical relationship with the cultural arena within which certain forms of identity are motivating.

Cultural-historical theory draws on key Vygotskian ideas about cultural development by placing a slightly different emphasis on mediation. Under a cultural-historical analysis there is an interest in the relationship between human consciousness and practical activity, an explicitly Marxist tenet: 'Consciousness does not determine life: life determines consciousness' (Marx and Engels 1845–6/1964: 37). Cultural-historical theory proposes that physical and psychological mediational tools are used to build cultures. Tool-use has a strongly historical dimension in that the tools have been imbued with meaning by past use and because new meanings can be embedded in them through present activity under evolving cultural conditions. Cultural tools therefore have a shaping function in terms of human activity but also can be re-shaped and cultures re-tooled. The historical development of human consciousness can therefore be traced through an analysis of cultural tools and the ways in which they function in a mediating capacity. This focus may concern both cultures and the settings that they provide for human action and individuals as they appropriate cultural tools through which to navigate their environments.

CHAT, like the cultural-historical line, takes on Vygotsky's interest in social and semiotic mediation but shifts the emphasis from individual to collective subjects. This shift is informed by the work of one of Vygotsky's students, A.N. Leont'ev, and his development of activity theory. Leont'ev distinguished between the individual subject's operations, the individual or group's goal-oriented actions and the level of collective activity given meaning by a shared object-motive.[1] CHAT might be distinguished from the broader cultural-historical line by both its collectivist perspective and its 'emphasis on action or intervention in order to develop practice and the sites of practice' (Edwards and Daniels 2004: 108). A major contribution to CHAT has been made by Yrjö Engeström, and it is Engeström's triangular representation of the activity system associated with his 'third generation' of activity theory that has often become associated with a CHAT perspective. However, key CHAT concepts can still be traced to Vygotsky's Marxist, developmental project, to Vygotsky's students and to Soviet philosophers such as Il'enkov (1977), who proposed that internal contradictions within activity systems might act as generators of change and the evolution of the system.

Presenting such 'potted' distinctions between members of the same family is risky in at least two respects: first, gross over-simplification; second, reifying the distinctions in unhelpful ways, especially when our concern in this book is with how a theoretical line that can be traced to Vygotsky is useful in thinking about the education, training and development of teachers. Rather, we see the differences as offering a rich 'conceptual tool box' (Edwards and Daniels 2004: 108) with which to answer some of the vexing questions about how teachers learn and how they might learn better. For consistency's sake, we have adopted 'cultural-historical' as the framework that best reflects the perspectives of the book as a whole and hence its place in our title. Across the various chapters, however, the different emphases are apparent; a few chapters are more sociocultural and others are written from a much more explicitly CHAT perspective. Regardless of which aspect of a Vygotskian approach they foreground, each author bases her or his research on the notion that human development relies on the appropriation of pre-existing cultural tools, that this appropriation occurs through social interchange, and that as a consequence of these dynamics, people grow into the frameworks for thinking afforded by the cultural practices and tools made available to them in the social settings of their development.

Key ideas in the cultural-historical line and their relevance to studying teacher education and development

The authors in this collection argue that the cultural-historical line provides the intellectual resources to develop a coherent view of how teachers at different stages in the professional life-course conceptualize their praxis. Some of these key ideas are:

- an understanding of historical processes as dialectical relationships between continuity and change and the reproduction and transformation of social structures and relationships, underpinned by a complex chronology of development;
- a recognition that expertise is distributed across systems and that learning involves being able to perceive, access and contribute to that expertise;
- a conceptualization of learning to teach as a continual, mutually mediating process of appropriation and social action, where practitioners take on the cultural practices that are valued in the social situations of their development – whether these settings are schools or universities – and employ them in turn to shape that social situation;
- an analytic interest in cultural and historical practices and mediational tools, and the values that underlie them, and how they inform particular notions of practice in each of the settings of learning to teach;
- a recognition of transitions between settings in teachers' learning as important foci of analysis;
- an understanding of the relationship between theory and method when taking a cultural-historical approach to studying learning and how this can help us formulate key questions about fundamental prob-

lems of design in teacher education programmes as currently conceptualized.

We hope that, in exemplifying and interrogating these key ideas in the chapters that follow, the book both complements and extends the work of other researchers who study teacher education and development using an approach emerging from the insights of Vygotsky (e.g. Johnson 2009; Tsui and Law 2006; van Huizen *et al.* 2005; Putnam and Borko 2000; Grossman *et al.* 1999).

The organization of the book

The book is organized thematically into sections that represent core concerns for researchers taking a cultural-historical perspective. Each chapter arises from the author's research in a culturally and historically distinctive setting. In part, the chapters' exemplifications of the key ideas we have elaborated above emerge from their analysis of the distinctively different material conditions of teacher education work around the world, whether in a relatively small, sparsely populated country like Iceland, a multilingual, politically complex city state like Luxembourg, a tightly prescribed, centralized bureaucracy such as the education system in England or locally controlled, conceptually ambiguous settings in the United States.

Part I: The social situation of teacher development (Chapters 2–6)

The social situation of development is, in Vygotskian terms, a learner's experience of the opportunities for action in an activity in a specific setting. The social situations of development in initial teacher education may be complex sites where the practices of school and the university intersect, or they may be discrete settings which reflect only the practices in which they are currently situated. However, they will certainly be experienced differently by each participant in them.

The chapters in this section examine the social situation of teachers' development from three starting points: teachers as learners (Douglas, Edwards, Smagorinsky); the school as an activity setting or arena which offers different learning opportunities though mentoring (Douglas) and through the pedagogical discourses available when the curriculum or children are discussed (McNicholl and Childs; and Hjörne, Larsson and Säljö); and teacher education as a product of societal expectations which have shaped educational practices (Edwards, Smagorinsky).

In the opening chapter Smagorinsky reminds readers of the distinctions to be made between the individual orientation of Vygotsky and the collective focuses of Leont'ev and Engeström. He turns to Lave's 1988 analyses of learning, and in particular her constructs of *arena* and *setting* where a setting is interpreted by the individuals who experience it, in ways that echo the description of the social situation of development just outlined. Douglas, in the next chapter, draws on his study of school-based mentoring to reveal how the social situation of development for student teachers is also shaped by how the practices in which the activity of mentoring are understood by the mentors. His analysis of how mentors used tools such as a course handbook combine a Vygotskian attention to tool use with an Engeströmian focus on the settings in which mentoring occurred. McNicholl and Childs continue the theme of subject departments as sites for teachers' learning by describing how science departments can operate as systems of distributed expertise which support the practices of student teachers and more experienced practitioners. Their cultural-historical analyses also lead them towards a critique of science teachers' dependence on 'pedagogic content knowledge' (Shulman 1986). In the next chapter Edwards looks more broadly at what the Vygotskian toolbox can offer those who design teacher-education programmes and calls for attention to the dialectical possibilities they afford, as teachers' responsibilities change in response to changes in national policies. In the final chapter in this section Hjörne, Larsson and Säljö continue the theme of teachers' changing responsibilities by examining conversations in one arena, where practitioners from different backgrounds discuss children as part of the development of a pupil health system. This chapter, with its analysis of the 'accounting for' pattern of individualizing children's problems in talk about children, makes a methodological bridge to the section that follows and concludes that these arenas and their potential for shaping new practices need to be understood better so that they can inform the development of more responsive pedagogies in schools.

Part II: A cultural-historical methodological perspective (Chapters 7–10)

Vygotsky's project was in large part a methodological contribution, a response to behaviourist psychology and a radical proposal for studying human activity holistically and paying attention to the processes of mediation. In one way, these interests are reflected in his emphasis on word meaning and the role of language in thinking and concept formation (Vygotsky 1986); in another, the 'zone of proximal development' (Vygotsky 1978) reflects a different emphasis on social mediation and the potential to study change by provoking it in a developmental space (cf. Moll 1990). The chapters in this section all address questions of method and show how a cultural-historical methodological perspective can be especially productive in understanding teacher learning and revealing the complexities of development. Key concepts in this section are analytic attention to the whole activity, the processes of mediation and the vital dimension of language.

In his chapter, Ellis explores the central importance of the 'double stimulation strategy' (Vygotsky 1978) as a methodological concept in the cultural-historical line. 'Double stimulation' describes the researcher's introduction of new tools as a way of stimulating work on the research problem. Rather than focusing simply on the outcome of the task, the researcher studies the complex semiotic activity that arises from what Vygotsky referred to as a 'second series of stimuli' (ibid). Boag-Munroe follows on from Ellis in focusing on the analysis of language-use in cultural-historical research designs. The relative merits of Conversation Analysis and Discourse Analysis as methods for analysing language are discussed in the context of Boag-Munroe's research into the construction of mentor–teacher identities in England. The chapter exemplifies important cultural-historical ideas about language and perception and the role of language in identity formation.

Jahreie and Ottesen's chapter takes a CHAT perspective on teachers' learning across the sometimes over-lapping but nonetheless distinct activity systems of schools and university departments of education. They refer to the spaces where the boundary-crossing work of teacher education takes place as 'learning spheres' and, drawing on their research in Norway, show that an analysis of participants' interactions and tool use reveals how the construction of knowledge is affected by historically-developed rules and division of labour. In the final chapter in this section, Sannino analyses how Italian student teachers developed specific understandings of the materiality of their individual students through a formative intervention known as the 5-D. Sannino methodologically expands on Leont'ev's notion of object and Davydov's ideas of abstraction and offers a form of analysis that allows her to conceptualize the learning of the student teachers as a movement from the abstract to the concrete. This chapter, like Ellis's, also underscores the transformatory potential of participatory, interventionist methodologies in the cultural-historical line.

Part III: Cultural-historical designs for teacher education (Chapters 11–14)

The third section features scholars who present studies of innovative, CHAT-informed teacher-education programmes in such contrasting locations as Iceland, China, Luxembourg and the USA. To begin, Jóhannsdóttir reports on an Initial Teacher Education distance-education programme in Iceland, focusing on the ways in which student teachers cross boundaries between their schools and the university. She finds that disturbances in both the schools and the distance education programme that follow from contradictions experienced during student teaching can serve as catalysts for change in each of these distinct activity systems. She considers how schools and teacher-education programmes can exploit these disturbances by capitalizing on shared motives for their work, even amidst the contradictory goals of the different settings of learning to teach.

Liu and Fisher then analyse the cultural factors involved during a shift in pedagogical policy in China. They examine the responses of teachers to traditional (based on the Confucian principles of deferring to the authority of elders) and liberal (based on Western principles of student agency and empowerment) teaching practices in English as a Foreign Language instruction. They find evidence of a 'boundary zone' for the members of the community to reflect, compare and voice opinions regarding the relationship between a national culture and how people most effectively teach and learn within that society. They conclude that this boundary-crossing opens up opportunities for intercultural learning as a central aspect of teachers' developmental trajectories.

Norton-Meier and Drake continue this attention to boundaries between settings for learning and interrogate the construct of the 'third space', an area in which 'official' school spaces intersect with students' own cultural routines to produce a medium that creates new opportunities for discourse and learning. They focus on pre-service teachers' incorporation of family and community resources into elementary mathematics and literacy instruction, and their integration of knowledge from these sources into formal and practical knowledge gained through their experiences in university and elementary school classrooms. Pedagogical learning, they find, is achieved through teachers' production of personal narratives of self as learner and teacher, their development of professional identities and practices as elementary school teachers, and their understandings of the mathematics and literacy practices and resources of children, families and communities.

Finally, Max outlines the Initial Teacher Education programme at the University of Luxembourg. This programme views student teachers' learning as a growing capacity to recognize the complexity of supporting children's learning and strives to interrelate academic concerns with school activities. This expansion takes place across various boundaries, including educational contexts, disciplinary communities and semiotic systems. Max draws on evidence of work in these learning spaces to analyse tensions emerging when those who are engaged in a joint learning-for-teaching activity move across institutional boundaries, and when learning in a boundary space is mediated through a collaborative inquiry task. He considers the innovative potential of such learning spaces at the boundaries of schools and universities for student teachers' learning and for generating change and development among the collaborating partners.

In an Afterword that concludes the book, Wardekker comments on the different lines of thinking that have emerged from Vygotsky's work in relation to the research reported in each chapter. For Wardekker, it is the very diversity of perspectives in the cultural-historical line that makes it such a powerful lens for understanding the problem of teacher education.

Concluding points

The contributors to this collection have all taken as given that teacher education has an important part to play in shaping the social situation of development of students in schools and, in particular, how what matters in society is mediated by teachers. While recognising that teachers are not always and easily positioned as agentic professionals within national systems of education, between them they point to how the conceptual resources of cultural-historical theory, which owes so much to the legacy of Vygotsky, offer tools for shaping teacher education, from the micro levels of mentoring conversation through to the more macro ambitions of restructuring national teacher-education programmes.

Note

1 The concept of 'object-motive' was developed by Leont'ev, a colleague of Vygotsky and a major contributor to activity theory. He explained it as follows:

> The main thing which distinguishes one activity from another, however, is the difference of their objects. It is exactly the object of an activity that gives it a determined direction. According to the terminology I have proposed, the object of the activity is its true motive.
>
> (Leont'ev 1978: 62)

The object motive, how the object of activity is interpreted by participants in the activity, directs activities. For example, a student teacher who sees teaching as a matter of maintaining control will operate differently in the activity of teaching a lesson from another student teacher who sees it as enthusing children as learners.

References

Cochran-Smith, M. and Fries, K. (2005) 'Researching teacher education in changing times', in Cochran-Smith, M. and Zeichner, K. (eds) *Studying teacher education: the report of the AERA panel on research and teacher education*, Washington, DC and Mahwah, NJ: American Educational Research Association, Lawrence Erlbaum Associates.

Cochran-Smith, M. and Zeichner, K. (eds) (2005) *Studying teacher education: the report of the AERA panel on research and teacher education*, Washington, D.C. and Mahwah, N.J.: American Educational Research Association, Lawrence Erlbaum Associates.

Edwards, A. and Daniels, H. (2004) 'Using sociocultural and activity theory in educational research', *Educational Review* 56, 2: 107–111.

Furlong, J., Barton, L., Miles, S. and Whitty, G. (2000) *Teacher education in transition: re-forming professionalism?* Buckingham: Open University Press.

Grossman, P.L., Smagorinsky, P. and Valencia, S. (1999) 'Appropriating tools for teaching English: a theoretical framework for research on learning to teach', *American Journal of Education* 108, 1: 1–29.

Il'enkov, E.V. (1977) *Dialectical logic: essays in its history and theory*, Moscow: Progress Publishers.

Johnson, K. (2009) *Second language teacher education: a sociocultural perspective*, London and New York: Routledge.

Labaree, D.F. (2004) *The trouble with ed schools*, New Haven, CT: Yale University Press.

Lave, J. (1988) *Cognition in practice: mind, mathematics and culture in everyday life*, Cambridge: Cambridge University Press.

Leont'ev, A.N. (1978) *Activity, consciousness and personality*, Upper Saddle River, NJ: Prentice Hall.

Marx, K. and Engels, F. (1845–6/1964) *The German ideology*, Moscow: Progress Publishers.

Moll, L.C. (1990) 'Introduction', in Moll, L.C. (ed.) *Vygotsky and education: instructional implications and applications of sociohistorical psychology*, Cambridge: Cambridge University Press.

Putnam, R.T. and Borko, H. (2000) 'What do new views of knowledge and thinking have to say about research on teacher learning?' *Educational Researcher* 29, 1: 4–15.

Shulman, L.S. (1986) 'Those who understand: knowledge growth in teaching', *Educational Researcher* 15, 2: 4–14.

Tsui, A.B. and Law, D.Y.K. (2006) 'Learning as boundary-crossing in school–university partnership', *Teaching and Teacher Education* 23: 1289–1301.

Van Huizen, P., van Oers, B. and Wubbels, T. (2005) 'A Vygotskian perspective on teacher education', *Journal of Curriculum Studies* 37, 3: 267–290.

Vygotsky, L.S. (1978) *Mind in society*, Cambridge, MA: Harvard University Press.

Vygotsky, L.S. (1986) *Thought and language*, Cambridge, MA: MIT Press.

Zeichner, K. (2009) *Teacher education and the struggle for social justice*, New York and London: Routledge.

Part I

The social situation of teacher development

Chapter 2

A Vygotskian analysis of the construction of setting in learning to teach

Peter Smagorinsky

Introduction: individualism and collectivism in the cultural-historical tradition

The cultural-historical tradition in psychology experienced a seismic transformation when, following the death of L.S. Vygotsky in 1934, Vygotsky's student and collaborator A.R. Leont'ev shifted the unit of analysis from individual, volitional, goal-directed, tool-mediated, and socially and culturally conditioned action to the mediated action of the collective. Bakhurst (2007: 63) observes that 'Despite his emphasis on the sociocultural foundations of psychological development, Vygotsky's thought remains centred on the individual subject conceived as a discrete, autonomous self.' Leont'ev turned his focus instead to the sources of the social and cultural patterns of action through which individuals internalize their understanding of the world. These recurring, routine actions contribute to collective conceptions of the trajectory of whole societies and therefore of individuals within them, and to the construction and maintenance of the cultural practices through which people and groups learn to help their presumed teleological destinations come about.

Vygotsky (1987) recognized and accounted for social and cultural mediation in his account of individual concept development. He nonetheless focused on individual internalization and externalization of patterns of thinking and the patterns of speech. These patterns reflect prior cultural practices and ultimately help individuals to construct them anew as they take on and reproduce their societies' ways of knowing. In his departure from Vygotsky, Leont'ev (1981) – the architect of what has generally been called 'activity theory' – took a more orthodox Marxist perspective on human labour and cognition by foregrounding the social group rather than the individual.

This shift was not necessarily based on purely scientific differences. The ascent of Vygotsky in the world of Russian psychology coincided with the founding of the Soviet Union and its basis in a highly centralized philosophy based on Marxist assumptions regarding social-class homogenization following from the demise of capitalism's class-based conflicts. The setting provided by the Soviet Union proved critical for the direction that science, including psychology, took between the early 1920s and early 1990s. First, as an explicitly Marxist state, the Soviet Union established a central and abiding ideology that suppressed the role of individuals, especially as they exercise capital-based control over one another. Vygotsky's interest in individual cognition did not fit within this perspective in spite of his emphasis on higher mental functions as developed through social transactions that are situated in cultural and historical practices for solving the problems presented by specific environments (Tulviste 1991). Vygotsky's foregrounding of the individual became increasingly at odds with official state ideology, a conflict that undoubtedly would have escalated had he lived to develop his research programme.

Second, the Soviet Union's Marxist emphasis took a totalitarian turn soon after its leaders came into power, and they reinforced its ideology with a stunning brutality during Stalin's reign from 1924–1953 (see Cole *et al.* 2006), a period that encompassed Vygotsky's career. Those who survived this era had few illusions about the perils of defying Soviet dogma. Zinchenko (2007: 213), for instance, observes that 'Vygotsky's commitment to Marxist beliefs did not save him from criticism. His works were banned, denounced, and declared to be vicious and even evil. He was lucky to have managed to die in his own bed in 1934.' Vygotsky, many commentators believe, would undoubtedly have met the same fate as Gustav Gustavovich Shpet, one of his mentors, who was dismissed from his academic positions on multiple occasions and subjected to 'brutal interrogation and execution in 1937' by Soviet authorities (Wertsch 2007: 184) due to his 'freedom and dignity and the independence of his thought from Marxist-Leninist ideology, which at the time was growing stronger and stronger' (Zinchenko 2007: 212).

Vygotsky's death in 1934 coincided with a ban on pedology – Vygotsky's field of the study of child development – by the Pedology Decree of 1936, the execution of Schpet and others during Stalin's Great Purge, the decline of intellectuals and rise of the proletariat in stature, the elevation of Soviet paranoia following the rise of the Nazis in Germany and the increase in violent repression as a systemic aspect of Soviet life. Even Stalin's successor and close associate Georgi M. Malenkov was disposed of within two years, eventually expelled from the party and sent to Kazakhstan to manage a hydroelectric plant for 30 years; life was lonely and perilous even at the top of the system. Reading Vygotsky and his colleagues was forbidden almost immediately following his death. Kozulin and Gindis note that 'discussion of Vygotsky's ideas was practically impossible from 1936 to the late 1950s' (2007: 334), and Daniels reports that Vygotsky's book *Pedagogical Psychology* was considered to be so politically unacceptable to the rulers of the Soviet state that one had to have a special pass from the KGB that would admit one to the restricted reading room in the Lenin Library where the book could be read.

(2007: 307)

Leont'ev's (1981) turn away from individual mentation and towards the collective came about in this climate. Cole and Gajdamaschko note that

It is certainly plausible that Leont'ev, like many others, sought to distance himself from ideas and associations that had led to the deaths of colleagues and friends. However, given the evidence, it seems more plausible to see his reformulation as an effort to place mediation in its cultural context.

(2007: 206)

Regardless of Leont'ev's motivation for shifting from Vygotsky's emphasis on individual internalization of cultural practices to the mediated actions of collectives, the bifurcated trajectories that their research took from a common point of origin has left the field of cultural-historical psychology with duel legacies, one centred on individuals' internalization of cultural means of mediation and one centred on larger groups working collectively towards shared ends. With activity theory often invoked for both of these foci, much confusion has followed regarding what constitutes a Vygotskian perspective, what sort of research represents activity theory, what a focus on either will do to frame and interpret research and much more (Smagorinsky 2009). Although Engeström's (1987) activity triangle has been employed to associate many studies with activity theory, the degree to which the research indeed follows from his Marxist appropriation of Leont'ev, rather than a Wertschian (1985) appropriation of Vygotsky's emphasis on individual internalization of cultural practices and mediational means, remains open to question.

In this chapter I enter this discussion by looking at what I call the construction of setting in learning to teach. My work is more Vygotskian than Leont'evian, focusing on individual internalization of cultural concepts and practices, and thus ways of thinking and acting on the world. Like Vygotsky, I see 'both the significance of autonomy and how we owe our status as autonomous selves to history, culture, and society' (Bakhurst, 2007: 74). As someone who has lived my whole life in the USA, I have grown up with and internalized a conception of the individual as the societal exemplar. This orientation is inscribed in US founding documents and is a central feature of much required reading in US schools, such as Ralph Waldo Emerson's 'Self-Reliance' and Henry David Thoreau's 'On the Duty of Civil Disobedience', in which he argues that 'any man more

right than his neighbours constitutes a majority of one already' (see www.
transcendentalists.com/civil_disobedience.htm). For people like me,
adopting a Vygotskian perspective on the development of individual mentation makes good cultural sense and fits well with established schemata
for viewing human activity.

Yet in the USA the term 'activity theory' has become nearly synonymous
with taking a Vygotskian perspective, a conflation that I increasingly find
inappropriate. Whether this confusion has come about because people
wish for their work to be affiliated with a 'hot' theory or whether it follows
from a careless reading of the scholarship, it has become a common phenomenon in US scholarship that claims a Vygotskian perspective (Smagorinsky 2009). In this chapter I hope to illuminate this problem and stake
out a position in which I argue that for most cultural-historical scholarship
conducted in free-market capitalist economies, Vygotsky's sociocultural
theory of mind (cf. Wertsch 1985) provides a more appropriate framework
than Leont'ev's Marxist activity theory (cf. Engeström 1987).

The construction of setting within educational arenas

With this perspective established, I next turn to two constructs, *arena* and
setting (Lave 1988), to introduce the manner in which the setting of one's
work as a teacher is an individual construction that follows from an internalized perspective. An arena has properties that are indisputable. These
may be readily tangible, such as the walls, desks, computers, curricula,
books and other physical materials that mediate and structure teaching
and learning in schools. They may also be less tangible, such as the speech
genres through which disciplinary ideas are conveyed (Wertsch 1991).

Within an arena, individuals construct settings by interpreting the arena
through their internal representations of the situation. Thus, while two
teachers may work at the same arena (e.g. a school or department within a
school), they may have distinctly different understandings of the school
setting based on their own goals, histories and activities within the arena.

The experiences of one university supervisor with a group of elementary school student teachers illustrates well how one activity setting is open
to multiple construals (see Cook *et al.* 2002). The university supervisor,
Imelda, was a native of the Philippines and was working towards a PhD in
mathematics education. Her style of supervision was to observe a class and
then, rather than providing an assessment of the lesson, to ask the student
teacher how the lesson had gone. She planned these sessions to get the
student teachers to reflect on the lesson and think about how it had
worked. Imelda said that American students do not like direct feedback
and prefer a less critical approach, and that if she were in her native
country, she would respond with a direct critical appraisal. Student teach-

ers, however, consistently said that they would have preferred a direct critical evaluation of the lesson that pointed out their mistakes and suggested methods for improvement. Even, then, with a shared motive that the university supervision was designed to provide feedback and improve the instruction, this setting produced multiple and conflicting constructions that undermined this broad motive, even with only two participants and a relatively clear agenda.

Arenas with greater complexity are amenable to even more radical differences in the construction of setting. A student teacher or early-career teacher may be enveloped in multiple and competing traditions of schooling that may complicate any effort to construct the setting in a consistent way. In our research, for instance, we have found that early-career teachers are often caught between two general approaches that pull them in opposite directions (Bickmore *et al.* 2005; Cook *et al.* 2002; Johnson *et al.* 2003; Smagorinsky 1999; Smagorinsky *et al.* 2002, 2003, 2004a, 2004b, 2008). Broadly speaking, these competing traditions have been described as designative and expressive (Wertsch 2000), teacher-centred and student-centred (Cuban 1993), product and process (Emig 1971), form and procedures (Anderson 1976), and others: one that invests authority in teachers and texts and emphasizes formal knowledge that is not open to dispute, and one that invests authority in students and emphasizes strategies and means for learning that may be reapplied in new situations in a constructive manner.

In this chapter I will focus on a single arena in the south-western USA, Sequoyah Middle School, set in Edmund, Oklahoma, a northern suburb of Oklahoma City. More specifically, the arena centres on the English Department in this school; that is, the collection of teachers who instruct students in language, literature, writing and related areas. Within this arena, Leigh Thompson began her teaching career amidst multiple centres of gravity (see Johnson *et al.* 2003 for the full report). In the section that follows, I detail how these centres of gravity provided settings for her to construct as the context of her teaching, each with its own values and attendant practices. Through this review I illustrate how an arena has no static properties to those who experience it, but rather how it serves as the area in which various settings may be construed by different participants and stakeholders.

One teacher's construction of her educational setting

Leigh was a highly regarded graduate of the teacher-education programme located in her home state's most competitive university, and so presumably was among the most accomplished beginning teachers entering the profession in Oklahoma the year she began her career. As a middle-school English teacher (grades 6–8), she was in the midst of a

number of different and often competing interests that pulled her in a
variety of directions and suggested to her how she should go about her
work. These competing interests provided her with potential settings for
her instruction and required her to orient herself to a relatively limited
construction of the setting in order to teach in a coherent and consistent
manner. Shortly I will review these settings and how they exerted influence on her conception of how to teach middle-school English, particularly the writing strand of the curriculum. First, however, I will provide
some background on Leigh herself.

Leigh's background

Leigh had been a successful high-school student, flourishing in the conventions that dominate US secondary education. In the area of writing
instruction, she had produced many five-paragraph themes, which provides a template for student writers that include an introductory paragraph, three body paragraphs, and a concluding paragraph. Leigh
accepted the logic behind this formula: that it teaches a fundamental
structure that students can extrapolate to serve most expository writing
needs, an assumption that has been widely critiqued by writing theorists
even as it undergirds much high-school writing instruction (Hillocks
1995). Leigh reported having been taught the five-paragraph theme
almost exclusively in high school. She felt comfortable with this format
and found it useful, saying that 'Overall, the five-paragraph essay really was
helpful for me as a student to organize my thoughts.'

With this 'apprenticeship of observation' – Lortie's (1975) term for
one's experiences as a student that establish a schema for one's understanding of what counts as appropriate and sensible school instruction – in
place, Leigh then attended a university teacher education programme that
we characterized as being 'structurally fragmented' (Zeichner and Gore
1990): the dispersal of courses around the university, random order in
which students enrolled in them and variety of instructors who offered
them did not allow for articulation across courses, leaving students without
a sustained focus or a unified conception of teaching.

Because students could go through the programme taking courses that
were not in dialogue with one another, they did not engage in the kind of
shared activity that gives an education programme a particular culture and
focus, and potentially enables the development of a conceptually unified
approach to teaching (Smagorinsky et al. 2003). Further, the programme
was literature-based, offering no specific courses on writing pedagogy (see
Tremmel 2001 for an account of this pervasive problem in US English
education programmes). Like many early-career teachers who were successful with the repertoires of their own high-school teachers and who
then are provided insufficient conceptual reinforcement to frame viable

alternatives in their teacher education programmes, Leigh began her teaching career with instruction in the five-paragraph theme as her normalized conception of proper and effective writing instruction. She ultimately employed this structure with her eighth-grade students, justifying her decision by saying, 'I also think it was helpful for my students who didn't know where to start' in composing their essays.

Leigh's student teaching served to reinforce the formalist emphasis of instruction in the five-paragraph theme. Mrs Hoover, her mentor teacher, was highly rule-bound throughout her teaching, saying in an interview that

> We have to be the same and we have to show them that we try to be fair and that we have to follow the rules. In a building of a thousand students we have to have rules.... This is a very important stage, and it's a very good age for them to learn certain values and morals.... We're having to show them there are certain things that they need to be responsible for.

Mrs Hoover emphasized grammar instruction and paragraph formation with her sixth-grade students. Rather than five-paragraph themes, Mrs Hoover stressed the more compact tool of the five-sentence paragraph for her students, who she felt were not ready for the rigors of writing five paragraphs all in one theme. Rather, they focused on writing, as Leigh explained, 'a topic sentence and then three supporting sentences and a clincher sentence'. These paragraphs were evaluated on students' ability to follow directions and use correct writing mechanics, which Mrs Hoover described as including such features as spelling, comma placement and writing within the margins of the paper.

Remarkably, Mrs Hoover's instruction took place in an open-classroom school, i.e. a school with no classroom walls, a design intended to encourage open-ended teaching, diversity in instructional approach, and attention to students' individual trajectories and learning practices. Tulviste's (1991) principle of *heterogeneity* helps to account for the ways in which, within the decentralized, liberatory, inquiry-centred environment suggested by the open classroom design, Leigh was apprenticed to view writing as a formal, authoritarian, rule-bound, linear process. Tulviste describes how overlapping social networks can present a learner with a variety of types of problems to solve, thus allowing individuals to develop a number of frameworks for thinking. Yet even with multiple frameworks available, individuals may construct a more limited setting under the influence of powerful mediators designed to produce particular social ends. Mrs. Hoover's mentorship provided a setting that superseded the school designer's intentions of creating a context conducive to freedom of movement and expression and reinforced to Leigh the formalist nature of learning to write. This mentorship served as a key experience for Leigh in learning to teach writing and reinforced what she had learned from her apprenticeship of observation about the formalist quality of writing instruction.

Leigh's construction of Sequoyah Middle School

Leigh accepted her first full-time teaching job at Sequoyah Middle School. Leigh said of this school, one of about 15 schools she had considered for a job, 'This was about the only one I came out thinking, "I would just die to have this job".' When asked why, she said:

> I just felt like I could work with all the other teachers that I spoke with and they are the ones that I would be working with, and [assistant principal] Dara. I liked the area. I liked the look of the school, the things they told me about the school … just as far as the teachers being real supportive of one another, getting along. They had just implemented a reading/writing workshop which goes along with the English curriculum that they were implementing…. I just really can't put my finger on it, but I really liked the people that I interviewed with and was impressed with them. It wasn't really like an interview. It was more like a conversation which seemed to go real well.

Leigh's construction of this school matched that of others who experienced it. It had been named a Blue Ribbon School, which is awarded only to US schools that reach the top 10 per cent of their state's testing scores over several years or show significant gains in student achievement; many consider it to be the highest honour a US school can achieve. My own impressions of the school as a visitor were very favourable; I found that it had a comfortable and well-maintained appearance, minimum of disciplinary problems and welcoming ambiance. As Leigh did in choosing it from among over a dozen other possible schools, I felt that it would provide an enviable location in which to undertake a teaching career.

The state curriculum and assessment

Leigh's teaching was affected by two state mandates. One was the slate of language arts objectives that middle-school students were expected to accomplish as part of the state core curriculum. In the area of writing, the curriculum required 'Narrative, descriptive, expository, and persuasive paragraphs and longer compositions that establish and support a central idea with a topic sentence; supporting paragraphs with facts, details, explanations or examples; and a concluding paragraph that summarizes the points.' To many interpreters, this structure suggests five-paragraph themes, even for narratives.

This core curriculum objective was aligned with the second mandate Leigh faced: the eighth-grade writing test that required students to write an essay on a given topic, which the scoring rubric treated as a five-paragraph theme. This assessment became a central consideration in Leigh's writing instruction, leading her to conclude that instruction in five-paragraph themes not only made intuitive sense but helped students to perform well on the state writing test, an assessment that eventually would reflect on the quality of her school and of her own teaching. In constructing the setting of her teaching, then, Leigh came to the inevitable conclusion that teaching five-paragraph themes constituted effective writing instruction. Early in the year, she acknowledged that

> They are going to be taking this writing test. They are going be going on to ninth grade. If I don't do my job at this point, they are going to be hurting.... I [teach] according to what's mandated by the state. I'm teaching to the test.

Leigh's acceptance of both the reality and the merits of the state writing test guided her instruction in writing.

Entry-year committee

Like all first-year teachers in the state, Leigh was supervised during her first year of teaching by a state-mandated entry-year committee consisting of one school-based administrator, one school-based mentor teacher and one university-based professor. I was appointed as the university-based committee member, allowing me to combine my site visits for the research with my required classroom observations for the committee, a dual purpose that I believe enriched my work on each. I visited her class on four occasions, interviewed Leigh before and after each observation (each recorded), recorded two of the three committee meetings, and conducted interviews with Dara and Katherine. I also maintained communication with Leigh via telephone and email during the year to discuss her teaching and occasionally sent copies of articles that I thought would stimulate her thinking about instructional issues. My mentorship was designed to help Leigh work comfortably according to the school's priorities while encouraging her to teach imaginatively within that framework.

The administrative member, Dara, was one of three assistant principals in the school. She was a former English teacher with an MA in English education who liked a 'noisy classroom':

> I get nervous when I walk down the hall and it's quiet, because to me, without even peeking in one door, what I can only imagine is that a teacher is somewhere – maybe at her desk or someplace – and kids are

doing worksheets. You know, that's just my imagination at work. And when I hear a certain level of noise, I know ... that's the sound of learning.

Dara, recognizing Leigh's anxiety about the state writing test, did not discourage her from teaching the five-paragraph theme. At the same time she encouraged her to see beyond its limitations. During a feedback session following one of Dara's visits to Leigh's class, Leigh told Dara that she was 'worried about this writing test'. Dara replied:

> We had like a 99% pass rate the first year. I read the kids' little essays ... and my gosh, I can't even decipher them, which leads me to believe that for 99% of our kids to pass, there must be a really lenient rate of assessment. So don't get, you know, don't get [inaudible]. By teaching them a real formula kind of writing that they can access when they need it, which is when they'll need that, that's the best you can do.... On the other hand, I don't want them to think that's the only way to write.

Dara downplayed the importance of the five-paragraph theme on other occasions as well. She recognized that teachers at her school with large student enrolments at times felt pressured to use formulaic instruction to reduce the demands on their time:

> I was talking to a teacher [who] has 140 kids, and she's concerned about their proficiency for that test, and just beyond the test knowing how to write, and I was just trying to share with her ideas of how she can teach them the real basics of a five-paragraph essay without writing a five-paragraph essay. Things like have them write the outline of it or just the kernel points of the whole essay, and give them a day and have them write the thesis, give them the thesis and have them write the supporting points.

Dara encouraged the teacher to teach the organizational principles of the five-paragraph theme without dedicating excessive time or attention to the actual writing of five-paragraph themes. As she said to Leigh – who at one point worried that 'I'm not even sure what I would do for another type of essay' – she preferred that students get experience with many and varied kinds of writing in their English classes. Dara's goal for students at Sequoyah, rather than to prepare for the state writing test, was for students to be 'comfortable with their language, so I'm comfortable with teachers taking it from different angles'.

Katherine, Leigh's assigned mentor teacher, was a 28-year veteran of teaching, and Leigh was the fifth novice teacher she had supervised.

Mentor teacher Katherine appeared to be more wholeheartedly approving of how Leigh prepared the students to write five-paragraph themes. At the year's final entry-year committee meeting Katherine lauded Leigh's teaching by saying that

> I know that she has done an excellent job of teaching writing skills because in my class I have my eighth graders do three assignments that involve writing a formal five-paragraph essay. And I always have my kids tell me what team they're on, and the students that have had her for English do a super job in writing paragraphs and writing five-paragraph essays. So I know she's done a really good job of teaching writing skills.

Colleagues

In addition to Katherine, Leigh worked with other colleagues as a member an eighth-grade teaching team, which consisted of four core teachers, supplemented by a special education, Spanish and lab teacher who served all three teams. Leigh turned to her middle-school team colleagues particularly for help with classroom management. More critical to her construction of setting were the two other eighth-grade English teachers in her department. Leigh typically sought advice from other English teachers for pedagogical or curricular assistance: 'The problems with the actual English curriculum and that kind of thing, I'd go to the English teachers.... They gave me a lot of ideas. A lot of the units I did I took from them.' These colleagues greatly influenced Leigh's decisions about how to teach writing.

Leigh revealed the kind of guidance provided by her colleagues when discussing her instruction in the five-paragraph theme:

> When they [the students] take the eighth grade writing test, that's what they [the assessors] look for is the five-paragraph essay format. And that's something that I've talked a lot to the other two eighth-grade English teachers about, and so they've helped me on that. But they just said, 'Give them lots of practice. Have them practice writing this essay as much as possible' ... because that's kind of the structure they look for when people grade these writing samples that they have to give.

Leigh's conformity to this instructional norm undoubtedly helped relieve the tension of being a first-year teacher entering an environment with established expectations. However, the motive of this new setting, which included the pressures produced by expectations accompanying the state writing test, also contributed to her experience of new tensions. Two recurring terms in Leigh's accounts of teaching the five-paragraph theme in preparation for this test were *pressure* exerted on her from without and the resulting stress she perceived in her colleagues and experienced herself. In an interview conducted in late September, she said that her students needed

> to learn to write because eighth grade takes that writing test in the spring, and that's a big thing with this writing test which all the teachers stress about.... I want them to focus on being able to write an essay. You know, giving me a thesis statement and backing up your thesis statement, and just your basic old boring essay.... I think more and more I'm focusing on structure so that they can write that.

By January, only weeks before the test took place, the pressure intensified and Leigh was feeling the stress to prepare her students:

> I don't feel like I can spend any other time on any other type of writing right now. I have all these other things I want to do as far as writing, but up until they take this test, I don't feel like I can do anything else.... I'm just trying to get them ready for this test. And I've told them a hundred times that's my goal and we need to work on this.

The pressure to teach to the test confined Leigh's instruction to the five-paragraph theme. She deferred any other more imaginative writing instruction until after the state writing test:

> I feel like I can't do as many fun activities and different activities. And maybe once I've, like I've said before, maybe once I have some more teaching experience and know what to expect with this writing test a little more and know what works and what doesn't as far as helping them write, then I can vary a little bit. But I think definitely because just like I said, I'm going to let them do some more creative projects in writing after this writing assessment test is over. Right now I feel like I'm just pounding it into them. It kind of stresses me out. This whole writing test stuff.

Leigh revealed that the stress she experienced came through her interactions with her colleagues. She said, for instance, that

> I've never heard like if they do awful, that you're going to be fired or anything like that, but I've heard it reflects on you.... One teacher commented to me, she said, 'Well, you're lucky you have honours kids because your tests will be higher than mine.'

In contrast to Dara's assurance that her students would pass the test even if she did not dedicate her writing instruction to the five-paragraph theme, Leigh's colleagues impressed upon her the precipitous nature of the test scores in terms of their reputations as teachers and the importance therefore of teaching to the test:

> The pressure of the writing test mainly came from my 8th grade English colleagues. I think they explained to me how important this was, so I naturally assumed the stress. The scores ... are reflected through the school as the results are published annually through the city newspaper. Our school has a history of doing extremely well in the writing test so that was always a nice reward to see the 98–99% passage rates.... My colleagues also taught the same writing method – there are three 8th grade English teachers at our school. They all felt the same pressure I'm sure. I didn't feel much pressure from the administration.... I'm not sure I ever discussed it with them, [though] I did discuss it with Dara my first year.

Although Leigh's colleagues may have pressured her to join them in teaching to the test, it seems there were forces acting collectively on Sequoyah Middle School's teachers to uphold the standards of their school and maintain the high passage rates the community had come to expect. One issued from the surrounding pressure from the state and community to teach to the test, which influenced the eighth-grade English teachers to emphasize the five-paragraph theme to the exclusion of other writing. This expectation in turn contributed to Leigh's gravitation to departmental norms when her colleagues impressed on her the importance of teaching the five-paragraph theme as a means to producing the highest possible test scores.

Leigh's construction of the setting, while of her own devising, appeared to follow from the greatest sources of pressure she experienced. The combined influences of state writing test, community values on high test scores and faculty response to those influences appeared to supersede whatever effect Dara's encouragement to minimize the impact of these factors had on her decision about how to teach writing. Leigh's construction of the setting, then, led her to adopt particular goals (achieving high test scores) and pedagogical tools to achieve those goals (exclusive instruction in the five-paragraph theme) in her teaching at the expense of Dara's priority to allow students to develop broader writing repertoires with greater joy and personal fulfilment.

Discussion

This chapter has taken a Vygotskian perspective on Leigh Thompson's construction of the setting of her early-career teaching in the arena of

Sequoyah Middle School. I have focused on the different trajectories her teaching might take given different constructions of her setting and the pressures she felt to adopt one to guide her instruction. In conjunction with her own 'deep processing' (Craik and Lockhart 1972) of the five-paragraph theme through her apprenticeship of observation as a successful high-school student and formalist emphasis during student teaching, Leigh foregrounded the state writing test and the stress induced by her colleagues and concern for her students' progress through the test-driven system to view the five-paragraph theme as an appropriate means of instruction for her eighth-grade students. She constructed this setting in spite of explicit guidance from her most immediate and influential school administrator, Dara, to teach in less authoritarian, more 'noisy', more student-centred ways. In Leigh's construction, the motive of the setting was oriented to producing passing scores on the state writing test scores so that her students could proceed to ninth grade and her school would show well in district comparisons. This construction was overwhelmingly mediated by her colleagues' continual referencing of the exam and the attendant pressures that Leigh felt to have her students perform well on it.

A Vygotskian perspective focuses on Leigh's internalization of this value through her volitional, goal-directed, tool-mediated action in the social context of the English department at Sequoyah Middle School and writing testing mandate of the state of Oklahoma. In contrast, an activity theory analysis would focus on the action of a collective, such as the eighth-grade English teachers, as mediated by an artefact such as the writing test or the five-paragraph structure. Or, in Engeström's interpretation, an activity theory approach might introduce a new artefact such as his mediational triangle and study collective action around using that artefact as a way to 'expand' learning through collective action towards the goal of changing, and presumably improving, group processes. Foregrounding the collective would require a very different sort of data collection and analysis and different unit of analysis than were employed for our study of Leigh and others in this research.

My purpose is not to assert that one focus is superior to the other, but to argue that research grounded in the frameworks provided by Vygotsky and Leont'ev produce attention to different units of analysis and thus different interpretations. A Vygotskian analysis might indeed conclude that I have internalized from my US setting a tendency to focus my attention on individual mentation, although with greater attention to sociocultural mediation than has been found in previous US approaches (e.g. the information-processing paradigm, which in general has focused on 'in-the-head' cognition with less attention to how that cognition is socially mediated; see Smagorinsky 1998).

Vygotsky and Leont'ev have on occasion been set at odds because of their different units of analysis. I see no reason to pit their foci against one another, and urge researchers working in the cultural-historical tradition to simply accept that the two orientations produce different sorts of research and to align themselves referentially with an appropriate framework for their goals and interests. The goal of research ought to be to produce insights rather than to establish that only one means of investigation and analysis can yield useful understandings. What a researcher regards as 'useful' should in turn determine what he or she decides to study and how those investigations should be conducted and interpreted.

References

Anderson, J.R. (1976) *Language, memory, and thought*, Hillsdale, NJ: Erlbaum.

Bakhurst, D. (2007) 'Vygotsky's demons', in Daniels, H., Cole, M. and Wertsch, J.V. (eds) *The Cambridge companion to Vygotsky*, Cambridge: Cambridge University Press.

Bickmore, S.T., Smagorinsky, P. and O'Donnell-Allen, C. (2005) 'Tensions between traditions: the role of contexts in learning to teach', *English Education*, 38: 23–52.

Cole, M. and Gajdamaschko, N. (2007) 'Vygotsky and culture', in Daniels, H., Cole, M. and Wertsch, J.V. (eds) *The Cambridge companion to Vygotsky*, Cambridge: Cambridge University Press.

Cole, M., Levitin, K. and Luria, A. (2006) *The autobiography of Alexander Luria: a dialogue with the making of mind*, Mahwah, NJ: Erlbaum.

Cook, L.S., Smagorinsky, P., Fry, P.G., Konopak, B. and Moore, C. (2002) 'Problems in developing a constructivist approach to teaching: one teacher's transition from teacher preparation to teaching', *The Elementary School Journal*, 102: 389–413.

Craik, F.I.M. and Lockhart, R.S. (1972) 'Levels of processing: a framework for memory research', *Journal of Verbal Learning and Verbal Behavior*, 11: 671–684.

Cuban, L. (1993) *How teachers taught: constancy and change in American classrooms 1890–1990* (2nd edition), New York: Teachers College Press.

Daniels, H. (2007) 'Pedagogy', in Daniels, H., Cole, M. and Wertsch, J.V. (eds) *The Cambridge companion to Vygotsky*, Cambridge: Cambridge University Press.

Emerson, R.W. (1841) 'Self-reliance', in Emerson, R.W. *Essays: first series*, New York: Hurst and Co. Online, available at: www.emersoncentral.com/selfreliance.htm (accessed 28 March 2009).

Emig, J. (1971) *The composing processes of twelfth graders*, Urbana, IL: National Council of Teachers of English.

Engeström, Y. (1987) *Learning by expanding: an activity-theoretical approach to developmental research*, Helsinki: Orienta-Konsultit. Online, available at: http://lchc.ucsd.edu/MCA/Paper/Engestrom/expanding/toc.htm (accessed 28 March 2009).

Hillocks, G. (1995) *Teaching writing as reflective practice*, New York: Teachers College Press.

Johnson, T.S., Smagorinsky, P., Thompson, L. and Fry, P.G. (2003) 'Learning to teach the five-paragraph theme', *Research in the Teaching of English*, 38: 136–176.

Kozulin, A. and Gindis, B. (2007) 'Sociocultural theory and education of children with special needs: from defectology to remedial pedagogy', in Daniels, H., Cole,

M. and Wertsch, J.V. (eds) *The Cambridge companion to Vygotsky*, Cambridge: Cambridge University Press.

Lave, J. (1988) *Cognition in practice*, Cambridge: Cambridge University Press.

Leont'ev, A.N. (1981) *Problems of the development of mind*, Moscow. Progress Publishers.

Lortie, D.C. (1975) *Schoolteacher: a sociological study*, Chicago: University of Chicago Press.

Smagorinsky, P. (1998) 'Thinking and speech and protocol analysis', *Mind, Culture and Activity*, 5: 157–177.

Smagorinsky, P. (1999) 'Time to teach', *English Education*, 32: 50–73.

Smagorinsky, P. (2009) 'The culture of Vygotsky', *Reading Research Quarterly*, 44: 85–95.

Smagorinsky, P., Cook, L.S. and Johnson, T.S. (2003) 'The twisting path of concept development in learning to teach', *Teachers College Record*, 105: 1399–1436.

Smagorinsky, P., Jakubiak, C. and Moore, C. (2008) 'Student teaching in the contact zone: learning to teach amid multiple interests in a vocational English class', *Journal of Teacher Education*, 59: 442–454.

Smagorinsky, P., Lakly, A. and Johnson, T.S. (2002) 'Acquiescence, accommodation and resistance in learning to teach within a prescribed curriculum', *English Education*, 34: 187–213.

Smagorinsky, P., Cook, L.S., Jackson, A.Y., Moore, C. and Fry, P.G. (2004a) 'Tensions in learning to teach: accommodation and the development of a teaching identity', *Journal of Teacher Education*, 55: 8–24.

Smagorinsky, P., Gibson, N., Moore, C., Bickmore, S. and Cook, L.S. (2004b) 'Praxis shock: making the transition from a student-centered university program to the corporate climate of schools', *English Education*, 36: 214–245.

Thoreau, H.D. (1849) *On the duty of civil disobedience/Resistance to civil government*. Online, available at: www.transcendentalists.com/civil_disobedience.htm (accessed 28 March 2009).

Tremmel, R. (2001) 'Seeking a balanced discipline: writing teacher education in first-year composition and English education', *English Education*, 34: 6–30.

Tulviste, P. (1991) *The cultural-historical development of verbal thinking*, Commack, NY: Nova Science.

Vygotsky, L.S. (1978) *Mind in society: the development of higher psychological processes* (M. Cole, V. John-Steiner, S. Scribner and E. Souberman, eds), Cambridge, MA: Harvard University Press.

Vygotsky, L.S. (1987) 'Thinking and speech', in L.S. Vygotsky, *Collected works* (Vol. 1, pp. 39–285) (R. Rieber and A. Carton, eds; N. Minick, trans.), New York: Plenum.

Wertsch, J.V. (1985) *Vygotsky and the social formation of mind*, Cambridge, MA: Harvard University Press.

Wertsch, J.V. (1991) *Voices of the mind: a sociocultural approach to mediated action*, Cambridge, MA: Harvard University Press.

Wertsch, J.V. (2000) 'Vygotsky's two minds on the nature of meaning', in Lee, C.D. and Smagorinsky, P. (eds) *Vygotskian perspectives on literacy research: constructing meaning through collaborative inquiry*, Cambridge: Cambridge University Press.

Wertsch, J.V. (2007) 'Mediation', in Daniels, H., Cole, M. and Wertsch, J.V. (eds) *The Cambridge companion to Vygotsky*, Cambridge: Cambridge University Press.

Zeichner, K.M. and Gore, J.M. (1990) 'Teacher socialization', in Houston, W.R. (ed.) *Handbook of research on teacher education*, New York: Macmillan.

Zinchenko, V. (2007) 'Thought and word: the approaches of L.S. Vygotsky and G.G. Shpet', in Daniels, H., Cole, M. and Wertsch, J.V. (eds) *The Cambridge companion to Vygotsky*. Cambridge: Cambridge University Press.

Chapter 3

What and how do student teachers learn from working in different social situations of development in the same school?

Alaster Douglas

Introduction

In this chapter I draw on one aspect of a long-term ethnographic study of school-based teacher education in England, and present analyses of the learning opportunities for student teachers as they take part in meetings with their supervising teachers (subject mentors) in two school subject departments. The student teachers were participating in a one-year Post Graduate Certificate of Education (PGCE) programme at one university and were placed in different departments in the same school.

Mentor meetings took place between mentors (subject specialists in the departments where student teachers work) and student teachers, as protected, timetabled time once a week, and were designed to help support the professional development of student teachers in the school. Meetings were expected to help student teachers to analyse and evaluate their teaching and any other lessons they had seen, to reflect on and evaluate their developing skills, and to arrange learning opportunities and plan activities. In this chapter I compare and contrast how learning is constructed across the learning opportunities of mentor meetings in the two departments, and consider the key features of the sessions. The analyses indicate how the learning opportunities are constructed differently in the two departments, even though they are in the same school and working within the same PGCE course. Analyses particularly illustrate how pedagogical practices in mentor meetings shape student teachers' experiences of school–university partnerships as training programmes.

There was very little communication between mentors in the different departments (in school and the university), and therefore the departments operated in relative isolation.

The research

As a former deputy head teacher in two large English secondary schools I have long been aware that departmental cultures can vary within schools and offer different learning environments for the teachers who work in them. The increasing involvement of schools in Initial Teacher Education (ITE) may mean that these differences have a relevance that extends beyond an individual school and its staff. Since the late 1980s in England, schools have been given some direct responsibility for the training of student teachers, with that responsibility increasing over the subsequent decade. Currently, two-thirds of any secondary PGCE course in England is based in school, and during this time the responsibility for student teacher learning is shared between schools and higher-education institutions.

There has been little research undertaken on how secondary school departments, rather than individual mentors, contribute to student teacher learning, but what has been described in the research literature on school departments is the complexity of their make-up. Some research suggests that deeper thinking about pedagogical and subject beliefs is often absent (Butcher 2000 (in Post 16 teaching), and Maynard 2001 (in the primary sector)). The diversity of opportunities available to teachers in their departmental experiences is highlighted in McLaughlin and Talbert's discussion on professional communities (2001). In their research, many departments are characterised as weak professional communities where thoughts and practices are kept private. Departments can also differ significantly in collegiality, and in beliefs about students, subject matter and good practice (Helsby 1996; Visscher and Witziers 2004). A lot of research indicates the importance of the role of the manager/subject

Table 3.1 Data collection

Nature of data	S1	S2	Total
School visits	59	21	80
School interviews	24	31	55
Lesson observations			
Department 1	9	2	11
Department 2	11	2	13
Department 3	9	2	11
Department 4	16	1	17
Total	45	7	52
Mentor meetings			
Department 1	9	4	13
Department 2	12	3	15
Department 3	11	4	15
Department 4	15	4	19
Total	47	15	62
University tutor interviews	0	6	6

Notes
S1/S2 – school placements 1 and 2
The data consist of field notes for observations, which captured snippets of conversation, and transcripts for all interviews.

leader in departments as learning communities (Busher and Blease 2000; Donnelly 2000; Eraut *et al.* 2000). However, there is limited understanding of how departments might support student teacher learning. This study aims to help fill that gap in ITE research by examining what is happening in the departments, and is therefore based on *what* is occurring and *how* it is occurring.

Table 3.1 outlines the data collection over the fieldwork year.

Cultural-historical activity theory (CHAT)

I was aware that without using a theoretical lens to examine data generated from fieldwork, there was a danger that my 'insider' viewpoint could 'lapse into ad hoc use of commonsense interpretations' (Silverman 2005: 236). Therefore, I approached the evidence using a sociocultural perspective and have in particular drawn upon cultural-historical activity theory (CHAT) (Cole 1996) to understand the mentoring situation, its processes and student teachers' learning opportunities in the school departments. Sociocultural approaches, drawing on Vygotsky, consider learning as social, mediated by social practices and cultural tools, and created by joint participation in activities. However, as subject departments in secondary schools are complex organisational settings for student teachers' learning, it was helpful to augment my focus on mediation with attention to the collective practices of the departments by drawing on activity theory. Activity theory is helpful because it enables a setting where people are working together on a shared task or object to be examined in order to see if it is a system that is conducive to learning. The unit of analysis in the discussion presented here is the ITE work in each subject department and not the departments and the variety of activities that occur there. For analytic purposes I have presented the activity of ITE in each department as an activity system, which reduces the focus of the research to the ITE work. Modelling the activity of ITE as systems allows for comparisons across departments; for example, what tools are used and how they are employed.

CHAT allows researchers to consider the practices identified in an activity system in a broad context, taking into account how and why these have developed in the past. Therefore, insights into why department staff work the way they do in ITE activities may be gleaned from questioning how their practices have developed over time, and in relation to other practices in the department. It was important to achieve a sense of the evolution of ITE activity in order to reflect on present practice and the construction of the current social situation of teacher development experienced by the student teachers.

I am using Engeström's activity system models to assist my cross-department analysis. I recognise that I am talking about ITE as an activity where its object is negotiated, unfolding and often indeterminable.

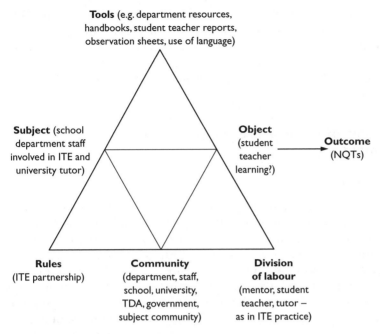

Figure 3.1 An activity system for school-based ITE.

The activity system heuristic is helpful in the present study because it allows an exploration of whether people share their understandings of objects and outcomes of systems by considering their use of tools. How tools, such as course handbooks and lesson plans, are used will indicate what the object of activity is and how it is interpreted. In brief, it can indicate how people make sense of a situation. In addition, one can question where, when and how the tools were developed, and the ideas that are brought into play as they mediate work on objects?

Despite recognising its debt to Engeström's activity theory, the study does not shape opportunities for action and thinking, by working on the object of the activity system alongside practitioners in the departments. Rather, the use of activity theory will be restricted to a 'framework that has considerable potential for researchers who are interested in how conditions for learning are created, and in what is learnt' (Edwards 2005: 55). The point of this research is not to change the system but to develop an understanding of the student teachers' opportunities for learning and how the departments are working in ITE.

Within the mentor meetings, mentors and student teachers work alone and therefore any systemic or outside factors may appear less visible. However, the department settings, social practices, tools and the attitudes shown towards the meetings' tasks influence the way the mentors and student teachers work, and this in turn will affect how they view the tasks that are the focus of the meetings. The history that each participant brings to the encounter will also be relevant. The interweaving of data from interviews and from observations of mentor meetings was therefore central to the analyses and the development of activity system models of ITE in each department.

An analysis of mentor meetings in two departments

Department I

There was one mentor and one student teacher in the department, and they rarely saw one another outside the mentor meetings. Owing to school pastoral commitments, the mentor was based away from the department setting. This necessitated extensive email contact and agenda items were kept until the one-to-one meetings. Therefore, the meetings were focused on issues brought by both parties. Nevertheless, the formality was not business-like. On the contrary, the mentor was careful to discuss points at some length by considering a variety of perspectives and questioning the student teacher in order to open out the discussion, ensuring that, for most pedagogical debates, there were no easy answers. The student teacher referred to her learning as 'a never ending journey through a tunnel' (Field notes – 25 April) highlighting a continual exploration. The student teacher acknowledged how she was made to think ideas through carefully, and how she was encouraged to take risks and challenge her own perceptions of what teaching involves:

> He does ask me to be specific about what went wrong in a lesson if I say that wasn't good. He doesn't like me just saying it was really rubbish. He wants me to tell him which bit was good, and why I think bits that didn't work should be analysed. It's a good hour I have with him.
>
> (Interview – 19 February)

If the evaluation of a lesson is seen as the main task of the activity in a session, then the mentor in asking the student to expand upon the lesson is trying to reveal the student teacher's thinking and expose their concepts to scrutiny and development. It was evident that the mentor was also considering issues afresh in their discussions, and this enhanced a genuine sharing of ideas. When talking about resources, the mentor borrowed and valued new materials as much as did the student teacher: '[Mentor] looks at sheet – this is really good, can I do a copy?' (Field notes – 10 January).

Consequently, both seemed to operate as learners, and although a novice, the student teacher appreciated that her learning was not predetermined but evolving. In that way the student teacher was positioned as a joint constructor of teaching tools with the mentor.

No agenda items were taken at face value in their meetings, and the mentor's constant questioning helped the student teacher to consider the reasons for doing things and for working in certain ways:

> Mentor: If they [the pupils] don't want to do it you need to explain why they are taking notes in that way. Does this help exam practice for example? Give the purpose for why they are doing it in that way.
>
> [The mentor considers the theory behind the practice. He suggests making pupils understand why they are doing tasks in the way they are doing them. This means that the teacher has to justify why she wants them done in this way. If the teacher can't justify that, then she should go back to her initial planning.]
>
> (Field notes – 17 January)

The mentor's asking for explanations helped to open out discussions and frequently extended the debate that ensued beyond the school context. The student teacher's previous experiences and home life influenced her understanding, and these were discussed along with the mentor's own beliefs and background. The relationship was therefore an open and personal one, further enhanced by the mentor adapting the course handbook schedule to meet the student teacher's specific needs. The handbooks were viewed and used very differently in the mentor meetings across the study. This mentor, unlike the others in the school, did not refer to the handbook regularly or let its list of suggested activities each week drive the meetings. However, the mentor was aware of the requirements embedded in the handbook but felt that the course 'is a bit full on' (Interview – 23 January) during the early weeks. His independent approach conveyed a confident stance to his mentoring. Consequently, the student teacher valued his flexible reading of the course expectations.

The mentor welcomed differences of opinion and considered personal issues to be relevant ('Have your children's teachers' attitudes to you changed since you started the PGCE?' Field notes – 10 January). This approach carried over to the student teacher's belief that her learning appeared continuous. Different styles of teaching were discussed and valued, with the student teacher not expected to mimic them, but to see in them opportunities for expanding her understanding of teaching. This openness to alternatives, curiosity and capacity for learning was also evident in the social practices of the department, and the student teacher was brought into these practices.

Collective learning and sharing of ideas was promoted, with the whole department involved at all stages in the compilation of the mentor's report on the student teacher's progress. These were also thoroughly reviewed in both mentor and the university tutor meetings. The lesson observation sheets from other teachers in the department were systematically collected and filed, and the mentor meetings provided an opportunity to use these as stimuli to talk about classes, with the student teacher candidly sharing her feelings about her learning along with other teachers' thoughts about this. If she disagreed with comments made, she felt comfortable in challenging them.

This intellectual approach (extensive debate and discussion from a variety of sources, including educational research literature) was demanding, and at times the student teacher felt daunted and in awe of the mentor's expertise and intellect. The mentor greatly valued academic engagement and had many links with the university for his own personal and professional development. He had worked extensively with the senior university tutor who had set up the PGCE course, and he was admired for the 'wisdom' he had brought to mentor meetings at the university over the years (Interview with tutor – 14 August). His perception of the PGCE course was therefore heavily influenced by its original principles or implicit rules such as debate without consensus, and the value in questioning all types of knowledge. Noticeably, the style of mentor meetings differed little from the student teacher's meetings with the university tutor when she visited the school. This seamlessness in the student teacher's experience reflected how the mentor saw himself as part of the broader activity of ITE and not simply as part of a department-based ITE activity.

In the social situation of development of the department, the student teacher's learning was enabled by the mentor encouraging the student teacher to respond to specific situations. He ensured they discussed and worked on tasks collaboratively whilst also focusing on educational issues from a broader perspective. The student teacher was guided in her thinking by constant questioning and discussion. She was not given answers or solutions to complex situations. Instead, she was encouraged to see these as learning opportunities, which could helpfully expose concepts to scrutiny and development.

Department 2

There was one mentor and two student teachers in the department, and the interaction with the student teachers was more regular than in Department 1. Sharing a small working space in the department team room enabled an almost continuous dialogue with regards to general progress and incidental and informal chats. A more focused discussion on the placement took place in the mentor meetings where one priority was the detailed preparation for the university tutor visits.

As an experienced teacher and mentor, like the mentor in department 1, this mentor worked with the student teachers on a personal as well as

professional level, but instead of debating their opinions on education
and the past experiences which informed these, she concentrated on their
experience as trainee teachers and the demands that came with following
a PGCE course. She was especially aware of the pressures of being seen
and evaluated (albeit informally) on a day-to-day basis, and was keen to
protect them from excessive criticism:

> They are being attacked and pressured from everywhere – their essays
> have got to pass, they have got to read up, fill in all this paperwork,
> they go into classes and they are being observed – everything and any-
> thing depending on whose room they are in might be pulled up on,
> what is not, may be pulled up in the next.
>
> (Interview – 10 January)

The student teachers sensed this caring approach and greatly appreciated the mentor's support and her praise of their teaching efforts. Their
discussions were characterised by talks on classroom management,
resources and lesson planning, with the mentor questioning the student
teachers on what they had observed and learned from their experience in
the classroom. The mentor was forthright in her opinions and used anec-
dotes to illustrate practice, frequently taking on a dominant role in meetings. The student teachers, who always met as a pair, listened carefully and
appeared content to take on the mentor's advice and contribute with anec-
dotes of their own. They particularly valued the discussion of resources in
the meetings and often spent an entire meeting discussing lesson materials
and sharing experiences of how they could be used effectively.

The mentor's self-deprecating humour and outspoken opinions were
enjoyed by the student teachers:

> Mentor: I have never done a plenary in my life. The bell rang on
> Monday afternoon and I said to the class, what is that? (Because this
> clock is broken and I never wear a watch.) I said what is that for? End
> of the day miss – and I had got 6 other activities I was hoping to do!'
>
> (Field notes – 10 January)

However, there was no indication that the mentor was considering her
learning anew. She did not expect the student teachers to emulate her
style of teaching but did believe they needed to grasp the basics and then
build their own style:

> I'm not saying I am right and they are wrong – you can only be true to
> a degree. You'll only be happy teaching if you are true to yourself
> rather than in a place that says you must be on page 20 by October.
>
> (Interview – 10 January)

The student teachers did not criticise the school department or mentor's point of view at all during the mentor meetings, but did at times critically evaluate some aspects of the department, for example a perceived over-emphasis on examination grades. It seemed that potential and contestable discussions did not occur in the mentor meetings due to a respect for the mentor and for what she and the department were doing in supporting the student teachers.

The style of mentoring reflected the social practices in the department in that the student teachers were made to feel part of a close-knit team by being allocated specific working space even in a cramped environment. They therefore worked closely with the teachers in the department and were party to general conversations and incidental discussions during informal gatherings in the team room. Their receptive responses to staff aided a feeling of being included, and enabled them to tap into teachers' ideas and support, which were happily given. A respect for the social environment suggested that a lack of tension was imperative in the smooth working of the department, and therefore any disagreements or tensions were avoided, with people keeping contentious ideas to themselves.

The relaxed nature of the interaction in the mentor meetings, the content of which was often initiated by the student teachers asking questions, tended to be unstructured with the mentor occasionally checking how much time was left. A communal feeling was established with each taking it in turns to buy food from the dining hall to accompany the hot drinks made in the team room. The mentor did not use the course handbook and structured the meetings around what the student teachers wanted to talk about, but 'still keeping an eye and making them keep an eye on the enormous amount of paperwork' (Field notes –10 January). Instead of treating the handbook as a jointly produced document and tool created through the school's collaboration with the PGCE course, she often used it to represent the university, and hence a somewhat idealistic document with academic intentions that were rarely realistic in the 'real world' of school:

STUDENT TEACHER 2: Questionnaire; a year 7 class in the autumn term – not done.
MENTOR: Drat I am going to ignore that feedback and just keep nagging you.
STUDENT TEACHER 1: There must be people who just don't do it.
MENTOR: Tick off what you have done – cobble some kind of survey together. You have to create a questionnaire so do one together.

[The student teachers are very negative, and the mentor does not attempt to change their minds in the value of the handbook tasks, only in the value of not getting into trouble for not doing them.]

(Field notes – 31 January)

In contrast to the avoidance of a task designed to take forward the student teachers' learning, were the meetings prior to the university tutor's visits where the emphasis was on detailed lesson planning for the tutor's observations. The nature of the interaction changed as assessment considerations took over. The tension in the build-up to the visits was palpable with an emphasis on classroom performance and delivery. A visit was regarded as an opportunity to show what the student teachers could do and to impress the tutor. Consequently, the student teachers were encouraged to create lessons that particularly highlighted their teaching skills and put into practice the modelling and routines that the tutor had introduced at the university. This placed the student teachers in the role of performers (often referred to as 'stars' by the mentor) with the tutor as a member of the audience. The mentor adopted a director's role, protective of the student teachers, wishing them success and willing them on.

The tension around the tutor's 'assessments' was conveyed to the student teachers very clearly in the mentor meetings. According to the university, the purpose of the tutor visits was to work with mentors to develop specific aspects of student teacher competence. It was stressed in the course handbook that these visits were not 'assessment visits'. One can therefore see the tutor visit as a tool for working on the student teachers' learning trajectories by exploring student teacher practice and expanding their understandings of teaching and learning. However, the visits were frequently referred to as 'assessment visits' by the teachers in the department, the student teachers and by some university staff.

This interpretation of the visits created a division between the student teachers' experiences of learning to teach in school, and the assessment requirements of passing the course. The objective of creating lessons specifically designed to meet the assessment requirements of the course acted as a rule in the ITE activity. The limitations of the mentor's appropriation of the visit as a tool (seen by the university as a means to work on the student teachers' learning) framed the rules for the student teachers' participation within the department and the activity system of ITE in the school:

> In Activity Theory terms, one might describe this relationship between the tool and rules for participation in the ... department community as an evasive movement around the object of the activity system, as slippage between tool and rule related to a contradiction in understanding the object of activity.
>
> (Ellis 2008: 19)

The contradiction lay in the development of student teacher learning versus managing the relationship between the university and the school in meeting the PGCE course requirements:

MENTOR: We'll sort [student teacher] out for Tuesday. We know [tutor] is
signing the thing. If you hadn't been so glaringly honest he would
have signed it. Just say thank you and stop talking. Let him find out
from trawling through the paperwork, which he won't do. Don't say
that some days you are not sure that the classes are learning, show
your mark book and say I am pleased, and here is the evidence.

STUDENT TEACHER: I have got to stop shooting myself in the foot [a phrase
that had been used by the mentor previously].

(Field notes – 28 March)

The mentor's advice gained from the experience of mentoring other
student teachers who had passed the course, and who were referred to
fairly regularly in mentor meetings, was prioritised by the current student
teachers who did not question the recommendations put to them for their
lesson plans. The mentor reports were written after the visits by the tutor,
thereby having lower status than those in department 1, and operated as a
rubber stamp on progress once this had been agreed with the university
tutor. Similarly, the lesson observation sheets used by the teachers in the
department when observing the student teachers were given a low status
and not looked at by the mentor at all. Instead, she valued talking to the
other teachers about the student teachers' progress in the team room,
anticipating that any concerns would naturally arise in discussions.

Consequently, the tools for taking forward student teachers' learning
were underplayed. They were superficially appropriated, which meant they
did not work in the way they were initially designed. Observation sheets
lost their potential as a tool for developing student teachers' learning, and
where they were used were employed in a routine and unreflective way.
The conceptual and theoretical basis on which the tools were conceived
was not apparent. A lack of theoretical resources and historical
understanding of the tools' purposes appeared to indicate why they were
underplayed. The informality of the mentor's practices as a mentor and
her aversion to paperwork meant that formal tools were sidelined in
favour of informal discourse and anecdote.

The mentor had worked with the tutor for many years and both regarded
one another highly. The mentor saw her role as defending hard-working and
competent student teachers, and she promoted their capabilities during the
tutor visits. Therefore, the student teachers, who were aware of this and the
relationship between the mentor and tutor, may not have wanted to jeopard-
ise such support by questioning and challenging school practices. However,
both student teachers were very happy with the support and advice they
received from the mentor, and respected the tutor for his research interests
and his analytical perspective when discussing their lesson observations.

Interaction in the mentor meetings in department 2 highlighted differences between the practice of the teaching placement and the expecta-

tions of the university. The student teachers appeared to be in accord with the mentor, and therefore remained loyal to the practices of the school. This was also reflected in their adoption of some of the language used by the mentor, the importance of 'drumming in' certain subject matter for example. This ventriloquising added to the suggestion that they all shared the same perspective, and was in contrast to the language used to describe the pedagogy of the university course, which was dominant in discussions about university tutor visits.

Comparing and contrasting the mentor meetings

The object of activity

The analysis indicates that the two mentors viewed the objects of the ITE activity systems differently. The object in department 1 could be seen as the problem space of student teacher learning, and questioning and challenging all aspects of pedagogy opened this for expansion. These experiences were in contrast to those in department 2, where the mentor did not appear to consider her own learning as continuing. Consequently, she questioned aspects of pedagogy less and concentrated on meeting the requirements of the course as a key objective, and saw the object of activity as the relationship between the university and the school, which needed to be managed carefully. Consequently, the student teachers in department 2 were given less opportunity to debate teaching and learning issues, as the mentor meetings emphasised simply satisfying course requirements and passing the PGCE. This restricted object of activity seemed to hamper recognition of the complexity inherent in teaching and learning situations, which is particularly important for student teacher learning (Edwards, this volume).

There was generally less evidence of argument and challenge in the second department in any of its activities, and one sensed that this was in part due to the protective nature of the teachers. Different opinions were accepted provided they were justified by what were considered to be successful school practices. Contentious issues in the activity of ITE were seen in terms of the differences between the university and the school practices, and these were mainly acknowledged outside the university tutor visits and not debated in great depth. The mentor explains:

> [Tutor] wants an extreme version of [teaching style], and I can see why. Many leave here and don't believe in [tutor's] way so will never do it again. Many struggle to plan a lesson to teach so as to get him to tick the box, and don't understand why they are doing it in that way, so they never do it again.
>
> (Field notes – 25 April)

This divide was not seen in department 1, as the mentor, like the student teacher, regarded himself as a learner too, and consequently viewed all ideas as contestable. His object of activity was student teacher learning, which he opened up by encouraging ongoing exploration and debate.

Activity can constantly change, and this is the result of a process that Vygotsky termed internalisation and externalisation: a learner absorbing what is around them, interpreting it (internalisation) and, consequently, acting in and on their social worlds in newly informed ways (externalisation). Hence, the mentor's view of the object as expansive in department 1 encouraged the possibility of changes in the ITE activity.

Tools

A key feature in the use of tools in department 1 was the relative formality in how they were utilized, as opposed to incidental team room chats, very little attention to paperwork and the relaxed sharing of experiences in department 2. The meetings in department 1 were more formal, especially as the opportunities for the mentor and student teacher to get together were fewer, and therefore there seemed to be a greater urgency to complete the mentor meeting 'agenda'. Reports and observation sheets were also used formally as tools to take forward student teacher learning. Debates on educational research literature from the wider academic community occurred with the mentor having read and commented on the student teacher's assignments. He also read academic literature out of interest and was aware of the research work happening at the university, emphasizing the extent to which he seemed to regard himself as part of a wider and more general activity of teacher education.

For example, although not using the course handbook on a week-by-week basis, his confidence in adapting the tasks to the needs of the student teacher came from a long-standing relationship with the department at the university and his work with the tutor. Their close working relationship meant a joint understanding, and reflected a shared history in the development of the activity. The similar language and educational terminology used in both the mentor and tutor meetings highlighted this familiarity.

For department 1, the tools that were designed for supporting the student teacher's learning were used explicitly for this. However, in department 2 the tools used specifically for the PGCE course (observation sheets, the course handbook) were sidelined in favour of more general support and personal interaction on issues arising directly from the teaching practice.

With a clear understanding of the university department's preferred teaching and learning methods, the mentor in department 2 emphasised the differences between these and those methods used in the school. Acknowledging the benefits and features of both, the student teachers were given clear alternatives, and conversations on the relative effectiveness of different teaching methods were frequent, especially when planning lesson observations for the tutor. These were reviewed in relation to past successful student teachers' lessons with advice as to how the tutor would evaluate them. Noticeable here was the contrast in language-use between the subject terminology associated with the university's advocated teaching methods, and the more informal terms forwarded by the mentor.

Concluding comment

Using CHAT as a framing for the study has revealed connections between action and meaning as it questions the smaller activities that comprise the activity of ITE in the two departments. Meanings are particularly important when examining work-based learning if it is considered to be more than just inducting new practitioners into the established practices of the workplace. If meanings are not explicitly explored in subject departments when student teachers are learning there, then their learning is likely to be of a more traditional apprenticeship nature, where skills are outlined and discussed in anticipation of them being copied and mastered.

Analysing how student teachers' relationships are managed with the social situation of the development of their learning indicates the kind of learning opportunities afforded. It is evident that there was difference in the ways learning opportunities were constructed in the mentor meetings in the two school subject departments. The student teachers from the second department did not participate in extensive pedagogical discussion, as this was not available to them. Consequently, they concentrated on those issues that were most central to passing the PGCE course. However, in department 1 there was a strong focus on debating aspects of pedagogy with an understanding that considering a variety of contestable issues and viewpoints from practitioners and researchers would enhance student teacher learning. The nature of the object of the ITE activity in department 1 allowed for development in the activity through externalisation, as the mentor and student teacher interpreted what was happening and worked in newly informed ways as a result of their interpretations. In department 2, the opportunities to act in newly informed ways in the department were more limited.

CHAT helped in this analysis in that it focused on the importance of the social situation of development for the student teachers. The analytic framework guided the analysis by highlighting the cultural history and social practices in the social situation of development and their relevance to current mentoring practices in the two departments. By considering the relationship between the tools and the object of the ITE activity systems, one was able to see how different motives were brought to the activity and how these differently constructed the object.

Meanings and values in education, and the societal goals that often affect teachers' motives, are constantly in transition, and therefore new teachers should not be seen as fixed entities but as practitioners who need to be able to respond to changing situations. The CHAT analysis reveals the opportunities for student teachers to work in a responsive way by questioning how their relationships are managed in the social situations of their development.

References

Busher, H. and Blease, D. (2000) 'Growing collegial cultures in subject departments in secondary schools: working with science staff', *School Leadership and Management*, 20, 1: 99–112.

Butcher, J. (2000) 'Subject culture, pedagogy and policy on an open learning PGCE: can the gap be bridged between what students need, and what mentors provide?', *European Conference on Educational Research*: Edinburgh.

Cole, M. (1996) *Cultural psychology: the once and future discipline*. Cambridge, MA: The Belknap Press of Harvard University.

Donnelly, J. (2000) 'Departmental characteristics and the experience of secondary science teaching', *Educational Research*, 42, 3: 261–273.

Edwards, A. (2005) 'Let's get beyond community and practice: the many meanings of learning by participating', *The Curriculum Journal*, 16, 1: 49–65.

Ellis, V. (2008) *Boundary transformation in a school–university teacher education partnership: the potential of developmental work research in DETAIL*. Sociocultural Perspectives on Teacher Education and Development: New Directions for Research, University of Oxford. Online, available at: http://ora.ouls.ox.ac.uk (accessed 29 June 2009)

Eraut, M., Alderton, J., Cole, G. and Senker, P. (2000) 'The development of knowledge and skills at work', in Coffield, F. (ed.) *Differing visions of a learning society Volume 1*, Bristol: Policy Press: 231–262.

Helsby, G. (1996) 'Defining and developing professionalism in English secondary schools', *Journal of Education for Teaching*, 22, 2: 135–148.

McLaughlin, M.W. and Talbert, J.E. (2001) *Professional communities and the work of high school teaching*, Chicago and London: University of Chicago Press.

Maynard, T. (2001) 'The student teacher and the school community of practice: a consideration of "learning as participation"', *Cambridge Journal of Education*, 31, 1: 39–52.

Silverman, D. (2005) *Doing qualitative research*, London: Sage Publications.

Visscher, A. and Witziers, B. (2004) 'Subject departments as professional communities?', *British Educational Research Journal*, 30, 6: 785–800.

Chapter 4

Taking a sociocultural perspective on science teachers' knowledge

Jane McNicholl and Ann Childs

The context: initial teacher education in England

The 1980s and 1990s in England saw increasing government control over initial teacher education (ITE). Within a series of amended Standards for Qualified Teacher Status (QTS), centralised views were articulated about the knowledge, understanding and skills that beginning teachers need to have acquired by the end of their training. Alongside this has been a move towards increased involvement of schools in ITE, often through partnerships with universities. In England the Post Graduate Certificate in Education (PGCE) programme, a post graduate one-year course designed for graduates in specialist subjects, is the major route into secondary school teaching. In line with most teacher education programmes elsewhere, student teachers in England will spend periods of time in both higher-education institutions and in school. In England student teachers on PGCE programmes will spend about one-third of their time in higher education and two-thirds of their time in school.

Government standards for QTS for science specify that all science teachers on gaining QTS for the 11–18 age range should have acquired the knowledge and understanding to teach all three sciences as laid out in the National Curriculum at what is called Key Stage 3 (11–14 age range), one science subject at both Key Stage 4/GCSE level (14–16 age range) and Key Stage 5/A level (post-16 age range). Ensuring that newly qualified science teachers are able to meet these standards is a major challenge, not least because many student teachers arrive with large gaps in their subject-matter knowledge. Student teachers entering a PGCE programme may not have studied one or more of the core sciences since they were 16 and even graduates sometimes lack a sound understanding of their degree subjects (Dennick and Joyes 1994; Lenton and Turner 1999; Lock 2001; Willson and Williams 1996). Furthermore, Sperandeo-Mineo *et al.* (2005) found that even sound knowledge of subject matter at degree level did not equip trainees with 'deep knowledge of some significant factors' for teaching the subject (2005: 260). This is not a problem confined to the English education system and has been reported elsewhere (Chaika 2000; OECD 2003; *Washington Times* 2003). Given the challenges that such students present, PGCE science programmes constantly grapple with the issue of developing student teachers' subject knowledge for teaching; while another complication is the limited time student science teachers spend within the university, just 60 days.

Subject-specific knowledge for teaching: pedagogical content knowledge (PCK)

Thinking about subject-knowledge expertise for science teachers, and consequently how ITE programmes tackle it, has been influenced considerably by Shulman and his associates (Shulman 1986, 1987; Shulman and Grossman 1988). In the 1980s they argued that in order to make the subject accessible to pupils, teachers needed a new knowledge base besides subject-matter knowledge and pedagogical knowledge. That base arose from the merging of the two to form pedagogical content knowledge (PCK) which comprised knowing what, when, why and how to teach using a reservoir of knowledge of good teaching practice and experience. In cultural-historical terms, PCK therefore operates as a secondary artefact (Wartofsky 1973). Cole (1996) explains that primary artefacts are those tools such as axes which are actually used in production; secondary artefacts are representations of primary artefacts and include recipes, beliefs and norms which preserve and transmit current ways of acting and thinking; tertiary artefacts, while still imbued by the human needs and intentions that shaped the other forms of artefact, operate more conceptually. Wartofsky (1973: 209) described tertiary artefacts as follows:

> The upshot, however, is that the constructions of alternative imaginative perceptual modes, freed from the direct representation of ongoing forms of action, and relatively autonomous in this sense, feeds back into actual praxis, as a representation of possibilities which go beyond present actualities.

Working in this more conceptually oriented 'where to' way demands a great deal of both teachers and pupils. PCK, we suggest, operates at the level of secondary artefact, a way of sharing the what, when, why and how, to teach a concept, and is therefore of use for those who need to follow recipes in areas where they have limited subject knowledge. However, the use of the term 'PCK' to characterise teachers' specialist subject knowledge for teaching has become especially powerful in science education possibly because of the use of various representations (analogies, models, metaphors), a key component of Shulman's definition of PCK, in what many believe is exemplary science teaching (Grossman and Richert 1988; Grossman *et al.* 1989).

The pre-eminence that PCK has had in a shared understanding around the world about what expertise means for science teachers is manifested in the number of studies that have looked at science teachers' PCK and their classroom practice. Most people are concerned about the relationship between PCK and subject knowledge. For example, it has been argued that secure subject-matter knowledge is a prerequisite to the development of PCK (Roth *et al.* 1986; Tobin and Fraser 1988, 1990; Garnett and Tobin 1988). It has also been reported that when teachers possess limited PCK there is a consequent negative impact upon classroom practices (Roth *et al.* 1986; Hashweh 1987; Garnett and Tobin 1988; Millar 1988; Tobin and Fraser 1990; Carlsen 1991, 1993; Geddis 1993; Sanders *et al.* 1993; Lee 1995; Osborne and Simon 1996; Harlen and Holroyd 1997; Clement *et al.* 1998). The importance that science teachers give to PCK continues with an entire edition of the *International Journal of Science Education* in August 2008 given over to research studies into PCK.

Developing the Oxford Internship Scheme through research

First research project

The science PGCE programme, part of the Oxford Internship Scheme, has for many years employed the notion of 'practical theorising', whereby student teachers draw on the expertise of both university teacher educators and teachers, where both forms of expertise are considered to be equally valid (McIntyre 1990). This model of teacher education gives prominence to ideas of a capacity for theorising practical experiences, practical principles and craft knowledge, which are both derived from and applicable to practice (Hirst 1979; Tom 1980; McIntyre 1991). Many pedagogical issues – for example, learners' needs, classroom management, behaviour management and so on – are dealt with in just this way. However, in terms of the development of PCK, practical theorising has been less well-conceptualised.

Our dissatisfaction with current understandings of the interrelationships between school and university contexts with regard to the development of PCK, and our concern with how to best help our student teachers navigate these contexts, prompted a small-scale study. This first research project focused on the challenges faced by secondary science teachers, including student teachers, when teaching outside their subject specialism and the strategies they used to develop PCK (Childs and McNicholl 2007). In line with the literature in this area, many of the teachers perceived that limited subject-matter knowledge had a negative effect upon their PCK and a consequent impact upon their classroom practice. However, this study demonstrated that many of the teachers felt that given a supportive working environment, they were capable of developing their knowledge and practice, including PCK.

Through this study we were able to identify some strategies that teachers employed when faced with the challenge of teaching new and unfamiliar areas of science. For instance, teachers related strategies for learning new PCK while they were planning lessons, such as reading science textbooks and teaching schemes, which made lesson planning time-consuming. However, the most significant form of help was from colleagues who were specialists in the area. For example, one respondent talked about how a colleague helped with practical work:

> I was planning with Year 8 and the chemistry teacher came to show me... just exactly how to manipulate the equipment which I'm not so familiar with. But then also as she was talking she was saying things that then led onto conversation about extinguishers and why you need to plug it up and all those sorts of things and just to make it more entertaining.

This earlier study also provided insights into material artefacts that teachers drew upon when learning PCK. In many cases these artefacts were schemes of work[1] that provided examples of resources and ideas for the classroom. Indeed, schemes of work were seen to be a key support in some cases: 'Well it's the looking for the links ... if scientists are going to teach outside their initial specialism, concentrating on having really good schemes of work to support staff is the most important feature.'

However, the presence of a scheme of work in itself was not the solution for teachers when teaching outside their subject specialism. Some of our respondents felt that an excess of choice of possible activities and resources in the teaching scheme was actually unhelpful. These teachers felt they did not have the knowledge to make an informed selection of a 'good' activity or resource in a way that they could when planning within their subject specialism. This finding points to the limits of secondary artefacts in responsive work and also resonates with Hashweh's (1987) concerns about the nature of teaching schemes within science departments; one teacher in our study questioned the whole development of teaching schemes within his department:

> after teaching mainly outside my specialism Year 7 and 8 or lower school science in my school and I got very, very frustrated because there is a scheme of work etc. that has been developed over time and there are resources but the problem is there is no ownership of that work scheme.... After you've taught the lesson and go to [an experienced teacher and say] 'That was an appalling lesson' and they'll say

'Yes, you're right yes, I wouldn't use those resources I'd use those resources that I've generated myself.'

What became clear from this study was that PCK can be developed in quite individual ways, very much in line with the analyses offered by Bishop and Denley (2007) in their study of science teaching. However, also emerging from our data was a strong sense that PCK is the product of a social process, something we had previously not recognised. In the study, the teachers often referred to PCK as being shared, distributed and held across people, material artefacts and social settings or, as others argue, a type of knowledge that is distributed among those interacting as well as stretched over material and cultural artefacts (Ellis 2007, Lave 1988; Rogoff 1990; Pea 1993; Salomon 1993). This view is more in line with the newer models for PCK development, that stress the interrelated nature of the aspects of PCK and the dynamic nature of 'pedagogical content knowing' (Cochran *et al.* 1993), and with Hashweh's view on the creation of PCK, as occurring in practice, through teachers' engagement in the inventive processes of planning and teaching (2005: 73).

Barnet and Hodson (2001) have placed emphasis on the interrelationship between context and teachers' PCK, and have coined a new term for such knowledge: 'pedagogical context knowledge'. If it is the case that PCK is personal or idiosyncratic knowledge that is also heavily embedded in the context in which it is put into action, we would argue that it is best generated and shared in practice through teachers' everyday actions of planning, teaching and talking with colleagues. Situated learning perspectives, where expertise is viewed as a situated phenomenon, where knowledge as embedded in practice and learning occurs via participation in practices, went some way to help us conceptualise the process at work in subject departments. However, a focus simply on practices did not go far enough in examining the interrelationships between the individual and the context, where context also includes the complexities of the cultural and historical bases that underpin the rules and norms of practice in the places where teachers work.

The study also raised questions about school as a place for teacher learning. Recently, the significance of school as a setting for teacher learning has been gaining ground. Some studies have made the link between learning environments and informal learning (Hopkins *et al.* 1998; Cofield 2000; Eraut *et al.* 2000; Williams *et al.* 2001; Eraut 2004; Hodkinson and Hodkinson 2005; Lohman 2006). Our small-scale study of PCK suggested that for the science teachers we interviewed the school subject department was an important site for their learning. Historically, in English secondary schools, the curriculum subject tradition has acted as a central, conceptual framework, encompassing issues of epistemology, affiliation and career progression (O'Neill 2000) and in terms of the everyday lives of secondary school teachers, the subject department is pre-eminent too (Siskin and Little 1995). Furthermore, the agenda of local and national accountability has also led to changes in school management, with the emergence of the subject department as a major vehicle in the pursuit of school improvement.

Hargreaves has described school science departments in particular as being isolationist and distanced from the rest of the school, and has referred to this separation as a form of 'balkanisation' (Hargreaves 1994). Our own experience with schools would lead us to agree, and also to concur with those who suggest that science departments can be isolated, individual and idiosyncratic (Siskin 1994; Donnelly 2000; O'Neill 2000). However, our study also suggests that an aspect of subject departments that has been less well recognised is that some can provide rich learning environments for teachers, including student teachers. As teacher educators it is quite common for us to witness departments as learning environments as science teachers sit together at break and lunch time, discussing teaching and learning. However, not all departments offer equally effective learning communities, and some might even inhibit teacher learning. For instance, if the pervading attitude towards learning and helping novices in a workplace is negative, then this will have detrimental effects upon teachers' learning (Lawrence and Valsiner 1993; Billett 1995, 2002; Rogoff 1995).

The interplay between the knowledge-laden practices of the departments we observed and the learning that was occurring there called for a sociocultural analysis. We were particularly concerned to ensure that our student teachers were acutely aware of the ways in which they could access the potential of the school context in order to learn. Introducing to them how they might start to understand the contexts in which they found themselves and successfully navigate their way through them became a priority. It became important to help them grasp much more about *what* needs to be learnt and *how* they can accomplish this within the school context. This we now see as our role as teacher educators. In doing this we aim to help student teachers to develop a more sophisticated understanding of metacognitive processes: knowledge and understanding of what they need to learn and how to go about doing this (Brown *et al.* 1983) and hence to become more effective and resourceful learners. In university sessions, we discuss with our student teachers the nature of the challenges they will face when planning and teaching difficult scientific phenomena and concepts. We have employed the version of Shulman's PCK framework offered by Summers *et al.* (1998: 171) and, with some further modifications, use it as a heuristic device to frame these learning challenges so that students begin to understand what sorts of knowledge they need.

For a science teacher, the definition of PCK we use is knowledge about:

- children's conceptions and preconceptions about science;
- simple technical knowledge of equipment to be used in children's investigations;
- the strategies most likely to be fruitful in developing the understanding of learners;
- the most useful analogies, illustrations, examples, explanations and demonstrations;
- appropriate scientific terms and language to use with children;
- how to deal with common questions asked and responses given by pupils;
- what to emphasise (not just what is the case but, critically, what is *not* the case);
- how to simplify validly what are often very complex ideas.

We help student teachers to develop strategies for learning both in the university and particularly in school. In university subject-knowledge sessions that deal with particularly difficult science topics, we help students to identify the scientific ideas and concepts that underpin effective PCK. In these sessions we focus both on how they identify and grasp these key concepts and the potential and challenges of this approach as they work in schools. Our goal is to empower our students to take ownership over their own learning and to encourage them to be both active learners who contribute to knowledge in their school departments now and in the future; in essence, to become effective life-long learners and colleagues within their schools.

While we acknowledge the critical importance of Shulman's (1986) notion of PCK and the extensive research built upon it, we share Hashweh's view that the creation of new subject specific pedagogical constructions occurs in practice, through teachers' engagement in the inventive processes of planning and teaching (2005: 73). For this reason we focused our subsequent research study to investigate the kinds of informal workplace learning that take place as teachers engage with colleagues. We were concerned to examine how the knowledge in these practices is made visible and shared within specific conversational practices in departments. For us, participation in practices was an insufficient explanation of what was happening when student teachers were developing understandings of PCK.

The second research project

The study asked the following research questions:

- What areas of PCK do science teachers focus upon in their everyday interactions in science departments?
- What facilitates these interactions?

The study was conducted over two weeks in science departments in two state-funded secondary schools. The two departments were selected on the basis of our knowledge of them as effective teaching, learning and mentoring departments. Two researchers spent two weeks in each department observing interactions; interviewing teachers; 'hanging out' at break times and after school; attending all department meetings and continuing professional development training events. Field notes were used to record what happened and what was said, and a running commentary was later added to these notes in order to clarify and to add a level of interpretation. Other evidence was gathered through semi-structured interviews with teachers and student teachers (11 teachers and two student teachers in one school and seven teachers and two student teachers in the other school). The interviews asked teachers to reflect upon what and how they learnt as they interacted with others and what helped this. Analysis was conducted in three phases. First, we coded the interview data through a more grounded approach in relation to our key questions. Second, we were then able to use these codes to begin to understand the observation data as it seemed that what the teachers were talking about in their interviews was closely related to what we were observing. This level of analysis allowed us to develop a series of categories to address the second research question. In the initial analysis, unsurprisingly, PCK emerged as a major category. However, in the initial analysis it was undifferentiated. Therefore, the final phase of analysis, to address the first research question, was to impose a framework developed from an examination of how PCK is conceptualised, especially drawing on the work of van Driel *et al.* (1998). The components of PCK that we used in the final phase of the analysis were knowledge of: subject matter, strategies, student learning and conceptions, general pedagogy, curriculum and purposes. Although there is considerable debate over the components of PCK, our purpose was to use these areas as a heuristic device to give greater clarity and structure to PCK as a knowledge category and to look at what, within this category, teachers were really attending to in their interactions. We now discuss the findings.

What areas of PCK do science teachers focus upon in their everyday interactions in science departments?

Nias *et al.* (1992) identified talk as a key feature of collaborative schools. In these schools, staff spent a great deal of time talking to one another, and their conversations were a mixture of small talk and more focused discussions. Others have described much of the collective knowledge shared in these kinds of discussions as 'teacher lore': a term used by Schubert (1992) to describe the powerful oral tradition by which ideas, perspectives, insights, images of pupils, teachers and teaching, and the everyday workable strategies they rationalise are passed on to initiates. Schubert and

Ayer (1992) assert that teacher lore is the principal means by which teachers construct, reconstruct and share their professional knowledge, and it is often atheoretical and even anti-intellectual. However, others suggest that teachers talking together can be effective learning forums where knowledge about the subject and its teaching and learning can be acquired not just by those actively participating in the talk but by the onlookers too (Williams 2003). Ross *et al.* (1992) refer to this type of talk as 'professional theorizing' and assert that it can lead to the development of a collective professional knowledge, which might be akin to what Barnett and Hodson refer to as 'pedagogical context knowledge' (2001).

In the second study, although there was a lot of lore sharing, a major part of teachers' talk was discussions about teaching and learning scientific ideas and phenomena. Our analysis showed that the most significant areas that teachers focused on were knowledge of strategies and knowledge of subject matter.

First, in terms of knowledge of strategies, there were many examples where teachers asked for ideas/strategies/analogies on how to teach a concept and other colleagues responded: 'SB then asks RG about potassium in plants and RG says she has a PPP [Power Point Presentation] that she will share with SB.'

There were also discussions in the team rooms where teachers shared their knowledge of strategies more widely, for example: 'LS then talks about the screaming jelly baby experiment – she's done this in Y7 and she lines up jelly babies of different colours and they all scream at different pitches and then says that actually "Jelly Teds" work better.'

There were instances where non-specialist teachers needed more advice from a subject specialist on a particular strategy: 'HR asks JK's opinion about a Y10 lesson on heart rate. HR wants to know if they should repeat the readings because the temperature today is very different from when the pupils did the first set of readings.'

Finally, there were examples where non-specialist teachers needed help in how to do practical work and demonstrations and this included advice on safety: 'JS then asks EN about safety screen for demo of alkali metals with water and whether pupils should wear lab glasses and EN says JS should use both.'

The second most significant area, knowledge of subject matter, revealed that respondents were rarely able to talk about subject matter without intertwining it with pedagogy. For example, this discussion took place:

RG asks JG about conductance – they then discuss the concept and clarify their understanding. They then discuss ways of learning to teach A level and RG asks JG about an easy way to explain Young's modulus. Again they work out their understanding of the concept and then JG gives RG some advice on how to teach it.

This phenomenon has also been noted by Lederman *et al.* (1994) when they said: 'with the benefit of experience and continual use of one's subject matter structure for purposes of teaching, the division between pedagogical knowledge and subject matter knowledge may become blurred' (Lederman *et al.* 1994: 143).

Other areas such as the 'where to' or tertiary artefact aspects of pedagogy, such as knowledge of student learning and conceptions, did not feature as a significant area in teachers' talk. This could be because most discussions were about the very immediate concerns *as non-specialists teachers* where they almost resembled novices (Childs and McNicholl 2007) who focused on their own needs rather than those of their learners. If they talked about learners it was generally in a more 'what' and 'how' way about behaviour management.

What factors facilitate these interactions?

The provision in both of the science departments of a team room as a shared common physical space seems to be a significant facilitating factor. Williams *et al.* (2001) have suggested that spontaneous collaboration is very valuable for teacher development, and it is environments which embody spontaneity and which have a capacity to generate collaborative situations in unpredictable and unplanned ways that support 'professional discussion [which] is probably the most powerful development tool' (2001: 265). The rooms were separate spaces populated solely by science teachers, student science teachers and science technicians. The discussions within these spaces were rarely planned formal knowledge-sharing events; instead the teachers' talk related to their immediate needs, often occurring when teachers were planning lessons, and especially when teaching outside their subject specialism.

There were many examples of participants, teachers and student teachers, also having a shared language, or what Rogoff (1995) has termed a measure of intersubjectivity, and that this too appeared to be a significant facilitator of meaningful interactions. Our evidence suggests that it is these interactions which build up shared language and meanings (about knowledge, aims and purposes) that relate to specific contexts (pupils to be taught and resources available), and which sustain teachers' professional learning as they work daily to meet the demands of teaching challenging areas of the science curriculum.

It became apparent that it was not simply the provision of a shared physical space that appeared to facilitate useful interactions between teachers. In line with Van Huizen *et al.* (2005) we observed interactions also being facilitated by the expectation of a shared and inclusive participation where individuals have 'an expanded notion of professional autonomy' (Edwards 2005) and where true collaboration can lead to the creation of distributed and shared knowledge of how to teach. Furthermore, the relationships that we witnessed were very much characterised by trust, care and mutual respect, comfortable in sharing doubts without feeling like a failure. Our findings also showed that the student teachers participated quite significantly at times.

In one school, one of the student teachers had a doctorate in physics. One of the newly qualified teachers (NQT) in physics, who had an Engineering degree, would often ask other physics colleagues to help her with explanations for pupils and this student teacher would often help too. One of these exchanges revealed very clearly how dependent non-specialist teachers are on the recipe, or secondary artefact, features of PCK. Having been asked for help by the NQT, the student teacher launched into a complex explanation of the physics concept. The NQT did not find the explanation helpful. The head of science, who happened to walk in at the time, then took the conceptually oriented physics explanation being offered and translated it into a secondary artefact by describing an analogy she would use in teaching this physics idea. So here we saw the student teacher contributing as subject expert to the expertise that was distributed in the team room, while the expertise in teaching of the head of science was brought to bear to translate the more conceptual tertiary artefact explanation offered by the student teacher, in order to help the NQT.

The head of science, a physics teacher herself, often deferred to this student teacher's obvious expertise in physics and often asked him questions, appreciating, as a subject expert herself, his conceptual knowledge. However, the same process of translating from tertiary artefact to secondary was evident in how she helped him work with pupils. She asked him to plan a project with sixth-form pupils on quantum cryptography. However, she oversaw the planning of the project quite closely and her input in the discussions we observed was always to challenge the student teacher to think about how these challenging concepts could be taught. In the end, through a process of negotiation, the topic was changed to one about black holes because both the head of science and the student teacher decided that quantum cryptography was too difficult. The translation process through discussions appeared vital. The student teacher recognised the value of these discussions in helping him access teachers' craft knowledge when he said: 'otherwise you can copy things that teachers do without understanding why and then they don't quite fit'.

We would also argue that value lay in helping him to learn how to transform his sophisticated conceptual knowledge to match the level of the pupils he was teaching and which was a constant challenge for him.

Interactions and collaboration were also facilitated by other factors. For example, various members of the department often acted as catalysts to trigger conversations. The NQT just mentioned, who felt insecure in her subject knowledge, very often asked questions about teaching which would then involve many members of the department. In her interview she talked about how she used questions with other colleagues to get feedback and advice so she could develop her teaching, and this often included advice about how to teach higher-level physics. She seemed to be someone who was being much more deliberate and conscious of the potential of the department to be a key source of professional learning and we would characterise her as a very resourceful learner in this scenario. Another key figure in one department was the head of science who constantly started conversations about a wide range of topics from what popular science non-fiction students should read to how to teach a low-attaining set about plate tectonics. In addition, she used the coffee table in the team room to dis-seminate articles from journals like *New Scientist,* new teaching resources and, in one example, her own school exercise books which generated a debate about the departmental marking policy!

Finally, a major facilitating factor in these departments seemed to be their participation in processes of change. For example, one department was implementing a new course, Cognitive Acceleration in Science Educa-tion (CASE), in its younger year groups. As the teachers started to teach these lessons they would discuss them in the team room and the lessons over a period of days would be chewed over, shaped and developed by the collective. One of the teachers' concerns was how appropriate some of the resources and activities were for lower-attaining pupils and there was much discussion about how the materials and activities could be adapted. These discussions raised two interesting points for us: first, these conversations allowed for a more ongoing and sustained collaboration which was very different from the more rapid and serendipitous exchanges mentioned above. Second, these were conversations where pupils as learners and their needs and understanding did seem to be discussed, in direct contrast with the faster, more furious exchanges mentioned above where pupils as learners rarely surfaced. This is, at present, a tentative finding but suggests that a move away from the secondary artefact work of PCK towards a more conceptually oriented approach to teaching science is possible when the right tools are offered to teachers.

Conclusions and implications

The internship experience of student teachers is, in ITE programmes in England, a collaborative and collegial undertaking. Programmes are usually jointly planned with mentors and, in school, mentors involve other members of their department with student teachers. However, what is much less clearly conceptualised is the nature of the collegiality in subject departments and how teachers, whether qualified or student teachers, become part of a system of distributed expertise. Indeed, there has been little research into the role of school subject departments as sites of teachers' learning. Reflecting Huberman's (1993) notion of the teacher as an independent artisan, much of the literature on teacher development to date has emphasised the individual learner. The two small studies discussed here indicate that the learning of student teachers, and more experienced teachers, is shaped by their interactions with other people and by the practices that constitute the work of their subject departments.

Van Huizen *et al.* (2005) argue for a more overarching framework for teacher education which draws upon a Vygotskian perspective. Picking up on Vygotsky's attention to externalisation alongside internalization in the process of learning, we would also argue that our student teachers, in school, are not only shaped by their surroundings but they shape them by their actions as they contribute to the knowledge that is locally distributed; and at the same time they learn a lot about teaching. We are not alone in emphasising the social dimension, collegiality and the culture of teaching in encouraging and constraining individual development (Bell and Gilbert 1993; Hargreaves 1994) while others have argued that effective teacher development is underpinned by collaboration and collegiality (Nias 1998; Day 1999). However, collegiality is often over-used and ill-defined (Hargreaves 1993; Darling-Hammond and McLaughlin 1995). Greater precision over the sort of collegiality required is crucial for establishing an environment in which teachers learn.

One can begin to identify some of the features of collaboration for learning in the departments we studied. They included a long-term and agreed focus on the quality of pupils' learning experiences in science classes; a recognition that expertise across the three areas of the science curriculum is distributed across a department and is a resource to be drawn on for the benefit of pupils; an acknowledgement that specialist expertise is not a function of professional status, i.e. student teachers and technicians can contribute to the distributed understandings drawn on by colleagues; and that asking questions does not diminish one's sense of self as a good practitioner. It was exactly this type of mutually supportive and non-judgemental environment we witnessed in the science departments we studied where teacher collaboration was the norm; where beliefs that knowledge can be jointly created and distributed were common; and where there was an acceptance that no one is capable of possessing all the scientific knowledge found in secondary-school science curricula. The complexity, depth and breadth of this knowledge necessarily requires it to be shared and distributed across and amongst teachers and material artefacts such as schemes of work and resources.

The studies are also a first step in beginning to understand the processes, the potential and the limitations of the learning of PCK in subject departments. What seems to emerge from the data we gathered is that the ways of learning we observed and that the teachers talked about represented an integration of the 'where to' aspects of in-depth scientific knowledge with the 'what, how and when' of practical ideas for presenting them to pupils. In addition, teachers' specialist knowledge and classroom expertise appeared to mediate the extent to which they were dependent on the recipes offered by the PCK that was distributed across the team rooms. The teacher learning reported here certainly suggests that starting with the practices of departments and understanding how they are enriched by task-focused discussions which also capture concepts to be taught is a useful way forward for thinking about enhancing the quality of the time that student teachers spend in schools. The talk we observed appeared to 'task-centred and task-appropriate' (Biggs 1993: 75–76) and very much in line with what Billett has characterised as effective learning where new knowledge is both contextualised and grounded in one's own experiences and actions (2002: 460–461).

The next step is to carry out more longitudinal studies to help us understand why some schools within ITE partnerships are better at facilitating teacher learning than others. Our studies, and the Vygotskian line we have been following, take us beyond attention to context as sets of knowledge-laden practices. Instead we have studied departments as local systems of distributed expertise. This focus has, in turn, called for an examination of how the knowledge in practices is made visible, drawn upon and developed as teachers participate in the practices of supporting pupils' learning.

Note

1 Schemes of work are taken to be the documents a science department uses to support planning or teaching. These documents can be published schemes of work with accompanying textbooks or, at the other extreme, in-house developed material. Schemes of work can be as detailed as lesson-by-lesson plans with details of worksheets, practical activities, differentiation ideas, ideas for the use of ICT and assessment.

References

Barnett, J. and Hodson, D. (2001) 'Pedagogical context knowledge: towards a fuller understanding of what good science teachers know', *Science Teacher Education*, 85 (4), 426–453.

Bell, B. and Gilbert, J. (1993) 'Teacher development as professional, personal, and social development', *Teaching and Teacher Education*, 10, 483–497.

Biggs, J. (1993) 'From theory to practice: a cognitive systems approach', *Higher Education Research and Development*, 12 (1), 73–85.

Billett, S. (1995) 'Workplace learning: its potential and limitations', *Education and Training*, 37 (5), 20–28.

Billett, S. (2002) 'Workplace pedagogic practices: co-participation and learning', *British Journal of Educational Studies*, 50 (4), 457–481.

Bishop, K. and Denley, P. (2007) *Learning science teaching: developing a professional knowledge base*, Buckingham: Open University Press.

Brown, A.L., Bransford, J.D., Ferrara, R.A. and Campione, J.C. (1983) 'Learning, remembering, and understanding', *Handbook of child psychology*, New York: Wiley, pp. 77–166.

Carlsen, W.S. (1991) 'Effects of new biology teachers' subject-matter knowledge on curricular planning', *Science Education*, 75, 631–647.

Carlsen, W.S. (1993) 'Teacher knowledge and discourse control: quantitative evidence from novice biology teachers' classrooms', *Journal of Research in Science Teaching*, 30 (5), 471–481.

Chaika, G. (2000) *Education World*. Online, available at: www.education-world.com/a_admin/admin143.shtml (accessed 25 June 2009).

Childs, A. and McNicholl, J. (2007) 'Science teachers teaching outside of subject specialism: challenges, strategies adopted and implications for initial teacher education', *Teacher Development*, 11 (1), 1–20.

Clement, J.J. (1998) 'Expert novice similarities and instruction using analogies', *International Journal of Science Education*, 20 (10), 1271–1286.

Cochran, K.F. (1993) 'Pedagogical content knowing: an integrative model for teacher preparation', *Journal of Teacher Education*, 44 (4), 263–272.

Cole, M. (1996) *Cultural psychology*, Harvard: Belknap Press.

Darling-Hammond, L. and McLaughlin, M. (1995) 'Policies that support professional development in an era of reform', *Phi Delta Kappan*, 76, 597–604.

Day, C. (1999) *Developing teachers: the challenges of lifelong learning*, London: Falmer Press.

Dennick, R. and Joyes, G. (1994) 'New science teachers' subject knowledge', *School Science Review*, 76 (275), 103–109.

Donnelly, J. (2000) 'Departmental characteristics and the experience of secondary science teaching' *Educational Research*, 42 (3), 261–273.

Edwards, A. (2005) 'Let's get beyond community and practice: the many meanings of learning by participating', *The Curriculum Journal*, 16 (1), 53–69.

Ellis, V. (2007) *Subject knowledge and teacher education: the development of beginning teachers' thinking*, London: Continuum.

Eraut, M. (2004) 'Informal learning in the workplace', *Studies in Continuing Education*, 26 (2), 247–273.

Eraut, M., Alderton, J., Cole, G. and Senker, P. (2000) 'Development of knowledge at work', in F. Coffield (ed.) *Differing visions of a learning society*, Bristol: Polity Press.

Garnett, P.J. and Tobin, K. (1988) 'Teaching for understanding: exemplary practice in high school chemistry', *Journal of Research in Science Teaching*, 26 (1), 1–14.

Geddis, A.N. (1993) 'Transforming subject-matter knowledge: the role of pedagogical content knowledge in learning to reflect on teaching', *International Journal of Science Education*, 15, 673–683.

Grossman, P.L. and Richert, A.E. (1988) 'Unacknowledged knowledge growth: re-examination of the effects of teacher education', *Teaching and Teacher Education*, 4 (1), 53–62.

Grossman, P.L., Wilson, S.M. and Shulman, L.E. (1989) 'Teachers of substance: subject matter knowledge for teaching', in Reynolds, M.C. (ed.) *Knowledge base for the beginning teacher*, New York: Pergamon.

Hargreaves, A. (1993) 'Individualism and individuality', in Little, J.W. and

McLaughlin, M.W. (eds) *Teachers' work: individuals, colleagues and contexts*, New York: Teachers' College Press.

Hargreaves, A. (1994) *Changing teachers, changing times: teachers' work and culture in the postmodern age*, London: Cassell.

Harlen, W. and Holroyd, C. (1997) 'Primary teachers' understanding of concepts of science: impact of confidence and teaching', *International Journal of Science Education*, 19 (1), 93–105.

Hashweh, M.Z. (1987) 'Effects of subject-matter knowledge in the teaching of biology and physics', *Teaching and Teacher Education*, 3 (2), 109–120.

Hashweh, M.Z. (2005) 'Teacher pedagogical constructions: a reconfiguration of pedagogical content knowledge', *Teachers and Teaching: Theory and Practice*, 11 (3), 273–292.

Hirst, P.H. (1979) 'Professional studies in initial teacher education: some conceptual issues', in Alexander, R.J. and Wormald, E. (eds) *Professional studies for teaching*, Guildford: Society for Research in Higher Education, pp. 15–27.

Hodkinson, H. and Hodkinson, P. (2005) 'Improving school teachers' workplace learning', *Research Papers in Education*, 20 (2), 109–131.

Hopkins, D., Beresford, J. and West, M. (1998) 'Creating conditions for classroom teacher development', *Teachers and teaching: theory and practice*, 4 (1), 115–124.

Huberman, A.M. (1993) 'The model of the independent artisan in teachers' professional relations', in Ross, E.W. Cornett, J.W. and McCutcheon, G. (eds) *Teacher personal theorizing: connecting curriculum practice, theory, and research*, Albany, NY: State University of New York, pp. 257–272.

Lave, J. (1988) *Cognition in practice: mind, mathematics and culture in everyday life*, Cambridge: Cambridge University Press.

Lawrence, J.A. and Valsiner, J. (1993) 'Conceptual roots of internalisation: from transmission to transformation', *Human Development*, 36, 150–167.

Lederman, N.G., Gess-Newsome, J. and Latz, M.S. (1994) 'The nature and development of pre-service science teachers' conceptions of subject matter and pedagogy', *Journal of Research in Science Teaching*, 31, 129–146.

Lee, O. (1995) 'Subject matter knowledge, classroom management and instructional practices in middle school science classrooms', *Journal of Research in Science Teaching*, 32 (4), 423–440.

Lenton, G. and Turner, G. (1999) 'Student-teachers' grasp of science concepts', *School Science Review*, 81 (295), 67–72.

Lock, R. (2001) 'A-level biology teachers subject knowledge', *Science Teacher Education*, 31, 10–13.

Lohman, M.C. (2006) 'Factors influencing teachers' engagement in informal learning activities', *Journal of Workplace Learning*, 18 (3), 141–156.

McIntyre, D. (1990) 'Ideas and principles guiding the Internship Scheme', in Benton, P. (ed.) *The Oxford internship scheme: integration and practice in initial teacher education*, London: Calouste Gulbenkian Foundation.

McIntyre, D. (1991) 'The Oxford University model of teacher education', *South Pacific Journal of Teacher Education*, 19 (2), 117–129.

Millar, R. (1988) 'Teaching physics as a non-specialist: the in-service training of science teachers', *Journal of Education for Teaching*, 14, 39–53.

Nias, J. (1998) 'Why teachers need their colleagues: a developmental perspective', in Hargreaves, A. Lieberman, A. Fullan, M. and Hopkins, D. (eds) *International handbook of educational change*, Dordrecht: Kluwer Academic Publishers, pp. 1257–1271.

Nias, J., Southworth, G. and Campbell, P. (1992) *Whole school curriculum development in the primary school*, London: Falmer Press.

O'Neill, J. (2000) ' "So that I can more or less get them to do things they really don't want to": capturing the "situated complexities" of the secondary school head of department', *Journal of Educational Enquiry*, 1 (1), 13–34.

Organisation for Economic Co-operation and Development (2003) *Education at a glance*, Paris: OECD publishing.

Osborne, J. and Simon, S. (1996) 'Primary science: past and future directions', *Studies in Science Education*, 26, 99–147.

Pea, R.D. (1993) 'Practices in distributed intelligence and designs for education', in Salamon, G. (ed.) *Distributed cognition*, Cambridge: Cambridge University Press.

Rogoff, B. (1990) *Apprenticeship in thinking: cognitive development in social context*, New York: Oxford University Press.

Rogoff, B. (1995) 'Observing sociocultural activities on three planes: participatory appropriation, guided appropriation and apprenticeship', in Wertsch, J.V., Del Rio, P. and Alverez, A. (eds) *Sociocultural studies of the mind*, Cambridge: Cambridge University Press, pp. 139–164.

Ross, E.W., Cornett, J.W. and McCutcheon, G. (1992) *Teacher personal theorizing: connecting curriculum practice, theory, and research*, Albany, NY: State University of New York.

Roth, K., Anderson, C. and Smith, E. (1986) 'Curriculum materials, teacher talk and student learning: case studies in fifth grade science teaching', *Research Series #171*, Michigan State University: The Institute for Research in Teaching.

Salomon, S. (1993) *Distributed cognitions: psychological and educational considerations*, Cambridge: Cambridge University Press.

Sanders, L.R., Borko, H. and Lockard, J.D. (1993) 'Secondary science teachers' knowledge base when teaching science courses in and out of their area of certification', *Journal of Research in Science Teaching*, 30 (7), 723–736.

Schubert, W.H. (1992) 'Personal theorizing about teacher personal theorizing', in Ross, E.W. Cornett, J.W. and McCutcheon, G. (eds) *Teacher personal theorizing: connecting curriculum practice, theory, and research*, Albany, NY: State University of New York, pp. 257–272.

Schubert, W.H. and Ayer, W. (1992) *Teacher lore: learning from our own experience*, New York: Longman.

Shulman, L.S. (1986) 'Those who understand: knowledge growth in teaching', *Educational Researcher*, 15 (2), 4–14.

Shulman, L. (1987) 'Knowledge and teaching: foundations of the new reforms', *Harvard Educational Review*, 57, 1–22.

Shulman, L. and Grossman, P. (1988) *The intern teacher casebook*, San Francisco, CA: Far West Laboratory for Educational Research and Development.

Siskin, L. (1994) *Realms of knowledge: academic subjects in secondary schools*, London: Falmer.

Siskin, L. and Little, J. (1995) 'The subject department: continuities and critiques', in Siskin, L. and Little, J. (eds) *The subjects in question: departmental organization in the high school*, New York: Teachers' College Press.

Sperandeo-Mineo, R.M., Fazio, C. and Tarantino, G. (2005) 'Pedagogical content knowledge development and pre-service physics teacher education: a case study', *Research in Science Education*, 36, 235–268.

Summers, M., Kruger, C. and Mant, J. (1998) 'Teaching electricity effectively in the primary school: a case study', *International Journal of Science Education*, 20 (2), 153–172.

Tobin, K. and Fraser, B.J. (1988) 'Investigations of exemplary practice in Australian science classes', *Australian Science Teachers Journal*, 34 (1), 23–29.

Tobin, K. and Fraser, B. (1990) 'What does it mean to be an exemplary science teacher?' *Journal of Research in Science Teaching*, 27, 3–25.

Tom, A. (1980) 'The reform of teacher education through research: a futile quest', *Teachers College Record*, 82 (1), 15–29.

Van Driel, J.H., Verloop, N. and De Vos, W. (1998) 'Developing science teachers' pedagogical content knowledge', *Journal of Research in Science Teaching*, 35 (6), 673–695.

Van Huizen, P., Van Oers, B. and Wubbels, T. (2005) 'A Vygotskian perspective on teacher education', *Journal of Curriculum Studies*, 37 (3), 267–290.

Wartofsky, M. (1973) *Models: representation and scientific understanding*, Dordrecht: D. Reidal.

Washington Times (2003, July 16) 'Federal education report finds shortage of qualified teachers'. Online, available at: www.washtimes.com/national/20030715–114915–3853r.htm (accessed 14 January 2007).

Williams, A. (2003) 'Informal learning in the workplace: a case study of new teachers', *Educational Studies*, 29 (2/3), 207–219.

Williams, A., Prestage, S. and Bedward, J. (2001) 'Individualism to collaboration: the significance of teacher culture of newly qualified teachers', *Journal of Education for Teaching*, 27 (3), 253–267.

Willson, M. and Williams, D. (1996) 'Trainee teachers' misunderstandings in chemistry: diagnosis and evaluation using concept mapping', *School Science Review*, 77 (280), 107–113.

Chapter 5

How can Vygotsky and his legacy help us to understand and develop teacher education?

Anne Edwards

Taking stock

Where are we with teacher education? Cochran-Smith has described what she terms the 'new teacher education' in the United States as a 'public policy problem' (Cochran-Smith 2008: 271). Echoing Furlong's (2005) observation that teacher professionalism and the education associated with it has become increasingly managed by national governments to meet national policy aims, she argues that teacher educators should challenge the narrowest aspects of current versions of 'new teacher education' and should build on the opportunities they offer. In order to build on preoccupations with the 'ends' of education, she proposes questioning the purposes of education with the aim of including among them socioemotional development, participation in democratic processes and combating inequalities.

Government-funded education has long been a 'public policy problem' in the UK, whether the point was to educate the newly enfranchised or to prepare a civil service for an expanding Empire. But policy imperatives change, therefore the relationship between societal goals, the activity of schooling and the practices of teaching needs to be regularly scrutinised to identify disjunctions, outmoded legacies and unintended outcomes. The question driving the scrutiny has to be forward-looking, for example, 'What kinds of teachers for what kinds of learners?' However, the answer to this question won't ever be clear. As Vygotsky once put it: 'Questions of education will have been resolved when questions of life will have been solved' (1997a: 350).

Uncertainty is perhaps one of the few certainties facing education systems (Edwards *et al.* 2002). 'New teacher education' appears geared towards high stakes testing, which is seen to be linked to economic competitiveness (Cochran-Smith 2008). Yet, as I write, the US Congress is debating a bail-out of the Detroit car industry: survival in the changing conditions of the global economy may call for more than good test scores. In that context, teacher education systems that reduce the capacity of practitioners to respond to learners, to work with other professionals who support children's well-being or to adapt to changing socioeconomic conditions deserve to be revisited. The challenge, as the English Training and Development Agency for Schools (TDA) and National College for School Leadership (NCSL) now recognise, is to re-professionalise, as informed decision-makers, a profession trained for almost two decades in England in efficient curriculum delivery in ways that limited their responsiveness to learners (Edwards 1997, 1998; Edwards and Protheroe 2003, 2004).

In this chapter I discuss what Vygotsky's ideas, and their development into cultural-historical activity theory (CHAT), can offer an understanding of teachers' professional learning and development which is aimed at creating a professionalised workforce. I shall outline briefly how learning is conceptualised within CHAT; discuss how CHAT allows a questioning of legacy practices and an understanding of the production of new practices for new purposes; reflect on the insertion of values and motives into pedagogic settings; offer the idea of 'teaching as resourceful practice' based on CHAT principles; and consider the implications for teacher education. The message throughout these discussions will be that teaching as a responsive practice should be seen as part of a responsible professional activity which should be supported at a policy level. These sentiments find strong support in Mulgan's recent analysis of 'the art of public strategy':

> many of the best strategies are simple – they provide a framework within which smart, responsive and responsible people and units can work things out for themselves, supported by rapid feedback and easy communication. Over elaborate strategies that attempt to prepare for every eventuality are much more likely to fail.
>
> (Mulgan 2009: 6)

Aspects of a Vygotskian approach to learning

A more comprehensive introduction to Vygotskian approaches to learning can be found in the introduction to this volume and in, for example, Daniels (2001) and Moll (1990). Here I simply outline the concepts that inform the argument in the present chapter.

Learning, for a Vygotskian, is evident in learners' changing relationships with the social situations of their development and is a result of a process of internalisation and externalisation. In brief, relationships change as learners take in what is culturally valued, consequently interpret their social worlds differently and therefore act in and on them in newly informed ways, which in turn impact on the social situations. Vygotsky's learners are therefore not merely passive recipients of culturally valued concepts, but are actors in and on their cultures, being both shaped by and shaping the social situations of their development.

There are, of course, differences between learners and in the relative stability of social worlds. When learning is the induction of novices into relatively stable practices, such as a school curriculum, this interpretation of learning requires teachers to attend to the changing relationship by increasing the degree of challenge and by supporting learners' engagement with new demands. When learning involves doing something where practices are less defined, whether problem-solving in school or developing and taking forward new practices in the workplace, externalisation becomes more strongly evident and may involve questioning the rules of the broader activity in which learners are trying to work. For example, pupils collaborating through wikis may need to question their school's individually based assessment practices; or teachers who are expected to collaborate with social workers to support pupils' well-being may find themselves questioning the rules of schooling and creating new procedures or fresh 'tools' to enable that collaboration.

When we examine learning in practice, whether as a pupil or a teacher, a focus on the changing relationship between learner and social situation of development means that we should see minds as both encoding, i.e. efficiently storing understandings, and decoding, i.e. interpreting a problem to be worked on and identifying the resources that enable work on it (Edwards *et al.* 2002). Greeno, in his emphasis on pattern-seeking as part of his sociocultural account of cognition (1997), makes similar points. One sign that student teachers are learning is that they recognise the complexity to be found in tasks and how learners approach them, and become increasingly adept at identifying and using the resources available to them to help pupils engage with tasks. I shall be arguing that working in unpredictable classroom settings particularly demands attention to decoding and the development of resourceful responses.

However, we also need to attend to the encoding aspects of mind. Here the focus is the interaction between the sense-making of individuals and the meaning-making of the collectives with which they engage. As individuals we struggle to make sense of and accommodate understandings that are part of the meaning systems of activities in which we participate. When learners are dealing with a carefully described body of knowledge, such as a curriculum, this interplay can be seen as connecting the everyday understandings of novices with the more established understandings of experts carried in the curriculum, freeing the learners from the limitations of their everyday representations. Externalisation here may involve demonstration of understandings and questions that lead the learners to other areas of the curriculum.

The Vygotskian line that I am pursuing would suggest that when expert practices are less prescribed – for example, when teaching in complex settings such as classrooms – externalisations of understandings may have more impact. These consequences follow because, as we engage with public meanings through our questioning and prior understandings, we can contribute to and reshape them. For example, beginning teachers may want to question the amount of time spent on teaching to the test and move towards more problem-solving activities. This interplay between individual sense and public meaning offers teachers more than can be gained by reflection on practices for self-improvement, as it requires an interrogation of the meaning system of schooling, and the purposes and values that it encapsulates. Of course this interrogation is most likely to occur when encouraged by the practices of the school and, as Cochran-Smith indicates, the macro-political policies within which the practices are located.

My account so far as been largely cognitive, underplaying the affective aspects of learning. But this emphasis was not Vygotsky's intention. He was clear that emotion cannot be filtered out of analyses of how we act in the world, arguing that if emotion were ignored 'thought must be viewed … as a meaningless epiphenomenon incapable of changing anything in the life or conduct of a person' (Vygotsky 1986: 10).

In the last year of his life, he developed his ideas on the importance of emotion with a new unit of analysis, *perezhivanie* (Vygotsky 1994: 339), which can be equated with lived or emotional experience and was, for Vygotsky, central to how we engage with the world.

Perezhivanie was refined by Vasilyuk (1991) with the notion of 'experiencing' which involves living through personal crises in creative ways in order to restore meaning to life. Vasilyuk's examples of critical situations are often quite dramatic. Nonetheless, the attention he paid to the discomfort of personally experienced contradictions and the questioning of meaning in activities are useful reminders of what is involved in, for example, moving between university and school while learning to teach. Kozulin (1991), in his review of the English translation of Vasilyuk's book, suggests that it combines Vygotskian ideas about learning as processes of making sense and meaning as we engage in the world, with 'Western studies of the psychodynamics of the unconscious' (1991: 14). By making that connection between conscious thinking and the unconscious, Vasilyuk has helped us to see that coping with change is not simply a behavioural response, but also involves an affectively charged and relatively slow process of working through contradictions or 'crises' and gaining new forms of mental equilibrium which enable functioning.

Van Huizen *et al.* (2005), in their account of a Vygotskian perspective on teacher education, therefore rightly emphasise that teacher education should acknowledge and use the emotional experiences of student teachers. I have recently made a similar point (Edwards 2009a), suggesting that a Vygotskian view of teacher education should draw on Beach's idea of 'consequential transitions' in the development of identities (Beach 1999), in order to be alert to changes in the development of student teachers' professional identities which are 'consequential' for them, and to work with these as important opportunities for learning.

In summary, these Vygotskian ideas suggest that learning to become a teacher involves, among other things, developing a capacity to interpret and act on the workplace and to question meanings and the social practices that sustain them. Supporting student teachers therefore involves helping them to manage their relationships with the social situations of their development, to seek complexity in learners and tasks, and to recognise resources that will support their actions. All that while also attending to the emotional aspects of identity formation within the nested contexts of learning to teach.

Questioning and developing practices

The discussion so far has drawn mainly on Vygotsky's work and his attention to mind in action. It is now time to turn to the developments contributed by Vygotsky's contemporary A.N. Leont'ev, and more latterly by Y. Engeström. While Vygotsky's work focused on the cultural formation of mind, Leont'ev and later Engeström examined 'activities', their purposes and how they are culturally shaped. Engeström defines activities as 'systemic formations that gain durability by becoming institutionalised … [and] … take shape and manifest themselves only through actions performed by individuals and groups' (Engeström 2008: 204). The defining feature of any activity is what Leont'ev described as the 'object of activity' (or problem that is being worked on) in which is embedded the 'object motive' (or what calls forth the responses of actors).

The object of the activity of 'new teacher education', as outlined by Cochran-Smith, is curriculum delivery for test performance. However, the object motive may be high scores for the national good, or compliance to ensure the survival of training courses, or something else entirely. Cochran-Smith, although not using CHAT, has revealed a range of possible object motives for teacher education and has encouraged teacher educators to 'expand' the object of activity to include the broader motives of well-being, democracy and equity.

Expansive learning is a central concept in Engeström's work (Engeström 1999, 2008). Briefly, it involves the development of a simple idea into a complex object of activity and a new form of practice. He describes it as an expansive cycle which 'begins with individual subjects questioning the accepted practice, and it gradually expands into a collective movement or institution' (2008: 130). Expansive learning builds on Vygotskian ideas of externalisation to highlight the dynamic relationship that can exist between individuals and the social situations of their development, and particularly their capacity to change practices and reconfigure activities.

What can that dynamic mean for the education of teachers? Let us return to the question 'What kinds of teachers for what kinds of learners?' We know that new web-based resources, a valuing of inter-disciplinarity and peer support, and a focus on problem-solving are all raising questions about the roles of teachers and the assessment of learning that may lead to a reconfiguring of the activity of schooling. Schools in England are also being encouraged to look beyond their own tightly bounded social practices to collaborate with other practitioners to prevent the social exclusion of vulnerable children and young people, and engage them in education. All of these changes call for increased clarity about the longer-term purposes of education and the development of resourceful outward-looking practices that call into question the social practices of schools and related training programmes that focus primarily on induction into these long-established practices.

Let us illustrate that claim by examining the demands of inter-professional practice for the development of children's well-being. The 1990s saw a rethinking of the idea of disadvantage and the development of the concept of social exclusion, described by Room as: 'the process of becoming detached from the organizations and communities of which the society is composed and from the rights and responsibilities that they embody' (1995: 243).

Children who were 'at risk' of social exclusion were failing in school and unlikely to enter work (OECD 1998). The shift from disadvantaged to 'at risk' was regarded as helpful because it was future-oriented and allowed governments to consider how social exclusion might be prevented (France and Utting 2005). It also brought education quite firmly into the frame as part of the system that would prevent it.

Of course vulnerability to social exclusion is complex and may not be evident unless one looks across all aspects of a child's life: parenting, schooling, health and so on. Consequently, it was recognised that the services which work with children needed to find ways of enabling collaboration between practitioners (DfES 2003; Home Office 2000; OECD 1998). Currently, increased attention is being paid to engaging schools in preventative work because of the potential they afford for reaching large populations of children and young people (Demos-Hay 2004; Treasury/DfES 2007).

These demands mean that English schools are expanding their objects of activity to include well-being alongside curriculum coverage, and are employing staff who can focus on preventative collaboration and also work with teachers to support children's socioemotional needs. We have argued (Edwards *et al.* in press) that schools have accommodated these demands by establishing two activity systems: academic and welfare, which operate in parallel. Nonetheless, an expansion of the object of schooling as a broader activity to include children's well-being has meant that, while focusing on children as learners, teachers have needed to see themselves as part of a wider system of practitioners who are also working on children's developmental trajectories.

They have begun to recognise the conceptual and material resources that other practitioners can bring to support a child's development and to learn how to collaborate responsively with them (Edwards 2005, 2009b; Edwards *et al.* 2009). In other words, they have learnt to see other practitioners as resources and are able to be resources for others as part of systems of distributed expertise. But before they can start the fluid responsive collaboration needed to disrupt a child's trajectory towards social exclusion, they are having to learn to understand and respect the object motives of their potential collaborators and to expand their interpretations of children's needs. They are not relinquishing their primary concern as teachers with curriculum, but expanding the object of activity of schooling with insights from the practitioners with whom they are collaborating.

Our evidence suggests that the simple idea of 'a focus on the whole child', which emerged early in our discussions with teachers about the need to collaborate, was reformed into a complex object of activity by practitioners who questioned established practices and are currently producing new practices which are responding to that new complexity (Edwards *et al.* 2009). The challenge, we have argued, is now for education policy to recognise these reconfigured practices and support the conditions for their development in the demands that policies place on schools.

There are also implications for teacher development at both pre-service and in-service phases. Our experience of working with schools to expand understandings of the purposes of schooling suggest that Engeström's (2007a) focus on questioning and developing practices in cycles of expansive learning make it a potentially powerful tool for the development of the activity of teacher education. In particular its attention to the motives embedded in objects of activity takes us rapidly to concerns with professional values which is a central issue in the re-professionalising of teachers.

Values and motives in the practice of teaching

A major problem with the training of teachers in England over the last two decades has been the instrumental nature of its focus on curriculum and assessment. Over the first ten years of that period, we undertook a series of research studies on teacher education that focused on how student teachers learnt to teach while they were placed in elementary school classrooms to learn the practical aspects of teaching. There were some striking messages from the series of studies (Edwards 1997, 1998; Edwards and Collison 1996; Edwards and Ogden 1998; Edwards and Protheroe 2003, 2004) which confirm Cochran-Smith's concerns about a narrowing of focus in teacher education. Findings included the following:

- Student teachers very rarely interacted with other teachers while they were in classrooms learning to teach.
- Their work was guided by lesson plans, often supplied by the class teacher.
- Feedback focused on their delivery of the lesson and the pace at which children moved through the curriculum.
- Adherence to the lesson plans meant that student teachers became increasingly less responsive to children over the year of their training.

At the same time, in the elementary schools where this work was carried out, teachers were developing new forms of specialist expertise. Each school had specialists in work with children with special educational needs, and individual teachers were given responsibility for managing the schools' science, literacy and maths curricula. It was expected that schools would operate as systems of distributed expertise, where teachers could develop particular strengths in specific areas and could look for advice from colleagues with strengths in others.

Yet the student teachers we tracked were becoming polished performers in the art of curriculum delivery, unable to admit to any difficulty. They rarely sought help from other teachers and avoided situations which led them from their prepared lesson plans. They were not expanding the problems that they encountered in their teaching and thereby learning. Rather, the reverse: they turned away from anything that happened in their classrooms that they had not predicted in their plans. It was too risky for them to deviate from their scripts and perhaps produce a less-than-polished performance.

They did develop expertise in lesson planning, because they could work on the planned curriculum as an object of activity with their supervising teacher-mentors. But once in classrooms they were on their own and their teaching was limited to curriculum delivery. We argued that this process severely limited the development of their professional identities as responsive teachers who were able to exercise pedagogic expertise. We have, of course, been proved right as current concerns with re-professionalising indicate.

In one study (Edwards and Ogden 1998; Edwards and Protheroe 2003, 2004), we asked 24 student teachers to talk us through times when they felt they had helped children to learn in each of the 47 lessons we had just experienced with them. Most of the responses focused on how well they had presented the curriculum. The following response, from a student who had been working with six-year-olds, was one of the few that offered an account of an interaction with a child, and exemplifies the tyranny of the lesson plan and its negative effect on responsive teaching:

Daniel asked me for a word. It was a k and he couldn't find it in his word book. So I showed him there is j and k on the same page. But it wasn't planned.

The student teacher was apologising for deviating from a lesson plan to tell a young child how to find a letter in his vocabulary book. This focus on planned performance and lack of responsiveness reverberated into children's relationships with each other: only one of the twenty four student teachers mentioned helping children support each other as learners.

(Edwards and D'Arcy 2004)

The lesson plans were being used by the student teachers as 'what' and 'when' tools (Engeström 2007b) to deliver a pre-planned lesson, rather than more creatively as 'why' or 'where to' tools which were oriented to children's longer-term development as learners. To use tools like a lesson plan in future-oriented 'why' or 'where to' ways, teachers need object motives that stem from more than curriculum delivery. As Doyle back in the 1980s indicated, at the very minimum teachers need to be able to responsively connect learner, curriculum and task to take forward a child's understanding (Doyle 1986).

Doyle's analysis and Cochran-Smith's broader societal concerns suggest that more time should be spent in teacher education on how to interrogate the 'whys' and 'where tos' of teaching. There are at least two reasons for this suggestion. The first is that when managing learners' relationships with curricula, teachers need to be able to adjust demand to secure learner engagement. This factor is very much in line with Vygotsky's focus on learners' changing relationships with the social situations of their development through processes of internalisation and externalisation. In 1923, while still a teacher himself, he proposed that 'it is not so important to teach a quantity of knowledge as to inculcate the ability to acquire such knowledge and to make use of it'. Consequently the role of the teacher was to become the 'director of the social environment' (Vygotsky 1997a: 339).

The second reason for a focus on 'why' and 'where to' also arises from Vygotsky's analysis of teaching, which demands that teachers engage with what matters in society. As a result of that engagement, teachers bring the values that arise in society to inform how they structure the social situation of pupils' development. In doing so, teachers connect classroom experiences with broader societal concerns. The idea is that as learners work with and on the teacher-directed environment, they join in with and shape society. Vygotsky is quite clearly de-centring the teacher in this analysis and is instead placing the learner's processes of internalisation and externalisation centrally in education, which he sees as person-making in the Liberal European tradition. Describing the belief that education consists of a relationship between teacher and student as 'basically false' (Vygotsky 1997a: 347) Vygotsky was not diminishing the role of the teacher; rather, he was seeing it as, through the structuring of the social situation of devel opment, crucial to the formation of socially responsible learners.

By focusing on creating learning environments that are imbued with meaning and on managing learners' engagement with them, Vygotsky was highlighting the role of teachers as mediators of what is valued in society. He was also, though he would not have used that language, suggesting that learners need to recognise and work with societally formed object motives while in school. When teaching and, by association, teacher education are deconstructed along the lines suggested by Vygotsky, we can see just how much what is offered in schools and teacher training differs from his model and how much his concerns echo those of Cochran-Smith.

That is not to say that Vygotsky has provided a blueprint; his work was always a reflective searching for meaning which invites the engagement of the reader. Writing during a period of almost incomprehensible turmoil in Russia in the 1920s, and a victim himself of anti-Semitism, his writing on education appears understandably to aim at societal homogeneity in ways that may be uncomfortable for readers currently grappling with issues of diversity. However, his analysis would suggest that if, for example, diversity is a significant societal problem, it should be made evident as a problem in the learning experiences offered to pupils.

Resourceful teaching for resourceful learning

Mediation for Vygotsky primarily involved helping learners to use culturally valued tools, i.e. concepts and artefacts, in increasingly informed ways to help them take control of their worlds. Although internalisation was important, the purpose of education was ultimately to enhance externalisation:

> The person using the power of things or stimuli, controls his own behaviour through them, grouping them, putting them together, sorting them ... man subjects to himself the power of things over behaviour and makes them serve his own purposes ... He changes the environment with the external activity and in this way affects his own behaviour, subjecting it to his own authority.
>
> (Vygotsky 1997b: 212)

Resourceful learners are therefore those who recognise how tools such as ideas and artefacts can strengthen their own impact and are able to access and use them to turbo-charge their actions.

Resourceful teaching for resourceful learning is therefore more than curriculum delivery and teaching for successful test performance. It involves guiding the agency of the learner to actions that strengthen their understanding of tasks and their impact on them. That in turn means emphasising decoding alongside encoding so that the complexity of tasks is revealed and the potential for action offered by artefacts and ideas is recognised.

Resources, however, are not limited to material artefacts and the knowledge embedded in them: the expertise of others is also a potential resource. Elsewhere we have developed the concept of 'distributed expertise' (Edwards *et al.* 2009) and highlight the negotiations involved in working with others to accomplish tasks.

Being an expert practitioner, I propose, now also involves recognising that the expertise of others can be drawn on to enhance actions. I've already indicated that we found little evidence in our studies of teacher education of how pupils were encouraged to work together and to support each other's learning, and that there was little evidence of mentors working alongside student teachers to manage the environment in which the student teachers were learning. That lack of collaboration between student teachers and mentors while teaching denied student teachers the opportunity to recognise that other adults can be resources who can, with them, enhance the management of learning environments for pupils. I suggest that isolation is a particular weakness if we are preparing student teachers for the following situations, among others: team teaching for multi-disciplinary project work; working with learning support assistants; making the most of parent helpers in elementary school classrooms; peer coaching for staff development.

Seeing teaching as resourceful practice can potentially strengthen rationales for learning to teach in the practice of teaching. In particular it suggests that one role for teacher educators is to work alongside beginning teachers, reading and decoding the landscape of classrooms and identifying the possibilities for action within them so that they can share their readings and responses with student teachers. As I've already argued (Edwards and Protheroe 2003, 2004), the current focus on the polished performance of student teachers in the English system inhibits the in-the-moment interpretations of how learners are engaging with classroom tasks and the actions that might assist that engagement, which characterise a Vygotskian approach to teaching. School-based teacher-mentors are ideally positioned to be mediators of the professional knowledge that comprises their expertise in the act of teaching.

The implications for teacher education

Let's extend the scrutiny question to now ask 'What kind of teacher education for what kinds of teachers?' Van Huizen *et al.* (2005) make the case that the close association between action and meaning that is central to a

Vygotskian approach to teaching and learning means that student teachers need to orient themselves towards publicly accepted standards of teaching which reflect societal goals. They stress that this orientation is not about being recruited unquestioningly to local ideologies, but simply to recognise that teaching does involve the mediation of culturally valued meanings. Importantly, and very much in line with Cochran-Smith (2008), they argue that: 'the more firmly an emphasis is placed in teacher education [on] the instrumental aspect, the more the aspect of meaning is left implicit or dogmatically imposed and, consequently, is inaccessible to exploration, reflection and discussion' (Van Huizen *et al.* 2005: 276).

They proceed to suggest that student teachers need to be able to explore the meanings that shape professional practices and can only do so when these meanings are presented explicitly and modelled in practice. I would agree. Ellis' recent work (this volume), on a research partnership between a university department, English departments in schools and the student teachers who are trained in both settings, demonstrates clearly the advantages for both initial and continuing professional learning that arises when practice-based meanings are modelled and open to scrutiny.

There is, of course, more to teacher expertise than reflective awareness and the questioning that accompanies it. I've already suggested that teachers in British schools have needed to become adept at negotiating their work on children's developmental trajectories with the other practitioners who support the same children. They are also expected to negotiate the support of children's learning with parents 'who are the most direct influence on young people's outcomes' (DCSF 2007: 128). The Vygotskian view of classroom practice I've outlined also suggests that teaching is a process of negotiating task-engagement through mediating the use of resources that sustain productive engagement. A corollary of Vygotsky's de-centring of the teacher in the learner's relationship with knowledge is raised expectations for a responsive pedagogy which involves the adjustment of support and demand in the learning environment and the negotiating of appropriate resources into the repertoires of learners.

One implication for teacher education of this Vygotsky-based discussion of teaching is that student teachers are most likely to learn how to negotiate and make adjustments to support pupil learning alongside more expert teacher-mentors who make those aspects of their expertise explicitly available in classroom conversations. In addition, while in the classroom with student teachers, teacher-mentors can adjust demand and mediate resources to support the learning of student teachers.

Vygotsky strenuously highlighted the importance of internalisation for informed action; hence the argument being made is not for the teacher as a knowledge-free facilitator. Rather, the suggestion is that knowledge of curriculum content, appropriate sequences of delivery, and how to test is not enough. Cochran-Smith was right to remind us of the long-term dangers to society of a narrow version of the 'new teacher education'. Vygotsky's writing on teaching offers considerable support to her case. However, it also digs a little deeper into the implications of the case for what happens in classrooms where student teachers are learning to teach. A reflective awareness of the interaction between individual sense-making and publicly attested meanings needs to become the focus for pupils, student teachers, the mentors who support them in schools and those who design the learning experiences of student teachers in universities.

References

Beach, K. (1999) 'Consequential transitions: a sociocultural expedition beyond transfer in education', *Review of Research in Education*, 24: 101–139.

Cochran-Smith, M. (2008) 'The new teacher education in the United States: directions forward', *Teachers and Teaching: Theory and Practice*, 14 (4): 271–282.

Daniels, H. (2001) *Vygotsky and pedagogy*, London: Routledge.

DCSF (2007) *The children's plan*, London: DCSF.

Demos-Hay (2004) *Schools out: can teachers, social workers and health staff learn to work together?* London: DEMOS-Hay.

DfES (2003) *Every child matters*, London: DfES.

Doyle, W. (1986) 'Classroom organization and management', in M.C. Wittrock (ed.) *Handbook of research on teaching*, 3rd edition, New York: Macmillan.

Edwards, A. (1997) 'Guests bearing gifts: the position of student teachers in primary school classrooms', *British Educational Research Journal*, 23 (1): 27–37.

Edwards, A. (1998) 'Mentoring student teachers in primary schools: assisting student teachers to become learners', *European Journal of Teacher Education*, 21 (1): 47–62.

Edwards, A. (2005) 'Relational agency: learning to be a resourceful practitioner', *International Journal of Educational Research*, 43 (3): 168–182.

Edwards, A. (2009a) 'Becoming a teacher', in H. Daniels, J. Porter and H. Lauder (eds) *Critical perspectives on education*, London: Routledge.

Edwards, A. (2009b) 'Agency and activity theory: from the systemic to the relational', in H. Daniels, K. Guttierez and A. Sannino (eds) *Learning and expanding with activity theory*, Cambridge: Cambridge University Press.

Edwards, A. and Collison, J. (1996) *Mentoring and developing practice in primary schools*, Buckingham: Open University Press.

Edwards, A. and D'Arcy, C. (2004) 'Relational agency and disposition in sociocultural accounts of learning to teach', *Educational Review*, 56 (2): 147–155.

Edwards, A. and Ogden, L. (1998) 'Constructing curriculum subject knowledge in school-based teacher training in primary schools', *Teaching and Teacher Education*, 14 (7): 735–747.

Edwards, A. and Protheroe, L. (2003) 'Learning to see in classrooms: what are student teachers learning about teaching and learning while learning to teach in schools?' *British Educational Research Journal*, 29 (2): 227–242.

Edwards, A. and Protheroe, L. (2004) 'Teaching by proxy: understanding how mentors are positioned in partnerships', *Oxford Review of Education*, 30 (2): 183–197.

Edwards, A., Lunt, I. and Stamou, E. (in press) 'Inter-professional work and expertise: new roles at the boundaries of schools', *British Educational Research Journal*.

Edwards, A., Daniels, H., Gallagher, T., Leadbetter, J. and Warmington, P. (2009) *Improving inter-professional collaborations: multi-agency working for children's well-being*, London: Routledge.

Edwards, A., Gilroy, P. and Hartley, D. (2002) *Rethinking teacher education: an interdisciplinary analysis*, London: Falmer.

Engeström, Y. (1999) 'Activity theory and individual and social transformation', in Y. Engeström, R. Miettinen and R.-L. Punamäki (eds) *Perspectives on activity theory*, Cambridge: Cambridge University Press.

Engeström, Y. (2007a) 'Putting activity theory to work: the change laboratory as an application of double stimulation', in H. Daniels, M. Cole and J.V. Wertsch (eds) *The Cambridge companion to Vygotsky*, Cambridge: Cambridge University Press.

Engeström, Y. (2007b) 'Enriching the theory of expansive learning: lessons from journeys toward co-configuration', *Mind Culture and Activity*, 14 (1 and 2): 23–39.

Engeström, Y. (2008) *From teams to knots: activity theoretical studies of collaboration and learning at work*, Cambridge: Cambridge University Press.

France, A. and Utting, D. (2005) 'The paradigm of "risk and protection-focused prevention" and its impact on services for children and families', *Children and Society*, 19: 77–90.

Furlong, J. (2005) 'New Labour and teacher education: the end of an era', *Oxford Review of Education*, 31 (1): 119–135.

Greeno, J. (1997) 'On claims that answer the wrong questions', *Educational Researcher*, 26 (1): 5–17.

Home Office (2000) *Report of Policy Action Team 12: Young People*, London: Home Office.

Kozulin, A. (1991) 'Psychology of experiencing: a Russian view', *Journal of Humanistic Psychology*, 31: 14–19.

Leont'ev, A.N. (1978) *Activity, consciousness and personality*, Upper Saddle River, NJ: Prentice Hall.

Moll, L. (1990) 'Introduction', in L. Moll (ed.) *Vygotsky and education*, Cambridge: Cambridge University Press.

Mulgan, G. (2009) *The art of public strategy: mobilizing power and knowledge for the public good*, Oxford: Oxford University Press.

OECD (1998) *Co-ordinating services for children and youth at risk: a world view*, Paris: OECD.

Room, G. (1995) 'Poverty and social exclusion: the new European agenda for policy and research', in G. Room (ed.) *Beyond the threshold: the measurement and analysis of social exclusion*, Bristol: Policy Press.

Treasury/DfES (2007) *Policy review of children and young people: a discussion paper*, London: HM Treasury.

Van Huizen, P., van Oers, B. and Wubbels, T. (2005) 'A Vygotskian perspective on teacher education', *Journal of Curriculum Studies*, 37 (3): 267–290.

Vasilyuk, F. (1991) *The psychology of experiencing: the resolution of life's critical situations*, Hemel Hempstead: Harvester.

Vygotsky, L.S. (1986) *Thought and language*, Cambridge, MA: MIT Press.

Vygotsky, L.S. (1994) 'The problem of the environment', in R. Van der Veer and J. Vlasiner (eds) *The Vygotsky reader*, Oxford and Cambridge, MA: Blackwell.

Vygotsky, L.S. (1997a) *Educational psychology*, Boca Raton, FL: St Lucie Press.

Vygotsky, L.S. (1997b) 'Analysis of higher mental functions', in R. Rieber (ed.) *The collected works of L.S. Vygotsky, volume 4: The history of the development of higher mental functions*, New York: Plenum Press.

Chapter 6

Categorising children

Pupil health and the broadening of responsibilities for the teaching profession

Eva Hjörne, Pernilla Larsson and Roger Säljö

Introduction

Traditionally the social identity of the teaching profession rests on the responsibilities associated with instructing pupils in a classroom. Explaining curricular content, keeping order in the classroom, monitoring and evaluating student progress, and interacting with pupils within the school setting have been the traditional core duties of teachers since schools were first established in ancient Mesopotamia some 5,000 years ago (Gadd 1956; Kramer 1949). This image of instructing pupils as the core of what it means to be a teacher is reciprocated in the corresponding obligation of pupils to learn and to acquire specified curricular contents. When entering school, children are defined through the social identity of being a pupil, and the institutionally relevant entitlements and obligations when acting in this capacity are different from those that apply when acting as a child.

In recent decades, schools in many countries have been given wider responsibilities for the young generation and their socialisation and welfare. One sign of this at the institutional level is that pre-schools and after-school activities of various kinds have been introduced.

Another sign of this development, and the focus of this chapter, is that teachers and schools are assumed to take a broader responsibility for pupils and their social situation. For instance, schools and teachers are expected to establish and maintain in-depth contacts with parents (cf. Edwards, this volume) to monitor and support children's social, emotional and cognitive development, to intervene in cases of bullying in the school context and to cooperate with other social institutions when the need arises (Edwards 2004). Thus, schools, and teachers and other professionals, are becoming responsible not only for learning and curricular activities but also for the well-being and social adaptation of pupils. This widening of responsibilities in terms of socialisation that the institution of schooling has assumed can also be understood against the background of broader social changes that have to do with factors such as the increasing participation in the labour market of parents (and particularly of mothers), new demographic conditions (including migration and urbanisation), new family patterns and so on.

In the Swedish context, this development is obvious in curricular documents as well as in the emergence of new institutional practices within schools during recent decades (Hjörne 2005). One element of such changes is the focus on what is now officially referred to as 'pupil health' (Börjesson 1997). Although this term may appear vague, it nevertheless signals an explicit recognition of the politically formulated idea that schools should assume a broader responsibility for children's development and welfare; schools should actively seek to promote pupil health, and they will be held accountable for how they do this. In the particular case of Sweden, this development is a result of the directives from the government (SOU 2000) requiring that schooling should no longer be conceived as consisting of two parallel activities or responsibilities, where pupil-care initiatives were geared towards those who had special problems or learning difficulties, while the majority could engage in learning without such support. Rather, promoting learning and individual development should be conceived as one activity aimed at promoting what is referred to as 'pupil health'. This is an interesting reconfiguration of responsibilities in the sense that the output of education should not only be knowledge and skills, but also pupils who are in good health psychologically, socially and otherwise, and who are prepared for the strains of modern life.

The study to be reported here concerns how schools handle these institutional responsibilities of promoting pupil health and well-being. One institutional setting of particular relevance in this context in the Swedish school is the so-called 'pupil-health team' (cf. Hjörne and Säljö 2004, 2006, 2008). The terminology used here is interesting. Previously, these teams, operating in very much the same way, were referred to as 'elevvårdsteam', which literally translates into 'pupil-care teams'. The new terminology, however, is based on the metaphor of 'health', and the ideology of promoting health, which can be found elsewhere in society, emphasises preventive work and early intervention,[1] rather than care when the problems have already manifested themselves in a serious manner.

Pupil-health teams meet regularly and their institutional role is to discuss, analyse and take decisions on matters of pupil health and well-being in the school. The questions in focus in this presentation concern how this work is performed and how pupils' problems in school are understood and negotiated. What are the discursive resources the teams use when analysing pupil-health issues and when taking decisions on how to work with problems? How does this focus on health manifest itself in the practices and decisions of the team?

Pupil health in the decentralised school: the case of Sweden

In the 1980s and 1990s, the Swedish school developed into a more goal-and result-oriented organisation. 'Decentralisation' and 'deregulation' became the buzzwords of the day. This trend had clear consequences for management and for leadership (Lindensjö and Lundgren 2000). The reduction of central control, and the corresponding increase in local responsibility, resulted in a focus on the role of the professionals: head teachers, teachers, administrators and others in the local school and school district (Tideman 2000).

According to the present curriculum (Lpo 94: 1994), the 'school has a particular responsibility for pupils, [who] have difficulties reaching the educational goals' (1994: 6, our translation). Moreover, 'everybody who works in school is obliged to pay attention to and assist pupils in need of special support' (1994: 14, our translation). It is also stated that an important task for the school is to inform and co-operate with the parents concerning each pupil's situation in school and the development of his or her knowledge and skills.

The pupil-health team is the context sanctioned to deal with the various kinds of 'learning difficulties' or 'school-problems' that will appear in all schools. Such teams meet at regular intervals, usually every two weeks. Ever since the curriculum of 1962 (Lgr 62: 1962), all schools are obliged to have such a team with various kinds of expertise (SOU 2002: 38). Which kinds of expertise are present in the team vary somewhat depending on the size of the school and other factors. Normally the head teacher will serve as chair, and other members are vice head teacher(s), teachers, special educational teachers, school psychologist, school nurse, speech therapist and so on. In most cases the teams have six to eight members.

The task of the pupil-health team is to 'create a positive environment for learning and to promote the general development of the pupils; that is, to promote their emotional and social development and give support to pupils with special needs' (SOU 2000: 49, our translation). In addition, the pupil-health team is supposed to work preventively and to find pupils who for some reason need support. Hence, the purpose of the work of the team is to suggest and implement measures that will make it possible for the pupil to participate successfully in school activities. At present, and in contrast to what was the case earlier, there are no detailed descriptions from central authorities of exactly what pupils and what problems should be attended to. This is for the local school and school authorities to decide on.

From a historical point of view, it is interesting to see that such ambitions of using schools to promote health in the population are not new. Such strategies were part of the first attempts to establish a modern welfare state during the late nineteenth and the twentieth centuries, when there were special programmes in schools providing poor children with milk, free lunches, school baths and medical attention (cf. SOU 1947: 11; Börjesson 1997). In 1962, there was a dramatic change in the Swedish school system when the so-called parallel school system, which consisted of a basic school (*folkskola*) and various kinds of grammar schools, was reformed to a nine-year comprehensive school (*grundskola*). This reform also changed the responsibilities of schools towards the pupils. An explicit ambition behind the comprehensive school was to do away with the traditions of segregating students on the basis of their gender, class and intellectual capacity. The leading idea was formulated in the political slogan of having 'one school for all'; a school that would offer high-quality education irrespective of the background or capacities of the individual pupil.

The first national curriculum of the comprehensive school was heavily influenced by the thinking of the 1940s, with a clear emphasis on the duty of schools to 'foster' pupils. For example, the pupils received grades in Conduct and Order, respectively (Qvarsebo 2006), as evaluations of their personal behaviours and ability to keep order in their desks, be on time for class and so on. In the late 1960s, there was a significant change in the use of the term 'foster', which was considered too authoritarian and less suited to describing the responsibilities of schools towards children. Instead of fostering children, schools should, in the language of a more child-centred ideology, conceive of themselves as providing rich opportunities for pupils to develop their intellectual and social skills. It was in this Zeitgeist that terms that build on the metaphor of 'pupil care' were introduced. Through moves of this kind, the responsibilities of teachers for the socialisation of children become wider.

At present, and as a side comment, there is a tendency in the Swedish society of reintroducing the use of the term 'fostering' as an appropriate description of what the responsibilities of schools should be, and there has even been a political initiative suggesting that grades in Conduct and Order should be given again.

Categorising 'school problems' in the pupil-health team

From a sociocultural and political point of view, the pupil-health team meeting is an interesting context, since it is here one finds an open and collegial discussion about problems that occur in schools. At the team meetings discursive work that is consequential for pupils, for teachers and for the school gets done: problems are reported and described, explanations are offered, solutions to remedy problems are suggested and decisions on how to proceed are taken. A consequence of this is that collective learning takes place among the participants in the team, a culture of analysing and dealing with school problems will emerge and be reproduced within the institution.

Linguistic categories are central in this institutional practice. In order to perform their duties and to make decisions, the participants have to re-present problems and events in discourse. Issues such as deciding on what the nature of a pupil's difficulties is, and what interventions and resources are reasonable and productive in a particular situation, rely on discursive work (Bowker and Star 2000). In these practices, categories, which are perceived by members as informative, legitimate and productive when understanding what happens in school, will be put to use as part of the 'doing' of pupil health to use ethnomethodological language (Garfinkel 1967).

The activity that the team members engage in can be understood as a particular form of 'people processing' (Cedersund and Säljö 1993; Prottas 1979), and to do this kind of job they use a specific social language (Bakhtin 1986) suited to the needs of the institution and its concerns. According to Bakhtin, a social language has 'the "taste" of profession, a genre, a tendency, a party, a particular work, a particular person' (1981: 293). A social language is 'a discourse peculiar to a specific stratum of society (professional, age group, etc.) within a given social system at a given time' (1981: 430). Thus, in such a perspective, words, utterances and language are considered to be social in a very profound sense, and, following this line of reasoning, a social language is used for meaning-making within 'speech genres', which organise our speech. Speech genres are relatively stable modes of communication within institutions; for example, within hospitals, social services or schools. These genres are generally familiar to the persons involved in these activity systems, but they may be less transparent to an outsider. To be a competent user of a speech genre within a discourse community means that 'one must be more than just a routine reproducer of it; one must in a real sense also play a part in its creative reproduction and sustenance' (Shotter 1993: 16). The question in focus here is what kind of social language and what kinds of categorising practices the members in the pupil-health team consider productive for describing and dealing with the problems they encounter in their daily activities.

Method

The analysis in this chapter is based on empirical data generated from longitudinal case studies of authentic pupil-health team meetings in four schools (2000–2005). (A more detailed presentation of the procedures for data collection and the schools can be found in Hjörne and Säljö 2004, 2006, 2008). The pupils in the schools we have documented were between six and twelve years of age. The meetings have been audio recorded, and we also have access to a range of documentation produced in, and relevant for, the activities of the teams. The work builds on a micro-ethnographic approach (Mehan *et al.* 1986), where the talk and interaction in the pupil-health teams are documented and analysed.

Results

The pupil-health team meeting is an arena where school problems are collectively represented and negotiated, and where decisions are made concerning measures to be taken. This includes attending to, and deciding on, how the available resources are to be used. In other words, the categorical work of analysing and classifying problems is consequential in several respects.

During these meetings, events are presented and constituted in narratives as problems and dilemmas of concern for the members in the team. This is done through using different techniques and rhetorical devices. One example of such a technique that appears frequently is what Pomerantz (1986) refers to as 'extreme case formulations', which are expressions used in order to defend or justify a description or judgement. According to Pomerantz (1986: 222), 'interactants use extreme case formulations when they anticipate or expect their co-interactants to undermine their claims and when they are in adversarial situations'. In the first excerpt from our material, Mary is presented as a girl in 'serious difficulties'.

Mary, ten years old

SPECIAL EDUCATIONAL TEACHER: And, then, we are very concerned about Mary in fourth grade, sort of
PRINCIPAL: She stands out there in the corridor, doesn't she (?)
SPECIAL EDUCATIONAL TEACHER: Yes, she doesn't really know where to go, she has serious difficulties and I feel I haven't had the time for her and in the class she doesn't feel quite well so we try to work on it all the time but you don't manage to make it good enough cause there's complete chaos in her little brain.

The special educational teacher presents Mary as someone they all are *very concerned about.* By doing this she is also justifying why she is bringing the 'case' to the attention of the team meeting. Her introduction of Mary implies that this is something they have to discuss and solve in the team. She continues by presenting the girl as a pupil who does not only have difficulties in school; rather, she has 'serious difficulties' and she claims that 'there's complete chaos in her little brain'. The special educational teacher is not specifying what the girl's difficulties consist of, but she signals that there is something really problematic about her. From an analytical point of view, the special educational teacher uses extreme case formulations through expressions such as 'serious difficulties' and 'complete chaos' when accounting for school problems. Thus, she makes strong claims in a particular direction, and it is difficult for the rest of the team to question or argue with it. The special educational teacher also mentions that she has not 'had the time for her'. This implies that the girl is judged to have special needs, but the special educational teacher has been fully booked. When she adds, 'you don't manage to make it good enough cause there's complete chaos in her little brain', she seems to be legitimising her decision to not give the girl extra support during her learning activities. Through her argumentation she is putting the problem inside the child or, in this case, even more specifically into the girl's 'little brain'.

This claim can also be interpreted as a way for the special educational teacher to argue for her position as the expert in the field of special needs. What is presented is her professional judgement and nobody asks any further questions. What this excerpt illustrates is a clear pattern in the nature of the discourse and the social language that emerges in the teams we have followed: the child's problems are seen as residing inside the child. It is obvious that there is a tradition of adopting a social language that implies explaining school problems rather than describing them. It is interesting to observe that there are no further discussions of the girl's problems, and nothing is said about the learning situation in the classroom. Somewhat paradoxically, and in spite of the fact that most of the team members are teachers, the teaching and learning situation is seldom considered as a significant part of the picture when it comes to understanding pupils' problems in school. In a systematic manner, teaching practices and their potential consequences are made invisible.

The special educational teacher continues her argumentation in the same meeting by once again pointing out that she is 'concerned about Mary'.

Mary, ten years old (cont.)

SPECIAL EDUCATIONAL TEACHER: Well, I'm concerned about Mary, they were concerned when she went to pre-school 'cos then she was standing on the side and didn't play with the other children. Then she has sort of started to play a bit and has friends and so on, but on the other hand this sort of chaos she has, which gets her to do nothing and she doesn't know what she is supposed to do and her motor-function is extremely poor and she has extremely poor perception ehh, and now, she has learned to read, she got some support from me when she was little and 'boom' it started like that, very fast like verbally and from a linguistic point of view she's fairly, fairly strong, you can see it in the

lower grade when it came to breaking the code and so. But comprehension and thoughts that's really, that's really a chaos in this girl, and
as I mentioned she keeps standing in the stairs, she can stand there
for half a day if nobody is helping her and mostly nobody does, she's
not seen.

The special educational teacher continues to elaborate on 'this chaos
she has', and she uses this metaphor as a social fact about the child. In her
narrative, she describes 'this chaos' as something that 'gets her to do
nothing', and 'she doesn't know what to do'. The impression given is that
this 'chaos' is something that exists within Mary without any obvious relationship to her teachers, friends or the situations she encounters. It is
something 'inside' the girl and, according to the special educational
teacher, the problems are visible in her lack of 'comprehension and
thoughts'. Furthermore, the girl is described as having 'extremely poor
perception' and 'her motor-function is extremely poor'. It is worth noticing that none of the other team members asks for further clarifications or
goes into issues that concern contextual factors. Obviously, Mary has
learned how to read, and there seem to be no obvious learning problems
in a more conventional sense. There is no more detailed account of how
and when the problems appear, or how they impact her learning. Instead
the main problem is described as the 'chaos in her little brain', which is a
rather vague, but institutionally powerful, account. Thus, her problems
are not seen as responses to what goes on in school or what is happening
elsewhere in her life; rather they are placed 'beneath the skin and between
the ears' of the girl (Mehan 1993: 241).

In the next excerpt, the team members discuss Muhammed, who is
claimed to have some difficulties in school that need to be attended to.

Muhammed, six years old

TEACHER: Concerning Muhammed, it's difficult but it works you can say
he is attending every day, he likes it very much here in our school he
… but (.) what we have noticed is that he needs very much (.) much
clarity he needs

SCHOOL NURSE: Excuse me, in what class is he?

TEACHER: He is a pre-school child, in grade zero we can say, he has
difficulties to concentrate, he has difficulties, but I don't know really,
it's difficult to get a handle on what his difficulties are, but I don't
know really, but what we think then is that he cannot manage, you
soon observe that he certainly can, so, what you think at first is turned
upside down, but definitely he has big, big, big concentration-
problems to sit, he has very (..) sometimes you wonder if he understands what you mean, he has great problems with that.

The teacher describes Muhammed's problems by saying that 'it's difficult to get a handle on what his difficulties are'. Through this comment
she opens up for the team to explain and categorise what kind of problem
might be relevant to consider. It is unclear what the boy's difficulties
consist of. He is described as having 'difficulties to concentrate' without
any further details about what this implies. This type of rather vague
description is frequent in these meetings (see, for example, Hjörne and
Säljö 2004). What is interesting in this case is that it is the class teacher
who presents the boy and the problems he is claimed to have. Generally,
the teacher of a particular child is not present during the meetings, and
this implies that the team members often rely on what in the literature is
referred to as 'reported speech' (Vološinov 1973).

In spite of the fact that the teacher has first-hand information of
Muhammed's activities in school, she does not include issues of instruction, pedagogy or classroom activities in her analysis of his problems.
Instead her accounting strategy implies that the problems are placed
inside the child, which may be seen as accommodating to the social language that dominates the meetings. Furthermore, it is interesting to note
that the last expression 'sometimes you wonder if he understands what
you mean, he has great problems with that' is mentioned in passing and
only as a short comment. Considering that the boy obviously has an immi-
grant background, it is astonishing that this issue is not made part of the
problem of describing and analysing the difficulties that occur.

In the next excerpt, the team is invoking a neuropsychiatric diagnosis
as an explanation of educational difficulties.

Robert, seven years old

SCHOOL NURSE: Robert, at even the smallest difficulty then he needs extra
    time (.) and you need to explain very carefully (.) and carefully
    explain what could happen
PRINCIPAL: He needs long-term planning all the time (?)
VICE PRINCIPAL: The mother wonders if it could be ADHD[2] or something
    like that (.) she has also expressed that something is wrong ehh, with
    him (.) thus, it's [something]
SEVERAL: [mmm]
PSYCHOLOGIST: But then you might start a [screening] (.) around this
SEVERAL: [mmm]

The school nurse is describing Robert as a boy who 'needs extra time
(.) and you need to explain very carefully'. The vice principal adds that
'the mother wonders if it could be ADHD'. Thus, the problems immediately move into the child. In this case the vice principal is using a neuropsychiatric diagnosis as a relevant explanation for understanding the

problems observed. Following the logic of the social language developed in the context of special educational teaching makes the process quick. Additionally, the participants invoke a comment made by the mother as relevant when arguing for ADHD. This use of reported speech is very effective in this context, since it makes it clear that there will be no difficulties in getting consent from the parents to have Robert examined for a diagnosis. It is interesting to note how quickly the team members come to an agreement when the psychologist says that 'you might start a [screening] (.) around this'. At this stage, the members do not perceive that there is any need to elaborate this case any further and, for instance, go into what is happening in the classroom. They are now at a stage where they can initiate an examination for a suspected neuropsychiatric disorder.

Discussion

The main point of these short excerpts from our extensive material is to illustrate some features of the discourse that dominate the pupil-health teams, and to relate this to the overall ambition of promoting pupil health. In relation to our observations, we want to make some points. At first, a clear result is that school problems are individualised and become located 'beneath the skin and between the ears' (Mehan 1993: 241) of the pupil. Thus, the logic of the professional reasoning is that the problems end up inside the pupils as alleged personal deficiencies in intellectual, social or other capacities. The analytical work engaged in is rarely focused on the concrete difficulties that children have in class or in their life outside school. Relational problems between teachers and pupils are not considered as relevant for understanding school difficulties. Furthermore, the explanations used increasingly seem to draw on modern neuropsychiatric concepts, which also imply that the problems are placed inside the child. The flexibility of these concepts in interpreting behaviours makes them into important resources for reaching consensus in the team meetings. The process seems to be focused on explaining deviant behaviours/activities and to locate the causes inside the child, rather than describing and analysing them as contextual and relational problems and as occasioned by the teaching or what happens in class (or in other settings). Invoking neuropsychiatric categories seems to be a particularly clear illustration of the processes that the philosopher Ian Hacking (1995, 1999) refers to as '*the looping effects of human kinds*' (1999: 35, italics in original). In the discussions, the members are continuously engaged in 'kind-making' in Hacking's sense, and the neuropsychiatric categories appear as powerful resources that close the gap for the participants between the reports given and institutionally relevant categorizations.

Second, the nature of the discursive work engaged in by the teams can be understood in terms of the distinction suggested by Mason (2002) between providing accounts *for* and accounts *of* educational difficulties. Accounting *for* implies invoking explanations of what is observed, while accounting *of* implies analysing and describing problems in some detail before deciding on potential causes of what is observed. The teams are almost exclusively engaged in accounting *for* pupil difficulties by invoking explanations that individualise what happens; a particular personality trait is considered sufficient for understanding the roots of the problems. The problems are accounted for by claiming, as in the case of Mary (in excerpts 1 and 2), that she 'has serious difficulties, it's complete chaos in her little brain, her motor-function is extremely poor and she has extremely poor perception, from a linguistic point of view she is fairly, fairly strong, but comprehension and thoughts that's really a chaos in this girl'. Thus, the team members hardly ever inquire into the circumstances of when and how problems occur, how they develop and how one could deal with them. The problems accounted for are rarely contextualised as responses to pedagogical practices, teachers' activities or other aspects of life in the classroom. Instead, such contextual features are made invisible in the discussions, which are focused on giving explanations, i.e. accounting *for*, in Mason's terminology. Furthermore, there are hardly any discussions of in what sense pedagogical practices do not suit a particular pupil, or in what sense they could be modified so as to support pupils with difficulties. There is almost no account of what attempts have been made to rectify the problems.

Furthermore, the social language that dominates the discourse, and that is taken for granted by the participants as an unproblematic tool for reaching consensus, focuses on shortcomings of the children. Thus, the speech genre developed in this context mainly consists of negative descriptions of children's capacities, while the practices in school are never analysed in a critical fashion. Not even those team members who have a responsibility for developing pedagogical practices make use of the opportunity to suggest alternative strategies and modes of organising teaching and learning. In this sense, in organizational terms, the meetings seem to function in a conservative manner where alternatives to current practices are not considered.

Considering the purpose of the pupil-health team to promote health and well-being among the children, it is difficult to see how this could be realised within this accounting *for* strategy which implies moving the problems into the brains and personalities of children. By almost exclusively focusing on children's alleged intellectual and personal shortcomings, instead of analysing pedagogical issues and the role of the teacher and the family, the impetus for developing school practices is weak. In all important respects, these manners of explaining school difficulties are rooted in the traditional 'defective child' discourse that has been part of the institution of schooling for a long time. This furthermore implies that the attempts to broaden the responsibilities for pupil health that schools have been given are not visible in the discourse which is used in the pupil-health team for understanding problems that emerge. The social language employed implies naming and individualising children's problems; a multi-faceted and complex situation is transformed into a dysfunction within the child, rather than an opportunity for the school to adjust its pedagogical practices to support the child. It seems that the health team, instead of opening up conversations that can lead to paying attention to and assisting 'pupils in need of special support' (Lpo 94 1994: 14), by locating the problem within the child, avoided making additional welfare demands on the school.

These findings echo those from a study of pupil-welfare systems in England (Edwards *et al.* in press) where recent emphases on pupils' well-being have been absorbed into the roles of new specialist workers (cf. special educational teachers and special teachers in the Swedish system) and have led to a restricting of teachers' work to efficient curriculum delivery and assessment. These moves appear to be limiting the opportunity for teachers to learn from the expertise of the health team, and similar groups in the English system, and to encourage a less than responsive pedagogy.

As an activity system, schooling has to cope with very different, and sometimes conflicting, demands. Any normative claims as to how to deal with various dilemmas will have to take this into account. The creation of a pupil-health system of the kind we have studied is an important step in the process of instituting arenas where significant events and features in school are publicly and openly attended to. Knowing emerges from such collective practices. However, the potentials of these arenas as contexts in which practices of schooling, and responses by pupils to these, are critically explored do not seem to be fully exploited. To deepen the understanding of how to convert such knowing into viable pedagogical practices that are accepted by teachers and pupils is a task that requires organisational learning. To be productive, the reasoning has to be much more complex, innovative and strategic, and it must not reproduce the accounting *for* patterns of individualising children's problems that we have documented. This is a major challenge for the school in which the health team was working, but one which, if taken up, may lead to teachers' learning and more responsive pedagogies with pupils who have difficulties.

Appendix: transcript symbols

[ ]   simultaneous talk
        interruption, the speaker interrupts him/herself at the end of a word
...   untimed pause
(...)   indicates that some talk is left out
?   marks intonation of a question
!   indicates an animated tone

,   continuing intonation
UPPER-CASE loud talk
(()) comments on how something is said, for example 'inaudibly'
Underlining marks emphasis

Notes

1 There may be slight differences in the connotations of the terms 'hälsa' in Swedish and 'health' in English. The Swedish term is now used with very broad connotations in the context of health promotion, and a more informative translation of the expression 'pupil-health team' would probably be 'pupil-health-and-welfare team'. However, the term 'pupil-health team' (elevhälsoteam) has been consciously chosen by the authorities to point to the idea of health promotion and preventive work that is meant to alleviate problems before they become too severe.
2 The Swedish abbreviation used is DAMP, which is a diagnosis quite close to ADHD. DAMP was used previously but has now largely disappeared.

References

Bakhtin, M.M. (1981) The dialogic imagination: four essays by M.M. Bakhtin (ed. M. Holquist). Austin, TX: University of Texas Press.

Bakhtin, M.M. (1986) Speech genres and other late essays. Austin, TX: University of Texas Press.

Börjesson, M. (1997) Om skolbarns olikheter: Diskurser kring 'särskilda behov' i skolan – med historiska jämförelsepunkter [On differences between children: discourses about 'special needs' in the school – with historical comparisons]. Stockholm: Liber.

Bowker, G. and Star, S.L. (2000) Sorting things out: classification and its consequences. Cambridge, MA: MIT Press.

Cedersund, E. and Säljö, R. (1993) 'Bureaucratic discourse, conversational space and the concept of voice', Semiotica, 97, 79–101.

Edwards, A. (2004) 'The new multi-agency working: collaborating to prevent the social exclusion of children and families', Journal of Integrated Care, 12(5), 3–9.

Edwards, A., Lunt, I. and Stamou, E. (in press) 'Inter-professional work and expertise: new roles at the boundaries of schools', British Educational Research Journal.

Gadd, C.J. (1956) Teachers and students in the oldest schools. London: School of Oriental and African Studies, University of London.

Garfinkel, H. (1967) Studies in ethnomethodology. Englewood Cliffs, NJ: Prentice-Hall.

Hacking, I. (1995) 'The looping effects of human kinds', in D. Sperber, D. Premack and A.J. Premack (eds) Causal cognition: a multi-disciplinary approach. Oxford: Clarendon Press, pp. 351–394.

Hacking, I. (1999) The social construction of what? Cambridge, MA: Harvard University Press.

Hjörne, E. (2005) 'Negotiating the "problem-child" in school: child identity, parenting and institutional agendas', Qualitative Social Work, 4(4), 489–507.

Hjörne, E. and Säljö, R. (2004) The pupil welfare team as a discourse community: accounting for school problems, Linguistics and Education, 15, 321–338.

Hjörne, E. and Säljö, R. (2006) '"There is something about Julia": symptoms, categories and the process of invoking ADHD in the Swedish school', in

H. Lauder, P. Brown, J.-A. Dillabough and A.H. Halsey (eds) *Education, globalization and social change.* Oxford: Oxford University Press, pp. 602–616.

Hjörne, E. and Säljö, R. (2008) *Att platsa i en skola för alla. Elevhälsa och förhandling om normalitet i den svenska skolan* [*To qualify for 'a school for all': pupil health and the negotiation about normality in the Swedish school*]. Stockholm: Norstedts Akademiska Förlag.

Kramer, S.N. (1949) *Schooldays: a Sumerian composition relating to the education of a scribe.* Philadelphia, PA: The University Museum, University of Pennsylvania.

Lindensjö, B. and Lundgren, U.P. (2000) *Utbildningsreformer och politisk styrning* [*Educational reforms and political steering*]. Stockholm: HLS förlag.

Lgr 62. (1962) *Läroplan för grundskolan* [*Curriculum for the compulsory school*]. Stockholm: Kungliga Skolöverstyrelsen.

Lpo 94. (1994) *Läroplan för det obligatoriska skolväsendet, förskoleklassen och fritidshemmet* [*Curriculum for the compulsory school system including preschool and after-school centres*]. Stockholm: Utbildningsdepartementet.

Mason, J. (2002) *Researching your own practice: the discipline of noticing.* London: Routledge/Falmer.

Mehan, H. (1993) 'Beneath the skin and between the ears: a case study in the politics of representation', in S. Chaiklin and J. Lave (eds) *Understanding practice: perspectives on activity and context.* Cambridge, MA: Cambridge University Press, pp. 241–269.

Mehan, H., Hertweck, A. and Meihls, J.L. (1986) *Handicapping the handicapped: decision-making in students' educational careers.* Stanford, CA: Stanford University Press.

Pomerantz, A. (1986) 'Extreme case formulations: a way of legitimizing claims', *Human Studies,* 9(1): 219–229.

Prottas, J.M. (1979) *People-processing: the street-level bureaucrat in public service bureaucracies.* Lexington, IN: Lexington Books.

Qvarsebo, J. (2006) *Skolbarnets fostran: enhetsskolan, agan och politiken om barnet 1946-. 1962* [*Fostering the schoolchild: the comprehensive school, corporal punishment and the politics of the child 1946–1962*]. Linköping: Tema Barn, Linköpings universitet.

Shotter, J. (1993) *Cultural politics of everyday life.* Buckingham: Open University Press.

SOU (1947) *Utredning och förslag rörande vissa socialpedagogiska anordningar inom skolväsendet: Statens offentliga utredningar* [*Investigation and suggestions concerning social-pedagogical arrangements within school: the official investigations of the government*]. (SOU 1947:11). Stockholm: Esselte.

SOU (2000) *Från dubbla spår till elevhälsa i en skola som främjar lust att lära, hälsa och utveckling: statens offentliga utredningar* [*From double tracks to pupils' health in a school promoting the will to learn, health and development: The official investigations of the government*]. (SOU 2000:19). Stockholm: Liber.

SOU (2002) *Skollag för kvalitet och likvärdighet: statens offentliga utredningar* [*The Education Act for Quality and Equality: the official investigations of the government*]. (SOU 2002:121). Stockholm: Fritzes.

Tideman, M. (2000) *Normalisering och kategorisering: om handikappideologi och välfärdspolitik i teori och praktik för personer med utvecklingsstörning* [*Normalization and categorization: on disability ideology and welfare policy in theory and practice for intellectually disabled persons*]. Lund: Studentlitteratur.

Vološinov, V.N. (1973) *Marxism and the philosophy of language.* New York: Seminar Press.

Part II

A cultural-historical methodological perspective

Chapter 7

Studying the process of change

The double stimulation strategy in teacher education research

Viv Ellis

It is only in movement that a body shows what it is.

(Vygotsky 1978: 65)

This chapter focuses on one of Vygotsky's key methodological concepts: the double stimulation strategy (Vygotsky 1978, 1987, 1999), a radical re-conceptualisation of the behaviourist experimental method that makes the unit of analysis the process or activity of engaging with a task rather than merely the outcome or product. In such a re-conceptualisation, the researcher's analytic gaze is directed at the mediation of the subject's or participant's activity by physical or psychological tools. For Vygotsky, the psychological tool of principal interest was language, principally spoken but also written (Vygotsky 1986), although his work is characterised by attention at different times to social as well as semiotic mediation and the associated concept of the 'zone of proximal development' (Moll 1990; Vygotsky 1978). Moreover, this re-conceptualisation challenges the researcher to see psychological processes as historical and dynamic, 'undergoing changes right before one's eyes' (Vygotsky 1978: 61) and, further still, capable of being provoked by the researcher.

In illustrating the significance of this methodological concept in researching teacher education and development, I will refer to two examples from my work: first, a study of beginning English teachers' concept formation and conceptual development (Ellis 2007a, 2007b); and, second, a formative intervention into the organisational learning of a school–university teacher education partnership (Ellis 2008, 2007c). The argument of the chapter is that the double stimulation strategy is useful and productive in conceptualising and designing research into teacher learning that seeks to explain its complexity and to trace the history of its development. The two illustrations will also reflect the different emphases and shifts in Vygotsky's work from semiotic to social processes of mediation and the potential of the research method itself to stimulate positive change.

The power of stimulus-means to organise and reveal

In Vygotsky's texts, the double stimulation strategy is variously referred to as 'the functional method of dual stimulation' (e.g. Vygotsky 1987), 'the instrumental method' (e.g. Vygotsky 1978, 1999) and by other formulations (see Engeström 2007: 364). For consistency's sake, I will use the phrase 'double stimulation strategy' throughout this chapter to represent the way in which researchers give their research participants a means of working on a problem or engaging in a task. The task or problem Vygotsky referred to as the 'stimulus-end' (1978), and the potentially problem-solving tools donated as the 'stimulus-means'. In his own experiments, he used the double stimulation strategy to reveal the ways in which children made sense of the worlds they were acting in:

> We simultaneously offer a second series of stimuli that have a special function. In this way, we are able to study the process of accomplishing a task by the aid of specific auxiliary means: thus we are able to discover the inner structure and development of higher mental processes.
>
> (Vygotsky 1978: 74)

The ways in which the research subjects use the 'second-series of stimuli' or 'auxiliary means' to work on the object or problem-space – the 'first' stimuli or stimulus-end – revealed for Vygotsky the subjects' 'higher mental functions' (1987, 1997), how they construct and reconstruct the object of activity and the culturally and historically mediating function of the stimulus-means. The researcher's interest is in how they use the donated tools, the sense they make of them, the ways in which their activity is shaped by the tool-use and, potentially, the ways in which subjects re-shape the meaning of the tools – all of which is studied in relation to how the subjects perceive and are motivated by the object. An example relevant to the study of teacher learning might be a researcher's introduction of an unfamiliar lesson-planning template as a 'second series of stimuli' into the planning processes of teachers in order to reveal how they understand the concept of curriculum or the materiality of the students they are teaching.

Vygotsky distinguished between degrees of 'ready-made'-ness in stimulus-means and explained the distinction thus:

> we do not necessarily have to present to the subject a prepared external means with which we might solve the proposed problem.... In not giving the child a ready symbol, we could trace the way all the essential mechanisms of the complex symbolic activity of the child develop during the spontaneous expanding of the devices he used.
>
> (Vygotsky 1999: 60)

In other words, Vygotsky left open the possibility, taken up by Wertsch in his distinction between explicit and implicit mediation (Wertsch 2007), that less prepared or 'ready-made' means might be particularly effective in enabling the researcher to trace 'complex symbolic activity' by opening up more space for subjects' agency and providing greater opportunities for engaging in difficult but generative problem-solving activities.

Drawing the concepts of subject English

Teachers' subject (or content) knowledge continues to be of perennial interest to policy-makers and researchers, specifically in relation to measures of the 'effectiveness' of teaching (cf. Darling-Hammond and Youngs 2002; Poulson 2001; Wilson *et al.* 2002). Very often, in both the research literature and policy, knowledge is understood from an objectivist standpoint (Edwards *et al.* 2002; Ellis 2007b): subject knowledge becomes a 'thing', some sort of viscous fluid that can be poured from head-to-head, 'boosted', 'topped-up' and 'audited', all words used in the teacher education policy in England (DfES 1998a). The corollary in terms of teachers' learning is an acquisitive view where learning becomes the accumulation of various inputs, 'brick-by-brick', something Kelly referred to as 'accumulative fragmentalism' (1963). A cultural-historical activity theory perspective would instead propose a view of knowledge as something that is accessed and developed in joint work on a potentially shared object of activity, where object is defined, after Leont'ev (1978), as an aspect of the social world that is perceived as a need or motive, as a shared 'concern ... generator and focus of attention' (Engeström 2008: 3). Similarly, a cultural-historical perspective seeks to understand the situatedness of knowledge and the participatory nature of learning, not in terms of knowledge being relativistically situation-bound or learning merely as reproduction, but in trying to explain the relationship between local activity by human agents in specific settings and the historical, culture-making processes that allow ideas to travel (cf. Lave 1988; Toulmin 1999). This Vygotskian line of thinking suggests that knowledge exists as much among participants in a field as it does within them and that our 'conceptual inheritance is communal' (Toulmin 1972: 5).

In the early 2000s, I conducted an in-depth study of a small sample of high school English teachers through their one year graduate-level teacher education programme and into their first year of employment (Ellis 2007a). My interest was in tracing their conceptual development in relation to the subject they were teaching (English), particularly the knowledge that constituted the subject, and in trying to understand how this development was related to their movement across the multiple settings for teacher learning (in each case, a university-based programme and at least three different schools). Data were generated over a two-year period through a series of research interviews, narrative writing by the teachers, the collection of documents and artefacts, some observations and a drawing task. The drawing task took place during each of the research interviews and the teachers were asked to draw a picture of the areas of English subject knowledge and how they might be related. They were encouraged to speak as they drew, and after they completed the drawing, I introduced their previous drawings and asked them to reflect on the images they had produced thus far over the period of the research.

Grossman had used a drawing task in her research with a small sample of US English teachers in the late 1980s (Grossman 1990), also questioning the nature of teacher knowledge and development, and her work was influential on me. However, it seems that the task was only used once, and it is not clear what part, if any, these data played in Grossman's analysis. Drawing was conceptualised in my research design as a mediational means the teachers were asked to use to make sense of the research problem – the nature and constitution of English subject knowledge and its development in individual teachers. My interest as a researcher was in the process of mediation and how this process enabled the teachers to construct and reconstruct the problem or object. In this way, through attention to the relationship between mediational means and interpretation of the object, the use of drawing task can be understood as an instance of the double stimulation strategy. Asking these teachers to draw in the context of the research interviews did not arise from any belief that drawings would provide me with more 'natural' or authentic insights into the participants' thinking than their spoken language or that the affordances of graphical representation were greater. Nonetheless, it is interesting to note that drawing is a less 'ready-made' stimulus-means than the physical artefact of the lesson-planning template referred to in the earlier example, perhaps especially for subjects who do not draw every day.

This use of drawing in a double stimulation strategy also differs from uses of superficially similar research methods. It is not 'concept mapping' (Novak and Gowin 1984) in the cognitivist tradition, for example, and the teachers were not asked to produce a concept map, a graphical genre with which they might have been familiar. The teachers in my study had more relative freedom to interpret the invitation to draw as they wished. More fundamentally, the drawing of an image, whether a map or something else, was not conceptualised as a direct representation of the teachers' thinking, as in the concept-mapping tradition. And there was no interest on my part in judging the extent to which the organisation and hierarchy of concepts and ideas in the drawing corresponded to my own or any 'agreed' understanding of that organisation or hierarchy. In an example from ICT education research, drawings made by a large sample of children in the UK about their understandings of new technologies in their lives were regarded as 'externalised representations' of these children's minds (Mavers *et al.* 2002; Pearson and Somekh 2003). The researchers inferred associations between the complexity of the drawings and the complexity of the minds from which they had 'sprung'. In this research – and often in research that uses formal concept mapping as a method – the valorisation of linear connectivity (multiple connections between concepts – nodes – made by straight lines) reflects the assumption that the more lines between the nodes, the more sophisticated the subject's concept formation. Even at a purely representational level, this conception does not allow for complexity to be more than two-dimensional. The key methodological difference, however, is that these images are treated as products or outputs to study; there is no attention to the process of making the image and how this process relates to the meaning of the research problem. A drawing task of this sort, in other words, is not conceptualised as an opportunity to study semiotic mediation, as it was in my research design.

Through an analysis of the image-making in the research interview situation (i.e. through observing the process and studying the talk involved around the image itself), it was possible to understand the conceptual development of these teachers as arising out of dispositionally influenced, agentic participation in the practices of multiple settings, practices that stood in a dialectical relationship with the tools and resources of a cultural arena (English teaching) and a cultural identity (the figure of the English teacher) (see Ellis 2007a: 65–69, 148–151 for an account of the analytic procedures). In terms of the organisation of the drawn images, the development of my sample of teachers' images over the two-year period reflected a messy and non-linear understanding of development: there was a change in what I referred to as the image's 'organisational type' over the period, either from a bounded image to an un-bounded one or vice versa; the number of areas of subject knowledge in the drawings (the nodes or concepts) decreased over the period; and the measure of linear connectivity (a measure of the relationships between areas of the image represented by straight lines) also decreased (ibid.: 149).

To this extent, a traditional analysis of the images as concept maps might have concluded that the teachers' understandings were becoming less complex, less connected and more idiosyncratic. So, in order to try to understand the nature of these teachers' conceptual development it was necessary to pay attention to the process of drawing and the talk around the drawing process, as well as the image itself. In other words, the process of semiotic mediation in visual and verbal modes was of vital interest.

It was possible, over the period of the research, to notice how the teachers, having recalled from memory some aspects of images previously drawn, came to consciously manipulate the images at the level of organisation and iconography. One teacher referred to a previous image as 'more like a slice of pie' and another spoke in the interview just prior to the drawing task about eagerly anticipating her new opportunity to draw and having 'rehearsed it in [her] head'. In 'Ann's' case, she herself noticed the shift from an unbounded image to a bounded one over the first year of the research and subsequently to attention to the boundary of the image itself in year two (see Figures 7.1 and 7.2). She explained that the zigzag lines that form the boundary around the concepts (the boundary being named 'English') were intended to indicate 'where the definitions

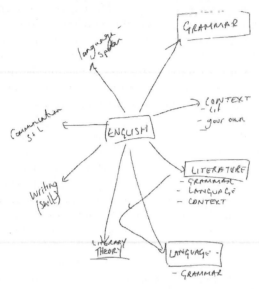

Figure 7.1 Ann: first image (source: Ellis 2007; reproduced by kind permission of Continuum International Publishing Group).

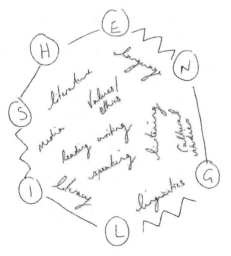

Figure 7.2 Ann: final image (source: Ellis 2007; reproduced by kind permission of Continuum International Publishing Group).

are slightly breaking down'. She recognised that by not making 'English' a strong boundary she was 'question[ing] the very concepts which create the complex question of what English does and what it should incorporate' (ibid.: 87).

Over the period of the research, it was possible to notice the increasingly conscious control of the tool of drawing by the teachers. Although there may have been some initial anxiety about the unfamiliarity of the mode (and continuing aesthetic dissatisfaction with the completed images at some times), the tool had become to a greater extent 'ingrowing' (Leont'ev 1997: 22), a word that describes the taking over and manipulation (the appropriation) of the mediational means in coming to understand the object. Indeed, the teachers developed affective responses to their drawings that reflected the ways in which they constructed this object – their concept formation and development in relation to the subject 'English'. In the case of 'Liz', she described the image she produced in the final research interview at the end of year two as 'floaty floaty' and was unhappy at what she perceived to be a lack of structure (see Figures 7.3 and 7.4). She said she preferred the image produced at the end of the first year: 'I feel like it ought to be more me, the togetherness, the structured' (Ellis 2007a: 132).

Yet she seemed reassured by the, for her, surprising continuity between the very first image she had produced and the last in the use of the heart icon, even though in the discourse of the interview it became apparent the heart meant different things at different times. In the final interview, the heart icon was implicated in the shifting development of her identity as a 'sad ... English teacher' ('sad' in this context meaning deserving of pity, but in a self-knowing way): 'Well, I think your students start seeing you as sad as you talk about books all the time and say "here's ma'am going off on one"' (Ellis 2007a: 131). Tracing the meaning of the heart icon in Liz's drawn images was useful in trying to explain the relationship between the various subject concepts of English and her shifting cultural identity as an English teacher. Liz knew that the heart icon was something of a cliché but it became a meaningfully ironic part of the complex symbolic activity of her engagement with the research problem.

Conceptualising the drawing task as stimulus-means in a double stimulation strategy enabled me as researcher to focus on mediating processes as the tool of drawing 'grew into' the teachers' work on the research problem.

Methodologically, this study raises interesting questions about complex semiotic processes and interrelationships between visual and verbal modes. Substantively, the drawing task was useful in explaining the complex, recursive and affective nature of these teachers' conceptual development, elaborating an understanding of development as a 'twisting path' (Vygotsky 1987; see also Smagorinsky et al. 2003), constituted by a 'cacophony of

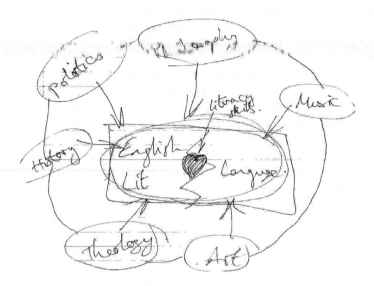

Figure 7.3 Liz: first image (source: Ellis 2007; reproduced by kind permission of Continuum International Publishing Group).

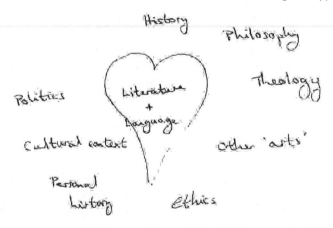

Figure 7.4 Liz: final image (source: Ellis 2007; reproduced by kind permission of Continuum International Publishing Group).

beckonings' (Britzman 2003: 250) from across the multiple settings for teacher learning.

The movement of these teachers across the different settings for practice (university programmes, school English departments) was significant or 'consequential' (Beach 1999, 2003) in terms of their English subject knowledge and their identities as English teachers. Indeed, my research conceptualised subject knowledge as a dynamic, sociohistorical phenomenon that was 'stretched over' (Lave 1988) the individual teacher, their environments and the communal inheritance of English teaching as a cultural field. The use of drawing within a double stimulation strategy was generative in revealing how these transitions across settings for practice were meaningful in terms of the research problem. The study also suggested the potential of these points of transition as spaces for teacher learning and it to this potential that I turn in the next section.

Developmental work research: provoking change to theorise practice – and improve it

England offers an interesting example of an essentially school-based form of teacher education where, at the graduate level, policy dictates that 24 weeks out of the 36-week course must be spent in the school setting (DES 1992). Schools and university departments of education are required to come together to form teacher education partnerships within which workplace mentoring of student teachers is provided by the school, and the university provides a related academic programme and takes lead responsibility for organisation and quality assurance. These partnerships might be described as 'hybrid organisations' (Pirkkalainen and Kaatrakoski 2007) in that they are occasions for joint work on a potentially shared object (the pre-service education of teachers) by constituent organisations (schools and universities) that have historically developed quite different and potentially contradictory motives, tools, rules and divisions of labour.

Recognising the 'consequential transitions' (Beach 1999, 2003) between these constituent parts as spaces for organizational as well as individual teacher learning led me to design a participatory intervention that drew on the Developmental Work Research (DWR) methodology of Engeström (1991, 1993, 1999, 2007). Engeström describes DWR as an explicit application of Vygotsky's double stimulation strategy where the stimulus-means of the conceptual tools of activity theory are donated to participants in order to help them work on a problem of practice (Engeström 2007).

The claims for DWR as a formative methodology are that it enables participants to do more than simply work on improving their own performance through action research methods or through participation in a researcher-led design experiment (ibid.). DWR claims to develop understanding among participants of how their existing practices and discourses have been shaped culturally and historically so that they might be worked on and developed at the level of the social system. This critical understanding, it is claimed, is stimulated by the power of the conceptual tools of activity theory (represented by the triangular image of the activity system) in helping participants to analyse how the object of their collective activity is constructed, how rules and a division of labour have emerged historically within a community of practitioners and how cultural tools are appropriated by members of that community – *and* how these might be changed for the better. Engeström has recently written for the first time at length about the methodology of DWR, and readers are encouraged to turn to his authoritative account for detailed procedures (ibid.: 370–382). In brief, the method can be summarised as depicted in Figure 7.5.

A data-driven, developmental workshop (Change Laboratory) of participating practitioners is facilitated by one or more 'researcher-interventionists'. Notes are taken of the group's interactions as well as a video-recording of the whole event. The researcher introduces evidence of current practices and discourses using one of three displays known as the 'mirror'. Readers will note from Engeström's diagram reproduced here as Figure 7.5 that data sources such as 'customer feedback' and 'statistics' reflect the use of DWR in commercial consultancy settings in Finland. The 'mirror data' presented – often in the form of video-recordings – are selected in order to highlight contradictions and disturbances in the activity systems.

Another display (labelled 'model, vision') is used for theoretical analysis of the data with the practitioners using the activity system triangle. The third display, 'ideas, tools', is used for recording key realisations or con-

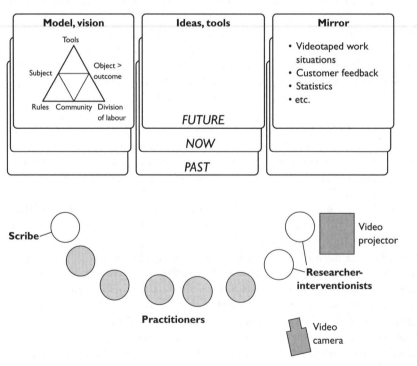

Figure 7.5 Prototypical layout of the Change Laboratory (source: Engeström 2007; reproduced by kind permission of Cambridge University Press).

cepts in the emerging analysis as well as potential 'solutions'. The displays have three historical layers – 'past, now, future' – and the researcher-interventionists begin with the present problem, seek the roots of this problem historically and then model or 'envision' future designs for a re-configured practice. Solutions and visions are not expressed in absolute terms but as partial and contingent, and the individual Change Laboratory is situated within a series of such workshops, part of a 'cycle of expansive learning' (ibid.: 372; see also Engeström 1991, 1996), a recursive process of interrogating current practices, modelling new designs, implementa-tion and further interrogation. Even from this brief explanation, it might be apparent that DWR, as initiated and elaborated by Engeström and his colleagues, has become increasingly systematised as a genre or 'brand' of research.

My own research design worked with the ideas of the DWR methodol-ogy in a considerably looser fashion but one which, I believe, remained true both to the spirit of the double stimulation strategy of Vygotsky's developmental project and to the collectivist, historicizing, change-oriented intent of Engeström's version of activity theory (see Ellis 2008 for a discussion of the design and analysis). Over an initial period of two years, I worked with a group of four high school English departments in the context of a pre-service teacher education partnership. Each English department was asked to identify a problem of professional practice that it wished to work on, something that was meaningful and significant on its own terms and that would form the basis of some change-oriented work with pre-service teachers and myself as the university-based teacher educa-tor. The publicised invitation was to develop the teacher education part-nership as well as the specific practices chosen by the four constituent English departments. The aim was to open out practice for examination in the spaces between the constituent parts of the hybrid organisation of the teacher education partnership so that the organisation itself could learn and its work on teacher education could improve.

The Change Laboratories of the DWR methodology were therefore conceptualised as mediating communicative spaces or 'boundary zones' (Engeström 2007; Wenger *et al.* 2002) *with* which and *in* which to work on the research problem (conceptualised as the problem of practice). Change Laboratories were held approximately every two months, although the first year of the intervention was principally used to build the sort of relationships and shared knowledge that would allow the project to have some chance of success. Mirror data of current practices and disturbances, contradictions and tensions were generated by the pre-service teachers and by a research assistant in each of the school settings. The Change Lab-oratories were facilitated by me with the research assistant as scribe. No video data were generated, and the Change Laboratories themselves were not video-recorded. I used flip charts and large sheets of paper as 'models, visions' and 'ideas, tools' displays, and either an overhead or digital projector to display mirror data (transcripts of lesson observations and interviews as well as visual images such as scans of documents or photographs of artefacts and situations).

There were therefore significant differences between my approach and Engeström's DWR methodology in its fullest, recent iteration. First, as the researcher-interventionist, I was implicated in the activity systems under study as I was also a participating teacher educator; second, the duration of the intervention was considerably longer than most DWR interventions in Engeström's research centre; third, the type of data generated was somewhat different in that I did not work with video and its different and perhaps enhanced affordances as data. Nevertheless, in working with participants on the analysis and development of practice using the conceptual tools of activity theory over time, I believe my design could still reasonably be described as DWR or, at least, as a variation of DWR. The first principle of the design of my research was the participatory use of activity theory tools in a double stimulation strategy to answer the practical question: 'What are we doing and why – and how might it be changed?' (Engeström 2007: 379).

Working with the conceptual tools of activity theory with teachers proved to be challenging, especially at the end of busy school days when a plethora of triangles threatened to overwhelm even the staunchest potential Vygotskian. However, it was interesting to note the ways in which these tools became 'ingrowing' (Leont'ev 1997: 22) for the participants' work in the Change Laboratories over time. Developing the conscious understanding that they were active agents in multiple, related yet potentially conflicting activity systems became meaningful for the participating teachers in interpreting the complexity of different motives for developing practice and also in understanding the historical, layered dimension of practice itself. Initially, the teachers gently parodied my facilitation of the workshops by referring to the 'triangle thing', but they gradually came to take up the concepts as tools with which to work on their understanding of the dynamics of their specific settings. In the following example from early in the first year of the intervention, the teachers are discussing a segment of mirror data, an extract from a transcript of an interview with one of their colleagues (who didn't participate in the Change Laboratories) in which she gave teacher recruitment as an important reason for joining a teacher education partnership; that is, joining the partnership creates a 'pool' of potential employees. I commented that this seemed a valid, pragmatic reason for joining in:

VE: It shouldn't be unexpected.
TEACHER 1: I don't think (.) I mean I know what you're driving at, that's an extreme, and there may be elements of that in some people, but I

do think that the school, the department, more people than that would suggest see the value of being involved in initial teacher training for its own sake and will articulate that.

TEACHER 2: And I wouldn't want that [()

TEACHER 3: No but it's an example] of tensions ((laughter)) in the ways of working and different ways of thinking about what an intern is.

TEACHER 4: Yeah and a lot of () isn't it, that they're just an extra, not really part of us.

(Change Laboratory 2, Episode 1 (lines 395–428))

The laughter from other participants occurs during Teacher 3's turn as she identifies a contradiction in the motives of schools for joining teacher education partnerships and names this contradiction as a 'tension', a word (like 'contradiction' itself) that she has picked up from the discourse of activity theory. Along with the parody of my language and the laughter, this playful, tentative appropriation of one of the conceptual tools was an early example of both the activity theory and the social space of the Change Laboratory beginning to act as a mediating means.

As the DWR intervention progressed, one of the schools, the Northtown School, chose to work on the teaching of writing to students being prepared for the high-stakes examination known as the General Certificate of Secondary Education (GCSE).[1] In generating data about this problem of practice in the school setting, the pre-service teachers and the research assistant noticed that the department as a whole was relying on highly specified plans (textual artefacts the teachers referred to as 'writing frames') to dictate the organisation and content of their students' writing. 'Writing frames' had been heavily promoted by the National Literacy Strategy (DfES 1998b) and the Secondary National Strategy (DfEE 2001) as a means of 'scaffolding' less fluent and independent writers into unfamiliar genres. Writing frames are associated with (Australian) genre theory (cf. Cope and Kalantzis 1993; Kress 1989) and involve specifying discourse-level features of certain recognisable types of text that are assumed to have intrinsic social and cultural capital (see Luke 1997 for a critique of these assumptions). In the Northtown School, the textual artefacts the teachers referred to as 'writing frames' had come to dominate the teaching of writing as the core of what Hillocks referred to as a 'presentational' pedagogy (Hillocks 1986): the teacher presented the 'writing frame' from the front as a template to follow and fill in. However, drawing on what they were learning in their university programme, the pre-service teachers noticed that these artefacts were not writing frames in the sense that policy-makers or Australian genre theorists would recognise. They were instead very detailed plans for what the students should write, in what order and for how many marks in the examination (see Figure 7.6).

Year 10 Original Writing Coursework

Task.
Imagine you were a passenger on board United Airlines Flight 93. Write a first person account of September 11th 2001, describing the events of the day, and your emotions, in as much detail as possible.

Remember:
- Avoid using too much direct speech as this can become boring and difficult to follow. Focus instead on your observations of the events and how you are feeling.
- When describing, remember to appeal to the sense of your reader: *Taste, touch, sight, hearing, smell.*
- You should write in the first person ("I") and in the past tense, as though the events have already taken place.
- You are being marked on your writing so spelling, punctuation and grammar are very, *very* important. If you are not sure about anything then put your hand up and ask, as I cannot tell you all of your mistakes when I mark your draft work.
- As with all of your coursework, but particularly with this piece, the mark you will receive is directly related to the amount of effort you put in when writing it.

Part 1: The beginning of the day.
Introduce your character, describe yourself leaving the house and your journey to the airport. Try to give the reader a sense of your character's background: family, job and anything else of interest.

Part 2: The Airport
Describe your thoughts, feelings and observations as you sit in the departure lounge. Try to give your reader a few clues about what is to come, without making it too obvious.

Part 3: The early part of the flight
What made it seem like a normal flight? Were you talking to anybody? Was anybody acting oddly? What were you thinking about?

Part 4: The Hijack
What happened? How were you feeling? What did you see? What were the other passengers doing? **Remember:** You do not yet know about the other planes.

Part 5: The End
What changed to make the passengers decide to take over the plane? Were you involved? Did you call anyone? What happened next? Try to write in such a way that your reader feels the same emotions as you did on the day.

In this piece of **English** coursework you are being assessed on **AO3 (EN3) writing.** You are expected to demonstrate your ability to:
1.   communicate clearly and imaginatively, using and adapting forms for different readers and purposes;
2.   organise ideas into sentences, paragraphs and whole texts using a variety of linguistic and structural features;
3.   use a range of sentence structures effectively with accurate punctuation and spelling.

Figure 7.6 Mirror data: the first page of a 'writing frame' from Northtown School English department.

In the following segment of data from a Change Laboratory towards the end of the first year, involving teachers from the four project schools, the Northtown School mentor is explaining to me, as other participants listen, how a tension in the activity system for teaching writing in her English department had been surfaced by the analysis of mirror data such as the 'writing frame' shown in Figure 7.6.

MENTOR: Well plans ... to some extent ... I mean, it depended in the member of staff, but some plans you know ... four bullet points per paragraph, you must address each one of these. Other ones were a bit more fluid and said 'in this paragraph you should discuss this'. And what came out of it was that most of the students didn't understand how to write it. Even though they had this writing frame, they didn't understand how to write it. Because they hadn't gone through the process of actually thinking

VE: Thinking ...
But how did that feel for you as teachers ... the English department? Because that could be quite embarrassing, couldn't it?

MENTOR: Oh absolutely.

VE: By saying your very helpful well intentioned plans//

MENTOR: //Which you took ages over//

VE: //which you took ages over are actually limiting what your students can do.

MENTOR: You know I think for some people it was like well I want them to get this grade so I need to talk about this, and it wasn't so much about the students independently gaining their own understanding of the text, or developing a skill, it was about some members of staff 'these are my results' you know 'my performance management is going to be based on this, therefore I will give them everything they need to put in a piece of coursework' ...
Because some of them are very much ... this is what the curriculum says, the literacy strategy says this, LEA [school district] says this – I must do that.

VE: So you make the link very strongly now with performance management.

MENTOR: Mm.

VE: Was it that strong?

MENTOR: Mm.... Performance management and the data that the school holds on you and your classes is now ... I mean it's practically in your mark book. You know you have all these children who are supposed to get all these levels, and then you get a nice little percentage where how many of them actually get ... it is a nightmare.

(Change Laboratory 7, Episode 1 (lines 654–721))

The tension that was being examined here was in the form of a contradiction about how the object of the activity system for teaching writing was being interpreted. This tension was, from Engeström's perspective, a primary contradiction between use-value and exchange-value (Engeström 1987), the motive of developing students' writing by providing a 'writing frame' and the motive of gaining good examination results that might satisfy a performance management target and result in additional salary. The research showed how this critical realisation and conscious awareness of the material conditions for her colleagues' work as English teachers had been developed in the social space of the DWR intervention and through the use of the explicitly mediating conceptual tools of activity theory. The tools had been used to analyse current practices, to understand how and why these practices had been shaped and to generate potential solutions or changes that might improve practice. In addition to revealing the difficulties of coming to a shared understanding of the object-motive, in this case, the intervention also revealed a secondary contradiction, how a superficial appropriation of the tool of the writing frame (the artefact shown in Figure 7.6 came to be understood as an over-specified plan rather than a writing frame) became instead a rule for participation in the activity system for teaching writing.

In stimulating change through an examination of current practices, the use of the DWR methodology in this research was associated with a better understanding of practice by tracing the talk of the Change Laboratory in relation to an activity theory analysis of the mirror data. This 'better understanding' was characterised as a multi-layered, historical awareness that Engeström explains as follows:

> An activity is not a homogenous entity. To the contrary, it is composed of a multitude of often disparate elements, voices and viewpoints. This multiplicity can be understood in terms of historical layers. An activity system always contains sediments of earlier historical modes, as well as buds or offshoots of its possible future. These sediments and buds – historically meaningful differences – are found in the different components of the activity system, including the physical tools and mental models of the subjects.
>
> (1993: 68)

It is through the identification of 'sediments' and 'buds' that possibilities for positive change were realised. Laclau described this process as 'reactivating the moment of sedimentation' (Laclau 1990: 34) – uncovering the historical traces of the routinisation of tool-use – and seeking to examine the processes by which the 'social was instituted' in order to stimulate a 'system of possible alternatives' (ibid.). In my DWR-framed research, the conceptual tools of activity theory worked as mediating means to stimulate a historicised understanding of practice. This understanding was also mediated socially through the negotiations and exchanges in the boundary zone of the Change Laboratory.

Conclusion: from tracing conceptual development to provoking conceptual growth

In this chapter I have used two examples from my research to illustrate the application of Vygotsky's methodological concept of the double stimulation strategy in the study of teacher education and development. I have argued that the double stimulation strategy has the potential to reveal how subjects construct and reconstruct the object of activity by analysing the processes of mediation. In seeking to identify how subjects' complex symbolic activity develops, it also makes space for their agency. The examples I have given reflect different priorities in conceptualising and designing research into teacher learning: the first example, involving the drawing task, sought to explain individual teachers' conceptual development and how it was mediated through cultural and historical channels of practice in specific settings; the second example, drawing on the DWR methodology of Engeström, sought to stimulate positive change in practice by better understanding current practices.

The second example was distinct from the first in being conceptualised as what Chaiklin refers to as 'practice-developing research' (Chaiklin 2008), the aims of which are explicitly conceptual growth (the propagation of 'good ideas'), practical change and the development of the theory of activity. The two examples also reflect the different emphases in Vygotsky's work which Moll (1990) refers to as a 'change of focus from sign mediated to socially mediated activity' (1990: 5). Indeed, the DWR methodology can be interpreted as a development of the double stimulation strategy in setting out to create a collective 'zone of proximal development' for the development of historically new forms of activity or 'societally significant practices' (Chaiklin 1993, 2008; see also Roth and Lee 2007: 206) through social as well as semiotic mediation. For Vygotsky, 'the search for method' was 'one of the most important problems of the entire enterprise of understanding the uniquely human forms of psychological activity' (Vygotsky 1978: 65). As this chapter has argued, the double stimulation strategy was a significant contribution to the enterprise, one of great potential in researching teacher education and development.

Note

1 Results of GCSE examinations are collated and published nationally (in newspapers and elsewhere) as 'league tables' at individual school level. At individual teacher level, GCSE examination results can be an important piece of evidence in applications for performance-related pay (known as 'threshold' payments).

References

Beach, K. (1999) 'Consequential transitions: a sociocultural expedition beyond transfer in education', *Review of Research in Education* 24: 101–139.

Beach, K. (2003) 'Consequential transitions: a developmental view of knowledge propagation through social organisations', in Tuomi-Gröhn, T. and Engeström, Y. (eds) *Between school and work: new perspectives on transfer and boundary-crossing*, Amsterdam and Oxford: Elsevier.

Britzman, D.P. (2003) *Practice makes practice: a critical study of learning to teach*, revised edition, Albany, NY: State University of New York Press.

Chaiklin, S. (1993) 'Understanding the social scientific practice of *Understanding Practice*', in Chaiklin, S. and Lave, S. (eds) *Understanding practice: perspectives on activity and context*, New York: Cambridge University Press.

Chaiklin, S. (2008) 'Practice-developing research: a cultural-historical approach', poster presented at the first UK and Ireland ISCAR Meeting, Bath, 17–18 July.

Cole, M. (1996) *Cultural psychology: a once and future discipline*, Cambridge, MA: Harvard University Press.

Cope, B. and Kalantzis, M. (1993) *The powers of literacy: a genre approach to teaching writing*, Pittsburgh, PA: University of Pittsburgh Press.

Darling-Hammond, L. and Youngs, P. (2002) 'Defining "highly qualified teachers": what does "scientifically-based research" actually tell us?', *Educational Researcher* (December): 13–25.

DES (Department of Education and Science) (1992) *Initial teacher training (secondary phase). Circular 9/92*, London: HMSO.

DfEE (Department for Education and Employment) (2001) *Framework for teaching English in years 7, 8 and 9 (Key Stage 3 National Strategy)*, London: DfEE.

DfES (Department for Education and Skills) (1998a) *Teaching: high status, high Standards: requirements for a course of initial teacher training (Circular 4/98)*, London: Author.

DfES (1998b) *The national literacy strategy: framework for teaching*, London: Author.

Edwards, A., Gilroy, P. and Hartley, D. (2002) *Rethinking teacher education: collaborative responses to uncertainty*, London: RoutledgeFalmer.

Ellis, V. (2007a) *Subject knowledge and teacher education: the development of beginning teachers' thinking*, London and New York: Continuum.

Ellis, V. (2007b) 'Taking subject knowledge seriously: from professional knowledge recipes to complex conceptualisations of teacher development', *The Curriculum Journal* 18, 3: 447–462.

Ellis, V. (2007c) 'More than "soldiering on": realising the potential of teacher education to rethink English in schools', in Ellis, V., Fox, C. and Street, B. (eds) *Rethinking English in schools: towards a new and constructive stage*, London and New York: Continuum, pp. 185–198.

Ellis, V. (2008) 'Exploring the contradictions in learning to teach: the potential of developmental work research', *Changing English: Studies in Culture and Education* 16, 1: 53–63.

Engeström, Y. (1987) *Learning by expanding: an activity-theoretical approach to developmental research*, Helsinki: Orienta-Konsultit.

Engeström, Y. (1991) 'Developmental work research: reconstructing expertise through expansive learning', in Nurminen, M.I. and Weir, G.R.S. (eds) *Human jobs and computer interfaces*, Amsterdam and Oxford: Elsevier.

Engeström, Y. (1993) 'Developmental work research as a test bench of activity theory: the case of the primary medical care practice', in Chaiklin, S. and Lave, J. (eds) *Understanding practice: perspectives on activity and context*, Cambridge: Cambridge University Press.

Engeström, Y. (1996) 'Developmental work research as educational research: looking ten years back and into the zone of proximal development', *Nordisk Pedagogy* 16: 131–143.

Engeström, Y. (1999) 'Innovative learning in work teams: analysing cycles of knowledge creation in practice', in Engeström, Y., Miettinen, R. and Punamaki, R.-L. (eds) *Perspectives on activity theory*, Cambridge and New York: Cambridge University Press.

Engeström, Y. (2007) 'Putting activity theory to work: the change laboratory as an application of double stimulation', in Daniels, H., Cole, M. and Wertsch, J.V. (eds) *The Cambridge companion to Vygotsky*, Cambridge and New York: Cambridge University Press.

Engeström, Y. (2008) 'The future of activity theory: a rough draft', keynote presentation to the ISCAR conference, 8–13 September. Online, available at: http://lchc.ucsd.edu/mca/Paper/ISCARkeyEngestrom.pdf (accessed 15 May 2009).

Grossman, P. (1990) *The making of a teacher: teacher knowledge and teacher education*, New York: Teachers College Press.

Hillocks, G. (1986) *Research on written composition: new directions for teaching*, Washington, DC: NCRE and ERIC Clearing House on Reading and Communication Skills.

Kelly, G.A. (1963) *Theory of personality: the psychology of personal constructs*, New York: W.W. Norton and Company.

Kress, G. (1989) *Linguistic processes in sociocultural practice*, 2nd edition, Oxford: Oxford University Press.

Laclau, E. (1990) *New reflections on the revolution of our time*, London and New York: Verso.

Lave, J. (1988) *Cognition in practice*, Cambridge: Cambridge University Press.

Leont'ev, A.N. (1978) *Activity, consciousness and personality*, trans. M. Hall, Englewood Cliffs, NJ: Prentice Hall.

Leont'ev, A.N. (1997) 'On Vygotsky's creative development', in Rieber, R.W. and Wollock, J. (eds) *The collected works of L.S. Vygotsky. Volume 3: problems of the theory and history of psychology*, New York: Kluwer/Plenum.

Luke, A. (1997) 'Genres of power: literacy education and the production of capital', in Hasan, R. and Williams, G. (eds) *Literacy in society*, London: Longman.

Mavers, D., Somekh, B. and Restorick, J. (2002) 'Interpreting the externalised images of pupils' conceptions of ICT: methods for the analysis of concept maps', *Computers and Education* 38: 187–207.

Moll, L.C. (1990) 'Introduction', in Moll, L.C. (ed.) *Vygotsky and education: instructional implications and applications of sociohistorical psychology*, Cambridge: Cambridge University Press

Novak, J.D. and Gowin, D.B. (1984) *Learning how to learn*, New York: Cambridge University Press.

Pearson, M. and Somekh, B. (2003) 'Concept-mapping as a research tool: a study of primary children's representations of information and communication technologies (ICT)', *Education and Information Technologies* 8, 1: 5–22.

Pihkalainen, J. and Kaatrakoski, H. (2007) 'Hybrid organisations', paper presented at the international workshop 'Making Connections: Relational Analysis, Boundary Concepts and the Future of Organisation Studies', 2–3April, Cardiff University, Wales.

Poulson, L. (2001) 'Paradigm lost? Subject knowledge, primary teachers and education policy', *British Journal of Educational Studies* 49, 1: 40–55.

Roth, W.-M. and Lee, Y.-J. (2007) ' "Vygotsky's neglected legacy": cultural-historical activity theory', *Review of Educational Research* 77, 2: 186–232.

Smagorinsky, P., Cook, L.S. and Johnson, T.S. (2003) 'The twisting path of concept development in learning to teach', *Teachers College Record* 105: 1399–1436.

Toulmin, S. (1972) *Human understanding. Volume 1: general introduction and part 1*, Oxford: Clarendon Press.

Toulmin, S. (1999) 'Knowledge as shared procedures', in Engeström, Y., Miettinen, R. and Punamäki, R. (eds) *Perspectives on activity theory*, Cambridge: Cambridge University Press.

Vygotsky, L.S. (1978) *Mind in society: the development of higher psychological processes* (M. Cole, V. John-Steiner, S. Scribner and E. Souberman, eds), Cambridge, MA: Harvard University Press.

Vygotsky, L.S. (1986) *Thought and language* (A. Kozulin, ed. and trans.) Cambridge, MA: MIT Press.

Vygotsky, L.S. (1987) 'Lectures on psychology', in Rieber, R. and Carton, A. (eds), Minick, N. (trans.) *The collected works of L.S. Vygotsky. Volume 1: Problems of general psychology*, New York: Kluwer/Plenum.

Vygotsky, L.S. (1997) 'Chapter 12: Self-Control', in Rieber, R.W. (ed.), Hall, M.J. (trans.) *The collected works of L.S. Vygotsky. Volume 4: The history of the development of higher mental functions*, New York: Kluwer/Plenum.

Vygotsky, L.S. (1999) 'Tool and sign in the development of the child', in Rieber, R.W. (ed.), Hall, M.J. (trans) *The collected works of L.S. Vygotsky. Volume 6: Scientific legacy*, New York: Kluwer/Plenum.

Wenger, E., McDermott, R. and Snyder, W.M. (2002) *Cultivating communities of practice*, Cambridge, MA: Harvard Business School Press.

Wertsch, J.V. (2007) 'Mediation', in Daniels, H., Cole, M. and Wertsch, J.V. (eds) *The Cambridge companion to Vygotsky*, Cambridge: Cambridge University Press.

Wilson, S.M., Floden, R.E. and Ferrini-Mundy, J. (2002) 'Teacher preparation research: an insider's view from the outside', *Journal of Teacher Education* 53, 3: 190–204.

Chapter 8

Investigating teacher language

A comparison of the relative strengths of Conversation Analysis and Critical Discourse Analysis as methods

Gill Boag-Munroe

Background

Learning, it is argued throughout this book, takes place through social interaction which, in turn, occurs through the mediation of the 'tools of tools' – language (understood in this chapter as signs, symbols and their organisation) which in turn may be understood as both an exchange, and a mutual development, of concepts between participants. If that is so, then part of our journey to understanding how learning happens must be through understanding how talk shapes learning, which leads to questions about how talk might be understood within activities. Within the school context, language is mostly in the form of text or talk and I aim to offer two ways in which language-use in schools might be explored, according to the level of activity at which language is being used. My aim in this chapter is to point to two methods of analysing language for two levels of activity – operation and activity – and to offer an example of how language at the level of activity was analysed to reach an understanding of the complexity of the work of a teacher-mentor in a secondary school in the English Midlands.

Vygotsky's exploration of the relationship between thinking and speech was first made widely available in *Thought and Language* (1962) and in the papers collected in *Mind in Society* (1978). He believed that thinking and speech had different origins, but that at some point in time they had become intertwined. In order to become speech, thought underwent a series of transformations. Thought, argues Vygotsky, is not only expressed through words, but comes into existence through words (Vygotsky 1986: 218), so that thought is a verbal process. Thought 'tends to connect something with something else, to establish a relation between things' (ibid.) and, though coming into existence through words, undergoes many changes as it turns into speech (Vygotsky 1986: 218–219).

The meaning of every word is a generalisation or a concept (1986: 212). Concepts emerge and take shape 'in the course of a complex operation aimed at the solution of some problem [and] for the process to begin a problem must arise that cannot be solved other than through the forma- tion of new concepts' (1986: 100). That is, concepts arise and evolve through activity. Words direct mental operations and the functional use of a word plays an important part in concept formation: real concepts are impossible without words (1986: 107). Although Vygotsky himself did not develop a means for further exploring the relationship between words and thought, several writers since have attempted to offer ways to understand the relationship between language and concept within a CHAT perspec- tive (e.g. Daniels 2008; Engeström 1995; Hassan 1996; Wells 1999; Wertsch 1991).

Leont'ev (1977: 9) argues that 'meanings refract the world'; that they are 'the linguistically transmuted and materialised ideal form of the exist- ence of the objective world' and 'the generalization of reality that is crys- tallized and fixed in its sensuous vehicle, i.e. normally in a word or word combination' (Leont'ev 1981: 226). If language is the material expression of meaning, and meanings are the expressions of ideal objective forms, an investigation of the language used in activity should reveal the meanings which those involved in ITE make within the activity. The problem becomes how to investigate the language in a systematic way.

Roth and Lee (2007) summarise ways that writers interested in how lan- guage in activity might be understood have conceptualised the relation- ship between language and activity, and suggest that the issue is problematised by the range of understandings that have been developed. They further point to how the choice of approach might be influenced by the unit of activity under investigation; that is, whether the activity is being explored at the collective (activity) level or at the individual (operational) level. For Roth and Lee (2007), Conversation Analysis (CA) offers a useful tool for understanding language-use at an operational level. In their understanding, speech appears to be a routinised operation (Leont'ev 1978) in which 'speech acts are constituted by components (operations) that conversationalists do not consciously choose: appropriate words emerge in response to the unfolding utterance by means of which the speaker attempts to achieve communicative goals' (Roth 2005: 207). At the activity level, however, CA may not be able to tease out meanings from text or multiple interwoven conversations, and I have suggested (Boag- Munroe 2004, 2007) that theories of Critical Discourse Analysis (CDA) might be a way to understand how language is used at this level.

Conversation Analysis (CA) and Critical Discourse Analysis (CDA): what can they tell the researcher about language in activity?

The aims and processes of Conversation Analysis and Discourse Analysis

CA is a method used to investigate conversations and how they are managed. Ten Have (2007) points to the purpose of CA as being 'not to explain *why* people act as they do, but rather to explicate *how* they do it' (2007: 9; emphasis in original). It focuses on the utterance (what is said within a turn in a conversation) as the smallest unit of analysis, and investigates it in the immediate context of the conversation. It uses transcriptions of recordings of speech which, unlike those used in CDA, include coding to signal prosodic and paralinguistic features – length of vowels, length of pauses, emphases and tone of voice – in order to understand how participants in conversations use speech to get things done (Wooffitt 2005). In particular, CA is interested in how the participants organise their conversation, explored through the management of turn-taking and content; and the organisation of turn-taking and repairs – that is, what happens when the conversation runs into difficulties (ten Have 2007).

The CA analyst begins the process by selecting a sequence of conversation and then characterising the actions contained in it before considering the form or 'package' (ten Have 2007) of the content and considering 'how the timing and taking of turns provide for certain understandings of the actions and the matters talked about'. Finally, consideration is given to 'how the ways the actions were accomplished implicate certain identities, roles and/or relationships for the interactants' (ten Have 2007: 123–124). CA looks at apparently random, decontextualised segments of conversations in their immediate social context with the aim of revealing understandings of the subject, subjects or immediate community and their relationships, ignoring the cultural and historical contexts that might shape participants' language choices. The focus for the analyst, then, appears to be on how participants in the conversation negotiated or managed an operation at a moment in time.

CDA, on the other hand, may be understood as a heuristic to help explain language in use in written and spoken discourses at word, sentence and text level, and in its cultural and historical context. The focus is on the *why* of language-use as much as on the *what* and *how*: it aims to describe, interpret and explain (Fairclough 1989: 26). Discourse

> involves social conditions, which can be specified as *social conditions of production*, and *social conditions of interpretation*. These social conditions, moreover, relate to three different 'levels' of social organization: the

level of the social situation, or the immediate social environment in which the discourse occurs; the level of the social institution which constitutes a wider matrix for the discourse, and the level of the society as a whole.... [T]hese social conditions shape the [members' resources] people bring to production and interpretation, which in turn shape the way in which texts are produced and interpreted.... So, in seeing language as discourse and as social practice, one is committing oneself not just to analysing texts, nor just to analysing processes of production and interpretation, but to analysing the relationship between the texts, processes and their social conditions, both the immediate conditions of situational context and the more remote conditions of institutional and social structures.

(Fairclough 1989: 25–26; emphasis in original)

Such an understanding directs the gaze to more complex interactions between layers of context than perhaps the CA approach is able to offer, pointing to more precise understandings of meanings and how they are negotiated, which in turn might lead to more delicate understandings of the object the participants are working towards.

CA proceeds from transcripts of language-in-action, that is, from transcripts of recordings of 'natural' conversation in everyday situations (there must be questions here around how 'natural' a conversation can be when participants are aware of being recorded for research purposes). It presupposes that participants to the conversation will want to, or are able to, take turns, though it interrogates points at which participants decline to take a turn that is offered (e.g. ten Have 2007; Wooffitt 2005). In studies that might include interview data, however, turn-taking is deliberately managed so that the interviewer may consciously ignore several points at which the turn might change in order to encourage the interviewee to keep talking about the selected topic. Interviews, then, are artificially constructed conversations that bend or ignore the usual rules of turn-taking and, while this rule-bending may in itself be of interest to researchers aiming to understand the structure of interviews as a genre, it is unlikely to assist the researcher interested in the conceptual tools and rules that the subject may be drawing on in activity, and may in the end only point to the underlying structure of the interview as genre.

What elements of activity might the two approaches reveal?

CA analysts are concerned with the rules that underpin the structures of language, rather than with the content of particular interactions. Billig (1999: 547–548) suggests that the programme of CA is 'to find general structures of orderliness' by following 'practices that direct analytic attention to issues which the participants do not overtly talk about'. CDA, on the other hand, is interested in the topic selected by the participants, which may point to the goal or object on which they are working, and in the kinds of language tool used which might point to concepts drawn on in that work.

CDA generally takes a critical stance to its investigation and concerns itself with issues of power by asking how ideologies are embedded in discourses, which makes it a useful tool for investigating power relationships in discourse. It begins from the standpoint that language reflects a priori a particular stance, both of the participants and of the analyst. Billig, for example, suggests that the 'specific tasks of CDA are frequently part of a wider analysis of social inequality' (1999: 576). A criticism frequently levelled at CA, however, is that it does not adequately account for power relationships within conversations, though Wooffitt suggests that such a perception is mistaken, and offers examples of how power relationships at the level of smaller interactions might be investigated (2005: 186–210).

CA is, according to Wooffitt (2005: 3), 'the best way to understand everyday conversation' as it emphasises 'the dynamic and action oriented nature of utterances [and] the highly patterned nature of interactional sequences', while, for Titscher *et al.* (2002: 107), CA seeks the 'generative principles and processes used to produce the structure and order of a situation'. They quote Sacks (1985: 13) as suggesting that CA is about 'finding and naming' rules and objects pointing to an approach which identifies and describes language-use in talk without going on to offer explanations of why particular language features might have been selected in that particular instance. Together with Roth's (2005) suggestion that language selection is in fact not consciously selected but routinised and unconscious, this idea points to an understanding of CA as a tool for accessing the rules within operations and actions within activity rather than for accessing language within the wider scope of activity.

Can the two methods address the ways that written text is used in activity?

CA focuses on speech and cannot offer understandings of written text in activity, which makes it unsuitable for analyses that seek to discover meanings created by the interweaving of documents and talk in activity. In investigations that seek to understand how participants may be interacting in operations or actions, the inability of CA to offer insights into text may not be important. To ignore the influence of written documents in activities, however, is perhaps to omit an important piece of contextualising data. For example, in the study outlined below, it was central to the project to understand how language in written policy documents fed into teachers' talk about their work which revealed their identities as teachers and teacher-mentors. Without a means to analyse both the relevant policy documents and talk about practice, it would not have been possible to understand how text and talk, policy and practice, were interwoven.

CDA investigates word, sentence and text levels of language in use and discursive practices – in the sense of particular patterns of language-use specific to a practice (education discourse, legal discourse, etc.) – through exploration of lexical choices, syntax and genres. CDA, then, is concerned with language-use at activity level rather than at the level of operations, and language may itself be understood as an activity that blends with practical activity (Boag-Munroe 2004).

CDA is concerned not only with spoken language but with written and multi-media texts and can therefore direct its lens to investigate language used in a range of situations within activity other than conversation. It offers the scope to explore how language enters activity through written documents as well as through conversations, though it may not always take account of the finer nuances of spoken utterances such as tone, pitch, pausing or emphases. Because it focuses the gaze at a wider level of interaction than conversation, it may offer greater insights into the conceptual tools in use in activity and into the division of labour. It allows for wider exploration of the interactions between subject and community than CA, because it analyses text as well as conversation and can encompass lengthier and wider communications between participants.

Summary

In summary, then, it may be said that CA's focus on structures might assist understandings of rules, and the ways that rules might mediate between the subject and the community and, in the process, offer understandings of subject and community identities. Because it focuses on conversation between two or more participants, and in particular on their structure, it may be a useful way of understanding how language is used intersubjectively in a narrowly populated interaction at the level of operations or actions (Leont'ev 1978), though the number of interactions that occur at the level of activity may mean that it is less useful in helping to understand the complexities of language-use at that level.

CDA might equally point to rules and identities formed and used in activity but, in addition, because of its interest in the wider contexts of human interaction, have potential to point to conceptual tools and highlight the relationship between them and language tools in use. Because it is a tool for analysing written as well as spoken text, it can offer ways to understand the interaction of documents and speech within activity, as for example in the research discussed below, where the ways that a policy document shaped the work of teachers was investigated. Further, CDA can, through its emphasis on critical analysis, suggest ways that power is distributed through the activity, pointing to an understanding of the division of labour. Finally, through the understandings it offers of the other elements of the activity, CDA can help to tease out understandings of the object, as well as the goals, being worked on.

Understandings applied to data

This section offers an example of how CDA was used as one analytical frame in part of one project, to investigate language within the activity of Initial Teacher Education (ITE). The aim was to understand how those teachers who worked as mentors to beginning teachers constructed identities that enabled them to work, apparently simultaneously, in two activities: classroom teaching and mentoring. Interview data were collected within four case studies of teacher-mentors working in two secondary schools in the English Midlands. Contextualising data were gathered from Course Tutors with whom they worked in partnership on Higher Education Institution (HEI) courses leading to the Post Graduate Certificate in Education (PGCE), a qualification leading to Qualified Teacher Status (QTS), which is essential to anyone wishing to teach in English state schools.

In addition, written data were collected from policy texts used to shape the activity (*Qualifying to Teach: Professional Standards for Qualified Teacher Status and Requirements for Initial Teacher Training* (TTA 2003) and the *Handbook of Guidance* (TTA 2004), together referred to as the Standards). Data were interrogated using a blend of activity theory, the CDA frame in Table 8.1 and a computer counting and concordancing programme, *Wordsmith* (for details, see references). However, for the purposes of this chapter, only data collected within one partnership – Midshires University (participant tutors Alan and Barbara) and Middlemarch School (two teachers: Celia and James) – are drawn on.

Language and conceptual tools

The main conceptual tools drawn on by policy-makers were outlined in the *Introduction* to *Qualifying to Teach* (TTA 2003). It was anticipated that concepts might be revealed through representational meanings within the text (Fairclough 2003); that is, through the ways in which the world was represented through agency and space–time. According to Fairclough (2003), representational meanings may be drawn out through an investigation of combinations of processes, participants and circumstances, or statements of who does what to whom (or what), when and where. Such an investigation fits with the CHAT theoretical focus on who (subject) does what to whom/what (object), in what circumstances (rules, community, division of labour, where and when).

Table 8.1 Frame (adapted from Fairclough 2003)

Values	Level		
	Vocabulary	Grammar	
Experiential: asks how the speaker's choice of words express her/his experience of the natural or social world	• What classification schemes were drawn on? • Were there words which were ideologically contested? • Was there rewording or overwording? • What ideologically significant meaning relations were there between words?	• What types of process and participant dominate? • Was agency clear? • Were processes what they seem? • Were nominalisations used? • Were sentences active or passive? • Were sentences negative or positive?	
Relational: expressing social relations	• Were there any euphemistic expressions? • Were there markedly formal or informal words?	• What modes were used? • Were there features of relational modality? i.e. does one participant have more authority than the others, as expressed through deontic modality? • If the pronouns we and you were used, how?	
Expressive: expressing social identities and evaluation of the reality the text relates to	• What expressive values do words have?	• Were there features of expressive modality? i.e. what was the author's evaluation of truth as expressed through epistemic modality?	
General	• What metaphors were used? • What binary oppositions emerge?	• How were sentences linked together? • Were complex sentences characterised by subordination or co-ordination? • How does the author refer inside and outside the text?	

A *Wordsmith* concordancing of the Standards document showed that a key discourse within the Standards is a managerial one, incorporating a market discourse and presupposing that all work is market-oriented and manageable. Key words within the discourse, drawn from Fairclough (2000), Mahony and Hextall (2000), and Walsh (2006), were identified and their use by all participants in ITE compared (see Table 8.2). The comparison in Table 8.2 suggested that market discourse, while used quite extensively within the Standards, was not at the time of the study being used by teachers and tutors, suggesting that these groups were constructing identities for themselves which were not yet aligned with those constructed by policy-makers.

Language in the Standards document helped construct the object of teacher training as the acquisition of a toolkit by masking agency through the use of nominalisation ('know' becomes 'knowledge'; 'understand' – 'understanding'; 'expect – expectation', for example, which hides the actor and changes the process to an object), passive voices and metaphor which might suggest a military approach to ITE. The presentation of the Standards as a list of skills and values that were possessed or acquired by the teacher contributed to the conceptualisation of teaching and teacher training as a mechanical practice rather than a nurturing process.

Five metaphors, which may be understood as having quasi-military connotations through their frequent use in military discourse, were particularly evident in the Standards document: 'deploy' (12 uses), 'train' and its lemmas ('trained',' training', 'trainee', 'trainer') (1029), 'objective' (50), 'target' (28) and 'hit the ground running' (1). Together they hinted at understandings of teacher education as the preparation of troops for battle and, within the market discourse, suggested a masculine and mechanistic understanding of classroom work which did not sit comfortably with the more nurturing conceptualisations of teaching and learning evident in teachers' and tutors' discussions of their work.

Teaching – and teacher training – was conceptualised as an activity that was capable of being inspected, managed and quality-assured, all processes which imply measurability, accountability and managerialist approaches. Teaching, then, was seen as an activity to which business or market concepts could be appropriately applied, which may entail that other aspects of the market – competition, for example – were part of the conceptualisation of teaching, though no argument was presented as to why or how these concepts might help pupil achievement. Teachers were presented in the Standards as skilled and knowledgeable professionals who used a toolkit of strategies to work with others on the object of pupil achievement. They drew on managerial concepts and were concerned with benchmarking and setting targets for their pupils. If language points to learning, then it might be anticipated that those learners and teachers involved in ITE might understand from the Standards document that teaching is a

Table 8.2 Occurrences of discourse markers in Standards document and participant interviews

Marker	Standards	Alan – Midshires HEI	Barbara – Midshires HEI	Celia – Middlemarch School	James – Middlemarch School
Total words	**43,184**	**12,816**	**8,395**	**6,382**	**11,117**
Account*	54	1	0	0	0
Achieve*	104	0	0	0	12
Assess*	255	1	1	0	0
Benchmark*	11	0	0	0	0
Choice*	16	0	0	1	1
Deliver*	15	0	2	1	1
Demonstrate	170	0	0	0	0
Design*	36	6	0	0	0
Effective*	99	2	0	1	0
Efficient	4	0	0	0	0
Goals	8	0	1	0	0
Manage*	70	2	4	1	18
Monitor*	34	0	0	0	0
New	19	4	16	3	7
Outcome*	10	0	1	1	0
Partnership*	73	10	4	0	0
Perform*	34	2	0	0	2
Target*	28	2	5	1	6
Train*	1,029	12	29	1	22
Total	**2,850**	**42**	**63**	**10**	**69**

Note
* Indicates that the root word and root + inflections have been counted.

managerial process. Interview data with teacher-mentors and tutors, however, suggested that they did not conceptualise teaching in the same managerial ways.

Rules and power distribution within ITE

In order to understand what constrained teachers in their work with beginning teachers, and thus in the identities they were able to form, I aimed to tease out the rules at play in the activity of ITE. These largely derived from the Standards document, though the interview data suggest that teacher-mentors additionally developed their own local rules which helped them to prioritise the different aspects of their work in teaching and mentoring. The document began by outlining a model of the teacher through a list of descriptors of skills, qualities and knowledge referred to as 'Standards'. Ownership of the Standards lay with the Secretary of State rather than with those who would implement it, and his power was asserted through the legal status of the document, set out at the beginning of the text on a frontispiece: 'The Standards in this document ... have the same legal standing [as an earlier document].... They set out the Secretary of State's Standards which must be met by trainee teachers.' Mentors were thus aware of the constraints on them in helping to shape the professional identity of beginning teachers, while HEI tutors and school mentors learned that they too had limited autonomy in guiding the development of new entrants to the activity of teaching.

Some rules in the Standards appeared to create tension for the HEI which understood that it must work with the schools who volunteered to work in partnership for ITE. There was no duty for schools to involve themselves in ITE, and HEI tutors were concerned that there was a shortage of schools who would work with them. This lack of duty on the part of schools became problematic for the tutors because they needed so many placement schools that they could not afford to turn away any volunteers. The HEI therefore felt that it had to make compromises in what mentors were asked to do with students, and emerged as potential tension for students between what the HEI wanted them to do and what the school wanted them to do. Alan, for example, was aware that

> we do get schools that tend to constrain significantly [what students can do but] because we are expanding our numbers we cannot afford to [not use weak mentors]. What we need to do is make weak mentors into proper mentors.

Barbara endorsed Alan's point of view. When asked whether she could move a student from a school where she was not getting the training Barbara hoped for, Barbara responded:

We haven't got enough schools to do it. We certainly haven't got enough placements given.... We don't have a surplus of schools so it really is not so much 'How do I select?' It is 'How do I try to improve ones I wouldn't otherwise have been using?'

In both these segments, the tutors reflect collegiate ways of working in their use of the pronoun 'we', which is then undermined by Barbara, the Midshires Science tutor, in her discussion of how local rules are created. Barbara aimed to involve the mentors in the writing of handbooks but saw it as her responsibility to take the initiative in writing and producing them:

So the focus for the mentor meeting this year has been ... 'I want us to focus on the issues between this part of the placement, this part of the year, and I have got a few questions to support it, but ultimately I want to take away what you're telling me and use that to go into a mentor handbook. If you see these as issues, let's see if we can get the advice and put that into the first section of the handbook.' So we've done that on two occasions. And I am putting these together.

An interpretation which draws on Fairclough (2003: 145–150) to understand Barbara's pronoun-use here may point to rules that appeared to underpin how she viewed the division of labour with mentors. Although on the surface she seemed to be trying to show how she worked in partnership by giving an example of how she and mentors have both contributed to the handbook ('we'), her shift to the use of the pronoun 'I' suggests that she saw it to be her job to manage and lead the group working on it. She said, 'I want us ... ', suggesting that she was taking the lead in the collaboration; then 'I want to take away ... ' and 'I am putting these together', pointing to processes in which she was the only actor. She shifts between 'I' and 'you' in a way that points to a division of labour in which she as Course Tutor has one role, and mentors have another. She then shifts to a more collegial perspective of the work, as demonstrated in her use of the pronoun 'we':

The first meeting we talked through all the issues and ultimately they said, 'Most of the stuff is in there somewhere. What we want is a two page laminate that says "Page ... Week one ... These are the key issues, this is where to find the stuff in the handbook. We don't want more. We don't want another handbook to tell us about it. We accept it is there somewhere. We just want the easy user guide, the way in.'

Celia and James both experienced difficulties in attending the mentor meetings held at Midshires, and, because Celia and Barbara both worked part-time, they were only rarely able to meet in school. Celia had no formal training to be a mentor and appeared not to have knowledge of the policy handbook which Barbara (Course Tutor, Midshires) thought that mentors relied on and which she had compiled as a substitute for a more interactive relationship. Consequently the process for Celia was directed by instinct rather than by any rules developed within the partnership or from other people's experience. She said:

> The first time I did it I literally went on gut feeling, and you don't ever know if that's right or wrong. I've never had any feedback if it's right or wrong but I'm doing what I think is best. But you just don't know, do you?

Her comment here suggested that Celia was looking for a more interactive relationship with her tutor and felt frustrated at not having the kind of contact that might foster her development as a mentor. It further pointed to ways the tutor worked and suggested that the tutor's focus was on the student and her own role in developing the student: Celia as mentor seemed to feel invisible to the tutor and as though she were not perceived as participating in the student's learning processes. Her use of the pronoun 'I' reinforces her position as isolated, on the fringes of the partnership.

Object

Within the Standards, the object of activity appeared to be to develop new entrants to teaching who understood the construct of a teacher and the profession of teaching through a managerialist discourse. For Barbara and Alan, the object that emerged was similar: a new entrant to the profession who was able to meet the Standards. However, they did not appear to understand the teacher to be operating in the managerialist discourse of the Standards (see the discussion of language above).

For Celia and James, the object of ITE tended to be aligned with other objects they were working on, and understood through the lenses of those other objects. For Celia, teaching and mentoring appeared to be undertaken as subordinate to being a mother, at least for the time being, and current work was understood to be part of her personal development. Much of what she did was guided by how she could sustain the image of herself that she believed she needed, not only to maintain her self-esteem, but also to be a mother who knew about youth culture:

> I think kids in high school keep you younger in a different way. Fashion. You know what the music is. You just kind of get.... And I think that's quite nice actually. You don't feel like you are completely boring. You have to keep up with them in a way.

Her use of the pronoun 'you' here suggests that she understands this aspect of her work to be common to most teachers.

In James' case, participation in ITE appeared to be guided by his difficulty in engaging with his pupils. If he was working with students, he could allow them to teach his classes while he completed administrative tasks: 'And I am thinking, "Great. They are going to come in and they could do that and that", and I am thinking, "I could get some of this done out of the way while they are teaching." '

Conclusions

This brief discussion aimed to show how CA and CDA might be used to understand language-use not only in the immediate context of its production, but in the wider context of the practice of which it forms part. Because CDA directs the gaze to language choices at word, sentence and text level, and because it draws attention to the ways in which it understands language as pointing to concepts, it proved to be a more useful tool for understanding the ways that policy-makers, HEI tutors and teacher-mentors interacted in their work in ITE. In addition, it drew attention to the ways that teacher educators were trying to grapple with changing discourses of education which were indicative of changing practices, and thus pointed to cultural and historical shifts in the work of teachers.

Whilst CA analysis, with its apparent focus on the ways that rules mediate communication between subject and community, could not have offered an understanding of the policy documents in use in the activity, it may have shed light on the operations and actions undertaken by the participants to achieve goals, and on the ways the participants negotiated work on the object. It might usefully have been drawn on, for example, to look in greater depth at the mentors' interactions with their student teachers in ITE to confirm or expand on the findings of the CDA analysis. Such an investigation might reveal the routines that mentors follow with their students in the school placement, and the operations they deploy to induct students into the practice of teaching, although CDA might draw out these routines and operations – perhaps less successfully than CA. A CA approach to understanding how the two mentors in this chapter conceptualised and organised their work in ITE might additionally have shed light on teachers' interactions with pupils and students by starting from classroom and mentoring transcripts to investigate pedagogical approaches.

Although this chapter has focused on the relative merits of just two approaches to investigating language in activity, there are others (see for example, Edwards and Potter 1992; Jones 2008; Lee 2001; Mercer 2000) which might equally be useful, and which need to be considered in the light of the aims of the research and in the light of understandings about the relationship between language tools and conceptual tools.

References

Billig, M. (1999) 'Whose terms? Whose ordinariness? Rhetoric and ideology in conversation analysis', *Discourse and Society* 10, 4, 543–558.

Boag-Munroe, G. (2004) 'Wrestling with words and meanings: finding a tool for analysing language in activity theory', *Educational Review* 26, 2, 165–182.

Boag-Munroe, G. (2007) *A commerce of the old and new: how classroom teacher mentors work in multiple activities*. PhD thesis. Online, available at: http://etheses.bham.ac.uk/38/ (accessed 25 June 2009).

Daniels, H. (2008) *Vygotsky and research*. London: Routledge.

Edwards, D. and Potter, J. (1992) *Discursive psychology*. London: Sage Publications.

Engeström, R. (1995) 'Voice as communicative action', *Mind, culture and activity* 2, 192–215.

Fairclough, N. (1989) *Language and power*. London: Longman.

Fairclough, N. (2000) *New Labour, new language?* London: Routledge.

Fairclough, N. (2003) *Analysing discourse: textual analysis for social research*. London: Routledge.

Hassan, H. (1996) *Ways of saying: ways of meaning*. London: Cassell.

Jones, P.E. (2008) 'Language in cultural historical perspective', in van Oers, B. Wardekker, W., Elbers, E. and van der Veer, R. (eds) *The transformation of learning: advances in cultural-historical activity theory*. Cambridge: Cambridge University Press.

Lee, D. (2001) *Cognitive linguistics: an introduction*. Oxford: Oxford University Press.

Leont'ev, A.N. (1978) *Activity, consciousness and personality*. Englewood Cliffs, NJ: Prentice-Hall.

Leont'ev, A. N. (1981) *Problems of the development of mind*. Moscow: Progress Publishers.

Mahony, P. and Hextall, I. (2000) *Reconstructing teaching: standards, performance and accountability*. London: Routledge Falmer.

Mercer, N. (2002) *Words and minds: how we use language to think together*. London: Routledge.

Roth, W.-M. (2005) *Talking science: language and learning in science classrooms*. Lanham, MD: Rowman and Littlefield.

Roth, W.-M. and Lee, Y.-J. (2007) 'Vygotsky's neglected legacy: cultural-historical activity theory', *Review of Educational Research* 77, 186–232.

Sacks, H. (1985) 'The interference-making machine: notes on observability', in van Dyke, T. (ed.) *Handbook of Discourse Analysis, vol. 3: discourse and dialogue*. London: Academic Press.

Ten Have, P. (2007) *Doing conversation analysis* (2nd edition). London: SAGE Publications.

Titscher, S., Meyer, M., Wodak, R. and Vetter, E. (2002) *Methods of text and Discourse Analysis*. London: SAGE Publications.

TTA (2003) *Qualifying to teach: professional standards for qualified teacher status and requirements for teacher training*. Online, available at: http://tta.gov.uk (accessed 9 September 2003).

TTA (2004) *Qualifying to teach: handbook of guidance*. Online, available at: http://tta.gov.uk (accessed 9 April 2004).

Vygotsky, L.S. (1986) *Thought and language* (A. Kozulin, ed. and trans.). Cambridge, MA: MIT Press.

Walsh, P. (2006) 'Narrow horizons and the impoverishment of educational discourse: teaching learning and performing under the new educational bureaucracies', *Journal of Educational Policy* 21, 1, 95–117.

Wells, C. (1999) *Dialogic enquiry: towards a sociocultural practice and theory of education*. New York: Cambridge University Press.

Wertsch, J.V. (1991) *Voices of the mind: a sociocultural approach to mediated action*. Cambridge, MA: Harvard University Press.

Wooffitt, R. (2005) *Conversation Analysis and Discourse Analysis: a comparative and critical introduction*. London: SAGE Publications.

Wordsmith concordancing programme. Online, available at: www.oup.co.uk/episbn/0–19–459400–9 and www. lexically.net/wordsmith/index.html (accessed 9 February 2008).

Chapter 9

Learning to become a teacher

Participation across spheres for learning

Cecilie Flo Jahreie and Eli Ottesen

Introduction

In this chapter we demonstrate how cultural-historical activity theory (CHAT) can be a highly productive theoretical and methodological lens for studying how student teachers learn to become teachers. Through the course of their initial teacher education, student teachers carry out actions that are organized in different ways and situations, located both at higher education institutions (HEIs) and schools. In order to grasp how student teachers learn to become teachers, we need a conception of how the relationships between interaction, learning and available cultural tools on the one hand, and the activity in which they are used on the other, can be conceived theoretically and pursued analytically (Arnseth and Ludvigsen 2006). In each of the places, or spheres, that constitute a teacher education course there are different participants with multiple backgrounds, interests and motives for their actions. This means that the student teachers face a variety of tasks and expectations across spheres. What counts as knowledge is, in other words, inherent in the different spheres, but is legitimized in the participants' situated interactions in situations (Ludvigsen 2009). What is considered methodologically important is to pursue an analysis that makes it possible to study how meanings of knowledge are constituted in talk between participants, and how the participants, through their actions, are responding to the institutional context they act in and thereby make it relevant (Roth *et al.* 2005; Arnseth and Ludvigsen 2006). In this chapter we will first explain how learning is conceived. In order to illuminate how student teachers become teachers, we will then direct attention to what characterizes participation over the course of a teacher education course. We will then describe how to pursue this analytically, and illustrate the description by an empirical analysis of participants' talk. Finally we discuss our methodological concerns and conclude with why this theoretical and methodological approach is conceived as relevant for teacher educators and researchers within the field.

The basic premise in CHAT is that humans' operations and actions are dialectically related to the collective activity (Leont'ev 1978). They presuppose each other. Thus, student teachers' actions and interactions are intrinsic to the activity system in which they are embedded. Research must encompass the functions of the educational institutions that constitute teacher education, as well as the educational tasks (the objects) that are worked on by subjects. We follow Engeström by describing activities as 'systemic formations that gain durability by becoming institutionalised ... [and] ... take shape and manifest themselves only through actions performed by individuals and groups' (Engeström 2008a).

The dialectic means that actors in teacher education produce and reproduce the conditions in which they live, but are also subject to those conditions. Student teachers interpret and act by using available cultural tools, and their actions will in turn impact on the activity. In this perspective, learning is seen as 'changing participation in ongoing but changing collective praxis' (Roth *et al.* 2005), a local and historical process of continuous movement, development and change. The purpose of this chapter is to suggest an approach for studying student teachers' changing participation across the spheres in which they learn to teach. As an illustration for our methodological concerns, we use data from a research project at the Department for Teacher Education and School Development at the University of Oslo, Norway. The student teachers in this program are enrolled in a one-year course after finishing their subject degrees. On campus, the student teachers attend seminars and lectures in their subjects and in educational theory. A portfolio with a collection of the students' tasks (case assignments) in pedagogy and subject matters forms the basis for an oral examination at the end of the course. In the oral examination the intention is to integrate subjects and pedagogy, but each is given a separate mark (ILS 2002). The marks are decided on after a joint assessment of the portfolio and the oral presentation. During the programme, the student teachers have two periods of internship: four weeks in the first semester and eight weeks in the second. In each school a contact person organizes the internship tasks for the students.

Participation trajectories in and across learning spheres

Our methodological concern is to understand student teachers' changing participation during the course of teacher education. This is considered important in order to design for coherent trajectories for student teachers. During the one-year course, the students participate in a number of different settings and situations, constituting their learning trajectories. To aid our analysis, we have 'chunked' the student teachers' experiences into learning spheres. The spheres are subordinate to the activity of teacher education and regulated by its unfolding object, rules and division of labour, but are too diverse and shifting to be considered as activity systems (Hyysalo 2005). Learning spheres are socially developed and patterned ways of interaction (cf. Scribner and Cole 1981; Engeström 2008b). They are both formal and informal and they intersect, overlap and co-exist. In this chapter, we are focusing on the formal parts of the student teachers' trajectories, e.g. mentoring sessions, lectures, seminar groups, assignments to be completed and exams. The borders between learning spheres are not impermeable; for instance, tools like the lesson plan template may travel between spheres (Jahreie and Ottesen in press). It is in and through actions in these spheres that cultural tools and actions may be constituted as important to the participants.

Historically evolved scripts codify and regulate standard procedures in the learning spheres. Although the script may be coded in written rules, they are often tacitly assumed in traditions and normative patterns (Engeström 2008a). Due to its rule-like character, the script is a peculiar cultural tool used by the participants in interaction. As they move between learning spheres, student teachers need to negotiate how to make use of, transform or resist using, scripts and other cultural and social tools. In the interaction, the participants can follow their scripted roles, or they can go beyond the confines of the given script, negotiating a joint understanding of how to conceptualize and solve it (Engeström 2008a). To address how student teachers learn to become teachers, we analyse student teachers' participation across learning spheres, each of the spheres offering possibilities of enriching their repertoire as teachers. Thus, it is important to study the ways in which participation is managed across the spheres and the connection between them; we analyse learning as participation trajectories (Lave and Wenger 1991; Dreier 1999; Rasmussen 2005). In their participation, student teachers do not move from peripheral to core participation (Lave and Wenger 1991); rather, within each learning sphere where students engage in interaction they experience a form of 'core' participation (Roth *et al.* 2005). The notion of a participation trajectory enables the researcher to analyse how interaction evolves over time within and across learning spheres, and the relationship between them. Also, it provides insight to the interconnections between activities as realized in situated actions, and agents are part of, and contribute to, the activity (Rasmussen 2005; Edwards and Mackenzie 2008). We are therefore suggesting that it is important to direct attention to participation trajectories across learning spheres to illuminate how student teachers become teachers. In the next section we account for how to pursue this analytically.

The relation between talk and the sociohistorical activity

Lately, there has been a growing awareness of agentic action in CHAT research (e.g. Edwards 2005; Engeström 2008). Daniels (2007), starting from the collective, argues that a theoretically powerful move in CHAT would be to understand how talk is regulated in terms of social, cultural and historical relations. His argument brings to the fore the need to examine how individuals work discursively, and to relate their talk to the conditions in which meaning can be made. These issues are central to our methodological approach (Jahreie and Ottesen in press). Inspired by Roth and colleagues (Roth *et al.* 1999), we have studied how individual and collective agency emerges as participants deal with the opportunities, resources and constraints of different learning spheres. Our concern is with the ways in which student teachers make sense of available tools in interaction with other participants across learning spheres, and how their actions are historically regulated by the activity.

In the examples in this chapter, we use interaction analysis in order to investigate how actions unfold and resources are used to perform actions and operations at particular moments (Jordan and Henderson 1995), as well as the ways in which in-situ actions are related to a sociohistorical activity. Ethnographic fieldwork, such as observations, video-taping, interviews and document analysis provided a background for the analysis of interaction, and the detailed understanding derived from the interaction analysis informed the ethnographic understanding (Jordan and Henderson 1995).

To study the relationship between subjective actions and sociohistorical activities requires intermediate concepts (Engeström 2009). We use concepts that are empirically grounded, but informed by key activity theoretical concepts (Hyysalo 2005). Our concern is to suggest intermediate concepts that will allow an analysis of the participants' talk to reveal their participation trajectory in relation to the historical activity they engage in. In the learning spheres of teacher education, students carry out goal-directed actions. However, goals are open and pliable and constructed in interaction (cf. Holland and Reeves 1996; Middelton 1998) through the participants' accounts. Accounts are specific forms of language-use – i.e. actions such as explanations, clarifications or justifications (Mäkitalo and Säljö 2002). By focusing on students' accounts, the attention is on what the students treat as relevant, as well as how they try to deal with these concerns in their talk. Their accounts relate not only to their experiences, but also to what is justified as legitimate within the context (Shotter 1984; Ottesen 2007).

What are considered legitimate in the learning sphere are understood as scripts and are resources that participants use to interpret the talk and actions of others and to guide their own participation. It can be seen as an orientation the participants come to expect after repeated interactions in learning spheres (Gutiérrez *et al.* 1995). In the interaction, participants choose to give accounts for the historical script, or for alternative scripts. For research in teacher education the whys and hows of student teachers' accounts are an important concern. In our studies we have shown how division of labour may constrain or afford possibilities for agency and action (Jahreie and Ludvigsen 2007; Jahreie in press). However, neither entitlement nor legitimacy is a 'given'; rather, they are negotiated in interaction as possibilities for actions. *Positioning* (cf. Holland *et al.* 1998; Daniels 2007) is a helpful analytical concept to unpack accounting practices. Student teachers' options for participation in learning spheres are regulated by their scripted roles. The script has the function of distributing roles and defining more or less clearly what is expected from each role (Engeström 2008a). However, position is situated and created in interaction. Holland *et al.* (1998) argue that, in situated action, there are spaces of authoring, moments that participants use for positioning rather than being positioned. In the flow of interaction, participants position themselves in accordance with, or as a reaction to, the script. Student teachers make accounts for what they will orient and position themselves in relation to. Positioning may imply that the student teachers adhere to the requirement to use specific concepts or theories in certain ways or to what are considered to be appropriate topics for talk in a seminar group, oral exam, etc. By using interaction analysis we are able to demonstrate how actors participate in learning spheres, how they make use of tools and resources in their argumentation, and how sociohistorical aspects are understood, dealt with and picked up. In the empirical analysis below (pp. 138–141) we show that what counts as knowledge, and which aspects of the practice the participants orient and position themselves in relation to, are managed by interaction, but are regulated in social, cultural and historical relations.

Empirical analysis

The empirical analysis in this chapter serves as an illustration of our methodological arguments. The data were produced as part of a larger study, which is built on extensive observations over a period of one year. One group of four student teachers was observed during their courses in educational theory, history and social science, and in their two periods of internship. In addition, one of the oral exams was observed. We have included extracts from three learning spheres: (1) an internship meeting between university teacher, contact person at the internship school and the student teachers at that school; (2) a sequence from the seminar in pedagogy; and (3) an oral examination. This selection of extracts allows us to follow the students' trajectories over time, and, important to our arguments, to follow the trajectories in different learning spheres.

Extract 1: internship meeting

The first extract is from a meeting held at the school in the first internship period with a university teacher in social science, eight student teachers and the school's contact person. In the meeting a number of issues of relevance to the teacher education programme are discussed. By asking questions directed at the students, the university teacher (UT) sets the agenda. However, the students are active participants, sharing their accounts of different aspects of the programme. The contact person (CP) does not play an active role in the discussion; the sequence that follows is the only time she was asked a direct question in this meeting. In the excerpt, the UT orients the talk to the students' case assignments. He is interested in the school's engagement in the assignments. According to the school–DTE partnership agreement, the school consents to be informed about the cases, to contribute to the students' work and to help in the process (PPU Directions 2002/2003).

[1]   UT: Does the school take any action regarding the case assignments?

[2]   CP: I haven't had anything to do with that. I've just read that it requires that we can help and contribute to the assignments, but I'm not familiar with the aims of the cases and their content [addressing the students]. But I'm sure that is something you have informed your mentors about.

[3]   GINA: We've got two hours with mentoring sessions each week with each mentor. During this time you are supposed to talk about what you are going to do in the following lesson, how it went, you have to talk a bit about the pupils, and the fact that you are going to observe one, maybe talk a bit about that. You don't have time to go more into it. And our mentors have heavy workloads, so to use them more is a bit difficult I think.

[4]   KRIS: Just to follow up on that. Most of the meetings we've had have been about lesson planning, the accomplished lesson, we have discussed structures in the class a lot, and things we should notice. And there the mentors have been quite pedagogical, they haven't been strict about what to do or not to do, but listened to what we've observed. I think it is our fault that we've focused a lot on these formal requirements, but I have to admit that I have stopped doing that. I have taken notes and then I'm going to see how they fit. (...). The requirements of the cases makes one feel a bit cramped.

[5]   UT: The main impression of what you're saying is that the mentors have let you loose. That is very professional.

The visit from the university teacher is a recurring meeting, taking place each year. The UT uses the script that is expected in this kind of visit: he asks questions and evaluates, and the CP and the students answer the questions. The UT sets the scene by asking a direct question to the CP. Since the schools are expected to be involved in the students' cases, this may be an effort to exercise control. The CP's response indicates that she knows what is expected, but that she regards this as a responsibility for the students and the mentors ('I'm sure that is something you have informed your mentors about'). In this way, through her account, she opts for a position as a responsible partner, although she does not herself get involved in the case assignments. Gina's account has the form of an explanation that legitimizes why they have not had opportunities to discuss the cases with the mentors. She refers to issues they are expected to cover in the sessions related to planning and teaching experiences [3]. Kris supports Gina, before adding that the students focus too much on the formal requirements. His final sentence might indicate that the case assignments take too much time and resources in the internship. He emphasizes that he has done what is required of him; thus, he is legitimizing his conduct both within the school (he is not focusing on the formalities any more) and the DTE (he has made notes that he will use when writing out the cases). In [5] the UT appears positive towards Kris's description of the mentors' role, seeing it as professional.

The participants in the meeting all follow the expected script and what is expected of them, but they give different accounts for it. Through his questions, the UT monitors the school's conduct, and the rules of the activity. The way he gives account for the script positions him as the university's representative. The CP, on the other hand, produces an alternative account of the rules and division of labour. She is aware of what is required of the school, but the student and mentors should deal with this. While the UT refers to the rules and divisions of labour of the partnership, the CP is positioned within the school; the students are expected to inform the mentors, and the mentors are supposed to help and contribute. The students' accounts indicate their 'in-between' position, trying to be accountable to both systems. Through their accounts, they position themselves both as *teachers* (recognizing the mentors' workload [3], not focusing on formal directives any more [4]) and as students (they have made observations and taken notes). This indicates the conflicts between expectations from the DTE (the students are supposed to just do observations in the first internship period), the choices of the school (giving the students lesson responsibilities) and the practical possibilities for accommodating to the intentions embedded in the regulations. Another conflict that appears is the institutional regulation of the mentors' role and how the UT positions them as 'professional'.

Extract 2: seminar in pedagogy – scientific language

This extract is taken from the last seminar in pedagogy where the focus is on preparation for the upcoming oral exam. A recurring theme during their talk is the use of scientific language. One student, Fiona, argues that one may be a good teacher, even if one does not 'know all the concepts'. Just before the conversation below takes place, the university teacher asked the students what they see as an alternative to scientific language. While Fiona agrees that everyday talk is not necessarily an alternative, she argues that the concepts used in teacher education are often given different meaning. Alex proposes an alternative.

[1] ALEX: Instead of asking 'what do you mean by Vygotsky's zone of prox-imal development?', I would explain what is meant by the concept and ask what do you mean by that difference, the development etc. That is the alternative. Instead of talking about his view, talk about what that view is, how you look at it. Maybe.

[2] GEIR: Isn't the point that you do not know Vygotsky like that, but that you can use, or compare with what you are doing when teaching? Or what it has to say about learning and teaching? I can reel off every-thing about Vygotsky, but (…)

[3] TEACHER: That is pretty irrelevant. Just to reel off and do namedrop-ping that is ridiculous. One is supposed to use it to reflect about prac-tice, and get a conscious relation to it, that is the point. Otherwise it makes no sense, so I totally agree with you.

Alex takes the teacher's invitation and proposes an alternative [1]. It is reasonable to assume that the impending exam situation is Alex's point of reference. He takes the position of a censor, suggesting how censors should pose their questions during the examination. Geir supports Alex's suggestion by saying that concepts should be used to reflect on learning and teaching. The teacher picks up on Geir's account, and characterizes namedropping as 'ridiculous'.

The interaction in this extract is a less rigidly scripted place (Gutiérrez *et al.* 1995) than the previous extract. Rather than following a script, they focus on a shared problem, negotiating what counts as knowledge in an exam situation. Through their accounts, the students challenge the teacher by positioning themselves as experts, teachers or censors. Alex's alternative account is based on his personal view: 'I would. .. ' Geir, on the other hand, orients his accounts to institutional regulations and to the teachers' accounts in the seminars. The teacher takes up their arguments, and in this way he acknowledges the students' positions as legitimate. What counts as knowledge in the forthcoming oral exam is to use theoret-ical concepts to reflect on practical experiences.

Extract 3: oral exam

In this extract we analyse Kris' oral examination in pedagogy and history. The students were asked to make a presentation for the exam. According to the information at the seminar referred to above (p. 00), the presentation should be an example from the student's internship. The teacher emphasized that this gives the students an opportunity to be active and have a voice in the exam (field notes 05/07–03). Kris chose to show a few minutes from a movie (*Saving Private Ryan*). His presentation was about a lesson he had planned for his internship, but decided not to carry out. Building on a dialogical perspective based on Bakhtin and Vygotsky, he focused on how experiences (as through a movie) may be a basis for verbalization and concept development. After the student's presentation, a more traditional examination takes place, where two teachers (in pedagogy and history) examine according to their specialisms. The teacher in pedagogy (TP) picks up on the student's decision not to use the movie in his history class. He talks about a teacher's role as a subject expert and as a person with some responsibility for the care and well-being of pupils, and asks Kris to elaborate on this. Kris talks about teacher professionalism, and the teacher follows up:

[1] TP. Teacher professionalism, I want to bring that a bit further because it consists of some components, do you know which components I have in mind?

[2] KRIS: Hmm, no, I'm thinking of, professionalism is about . . .

[3] TP: [Let me give you a clue so we don't spend time on this. Bergem classifies this, (. . .) and he puts up three categories for competence.

[4] KRIS: Ehmm (. . .).

[5] TP: Do you know what I have in mind?

[6] KRIS: I have to admit I (. . .)

[7] TP: [But you (. . .)

[8] KRIS: [I'm following you, it is something about, if you categorize something. If you give me the categories I will see if I, I'm thinking of knowledge production, you need to impart knowledge, he uses another term, ehm (. . .)

[9] TP: [Subject competence, pedagogical competence and competence of professional ethics.

[10] KRIS: Okay, then I'm with you. (. . .) A bit related to this are the three components of the development of practice theory [Kris goes on to explain the model of the practical triangle].

To give an appropriate analysis of this extract, it is necessary to see it in relation to the examination as a whole. In his presentation, Kris explains how to use experiences (through watching and talking about a movie) to

develop concepts and oral skills. The student seems to have been consciously attempting to integrate the subject matter and pedagogy in his
presentation. In the extract, the student answers questions from the TP.
Kris has just talked about teacher professionalism and the TP wants him to
mention three specific elements in relation to this [1]. Teacher professionalism is covered in different parts of the curriculum, and it is difficult
for Kris to know what the teacher has in mind. However, he tries to give an
account, but is interrupted by the teacher who explains that he wants him
to use Bergem's classification of competence [3]. This notion of competence is part of the curriculum. Kris is not able to reproduce Bergem's categories, but tries to make an account without remembering the exact
terms the teacher has in mind [8]. Again the teacher interrupts, this time
giving him the right answer. The 'naming' of the categories supplies Kris
with information that enables him to continue. In [10] Kris gives an
account for how he sees this classification in relation to another concept
in the curriculum (development of practice theory).

After the examination, the two teachers have a short meeting to discuss
the student's oral presentation and decide on a set of marks for each of
the two subjects. Based on the student's written portfolio, they have
decided the limits for adjusting the students' marks up or down. In the
following sequence they discuss the mark for pedagogy.

[11] TSD: But in between the limits that we have, I feel that he pushes the
borders quite a bit up.
[12] TP: yes? (…)
[13] TSD: Well, but I have (…)
[14] TP: I'm not sure.
[15] TSD: But you had this with the concept of competence that he was not
sure of and (…)
[16] TP: But he is quite good on learning theories, and that is an important
basis (…)
[17] TP: He could have done it better, I gave him the possibility to go close
to 2.4 or 2.3 but he does not live up to that, when he didn't manage
the concept of competence, he doesn't live up to that.

The teacher in subject didactics (TSD) seemed to think that the student
gave a better impression than in the portfolio [11]. The TP, on the other
hand, answers 'yes' in a questioning voice, and the TSD tries to explain his
view, but is interrupted by the TP who seems to disagree. The TSD
explains TP's uncertainty with the concepts that the student did not
remember. However, the TP emphasizes that the student displayed a good
understanding of learning theories, which he sees as important. The TP
seems quite uncertain about deciding on a mark; however, in [17] he
reaches a conclusion. He explains that he could have given him 2.4 or 2.3

but, since he did not know the required concepts about competence, he does not 'live up to that'. The focus is therefore on what the student does not know when assessing the student.

In the two sequences of interactions from the oral exam, the teachers and the student follow a traditional exam script. Historically, examinations are built on asymmetric relationships: students are expected to come up with 'right' answers in accordance to the curriculum, and the university teachers assess the quality of their response. In his opening presentation, the student accounts for the shared object, negotiated in the seminar: he uses a dialogical perspective to account for development of pupils' verbalization. The presentation is seen as good, but in the following examination the participants retreat from this unscripted space: accounts and student positions that are considered legitimate in the seminar no longer count. One possible explanation can be that the community does not have enough interactional experience in this unscripted space to mediate participation and, thus, to mediate a different understanding of teaching and learning (Gutiérrez *et al.* 1995). Appropriate accounts in this script are characterized by the 'right' answers. Both the student and the teachers produce appropriate accounts of what is expected in an exam script, the teachers position themselves as authorities and the student teacher as a student.

Discussion

A key characteristic of teacher education is its distribution across disciplines, sites and actors. For researchers aiming to study student teachers' learning, this poses a number of methodological challenges. CHAT provides a useful framework to meet some of these challenges: it facilitates investigation of the interrelationship between actors' situated actions, the cultural resources that are at play and the sociohistorical regulations that work on, and are worked on by, the actors. In this chapter, our aim has been to present a methodological approach to research that would enable us to disclose the agency of actors and the cultural-historic and systemic constraints that students confront as they learn to become teachers. Our approach has been to explore how knowledge is negotiated and accounted for in teacher education. Our investigation of interactions in institutional learning spheres allows us to pay close attention to different aspects of the students' learning trajectories (e.g. cultural resources at play and the students' agency and negotiations). Our findings indicate that, although the student teachers' learning trajectories provide a common motive for teacher education in schools and in DTE, these trajectories are often interpreted and constructed differently in different learning spheres. For example, in the analysis we have indicated how what counts as knowing differs in the seminar group and in the oral examination. Thus, a central concern in the analytic work is to illuminate the process of knowledge construction as a dynamic between individual agency and collective actions in different learning spheres, but also its relationship to the cultural-historical activity.

Complex activity systems, such as teacher education, may require intermediate concepts as heuristics for empirical analyses (Engeström 2008b). In this chapter we have demonstrated how actors adhere to cultural scripts in their construction of accounts. Scripts connect micro-processes in the different learning spheres to the cultural-historical activity of teacher education. The rules, tools and division of labour in the activity system are actualized in scripted roles in the learning spheres, legitimizing certain accounts or positions and proscribing others. The analytic concepts 'account', 'position' and 'script' aid the analysis in demonstrating how the participants' learning trajectories develop as individuals and collective movements, and their relationship to the cultural and historical development of the activity it is part of. The concepts make the agency of individuals transparent as they participate in collective actions. While participants are positioned as, for example, students, mentors or university teachers, based on the salient rules and division of labour of the activity system, actors also have the option to challenge or expand their positions. However, the legitimacy of their accounts varies between learning spheres, leading to disturbances and making evident contradictions inherent to the activity system. In the talk, student teachers and teacher educators make their ideas and understandings public, for example, as Alex's account about the use of scientific language in the oral examination in excerpt 2. Through his account he opens a space for negotiation. He can position himself as a 'virtual' censor, and make his account from that perspective. However, in the oral exam (excerpt 3), there is only one position available, that of a student. Kris' account is produced from that position; his agency is restricted. Using these analytical concepts, we draw attention to issues of power and influence in teacher education. We have demonstrated that objects often seem to arise from negotiations saturated with opposition and clashes of interests. Although the participants are working to construct the 'same' object across learning spheres, their motives may be different: for example, the participants' talk about scientific language that varied between the seminar group (extract 2) and the oral examination (extract 3). In the internship meeting (extract 1), student teachers produced different accounts that live side-by-side. The participants' accounts reflect the rules of two activity systems.

Conclusion

The quality of teacher education is a central concern for policy-makers around the world. Suggestions from the OECD point to the need for teacher education to be better adapted to teachers' changed roles, to rethink the role of field experiences, and to be better tuned to the interconnections between initial teacher education, induction and continued professional development in a perspective of life-long learning (McKenzie and Santiago 2005). In Norway, a recent White Paper (KD 2009) presents a number of efforts aiming to increase the quality in teacher education by strengthening the interplay of thorough reforms in teacher education and by strengthening partnerships between schools and HEIs for continued professional development of teachers. The methodological framework presented in this chapter is an important contribution to the field of research that might give further insight about learning in teacher education as well as workplace learning for teachers.

As part of our theoretical understanding, we accounted for how activity systems are reproduced or resisted in and through action. Our methodological argument has been that to understand how students learn to become teachers we need to study how the meanings of objects, tools and knowledge are negotiated in interaction between participants. Through their actions, the student teachers are responding to various features of the activity in which they act and thereby make them relevant. Seeing learning as a trajectory of participation in and across learning spheres makes it possible for teacher educators to reveal local disturbances in relation to contradictions in the institutional activity. This is important knowledge in order to prepare for transparent and coherent participation trajectories for student teachers.

Appendix: transcript notation

[ ] Text in square brackets represents clarifying information
[..... Simultaneous/overlapping talk
(...) Short pause in the speech

References

Arnseth, H.C. and Ludvigsen, S. (2006) 'Approaching institutional contexts: systemic versus dialogic research in CSCL', *Computer-Supported Collaborative Learning* 1, 167–185.

Daniels, H. (2007) 'Discourse and identity in cultural-historical activity theory: a response', *International Journal of Educational Research* 46, 94–99.

Dreier, O. (1999) 'Personal trajectories of participation across contexts of social practice', *Outlines: Critical Social Studies* 1, 5–32.

Edwards, A. (2005) 'Relational agency: learning to be a resourceful practitioner', *International Journal of Educational Research* 43, 168–182.

Edwards, A. and Mackenzie, L. (2008) 'Identity shifts in informal learning trajectories', in Van Oers, B., Wardekker, W., Elbers, E. and Van Der Veer, R. (eds) *The transformation of learning advances in cultural-historical activity theory*. Cambridge, New York: Cambridge University Press.

Engeström, Y. (2008a) *From teams to knots: activity-theoretical studies of collaboration and learning at work*. Cambridge: Cambridge University Press.

Engeström, Y. (2008b) 'Enriching activity theory without shortcuts', *Interacting with Computers* 20, 256–259.

Engeström, Y. (2009) 'The future of activity theory: a rough draft', in Sannino, A., Daniels, H. and Gutierrez, K.D. (eds) *Learning and expanding with activity theory*. Cambridge: Cambridge University Press.

Gutiérrez, K., Rymes, B. and Larson, J. (1995) 'Script, counterscript, and underlife in the classroom: James Brown versus *Brown* v. *Board of Education*', *Harvard Educational Review* 65, 445–471.

Holland, D. and Reeves, J.R. (1996) 'Activity theory and the view from somewhere: team perspectives on the intellectual work on programming', in Nardi, B. (ed.) *Context and consciousness: activity theory and human–computer interaction*. Cambridge: MIT Press.

Holland, D., Lachicotte, W., Skinner, D. and Cain, D. (1998) *Identity and agency in cultural worlds*. Cambridge: Harvard University Press.

Hyysalo, S. (2005) 'Objects and motives in a product design process', *Mind, Culture, and Activity: An International Journal* 12, 19–36.

ILS (2002) *Utfyllende retningslinjer og orientering om praktisk-pedagogisk utdanning. PLUTO projektet* [*Supplementary guidelines and orientation about the practical-pedagogical education. The PLUTO project*]. The Faculty of Education, University of Oslo.

Jahreie, C. (in press) 'Making sense of cultural tools in case work: student teachers' participation trajectory', *Teaching and Teacher Education*.

Jahreie, C.F. and Ludvigsen, S.R. (2007) 'Portfolios as boundary object: learning and change in teacher education', *Research and Practice in Technology Enhanced Learning* 2, 299–318.

Jahreie, C.F. and Ottesen, E. (in press) 'Constructions of boundaries in teacher education: analyzing student teachers' accounts', *Mind, Culture and Activity*.

Jordan, B. and Henderson, A. (1995) 'Interaction analysis: foundations and practice', *The Journal of the Learning Sciences* 4, 39–103.

KD (2009) 'Læreren, rollen og utdanningen' ['The teachers, their role, and the education'], White Paper no 11, 2008/2009.

Lave, J. and Wenger, E. (1991) *Situated learning: legitimate peripheral participation*. Cambridge: Cambridge University Press.

Leont'ev, A.N. (1978) *Activity, consciousness and personality*. Englewood Cliffs: Prentice-Hall.

Ludvigsen, S.R. (2009) 'What counts as knowledge: learning to use categories in computer environments', in Säljö, R. (ed.) *ICT and transformation of learning practices*. Amsterdam: Pergamon Press.

McKenzie, P. and Santiago, P. (2005) *Teachers matters: attracting, developing, and retaining effective teachers*. OECD: OECD Publishing.

Mäkitalo, Å. and Säljö, R. (2002) 'Talk in institutional context and institutional context in talk: categories as situated practices', *TEXT* 22, 57–82.

Middleton, D. (1998) 'Talking work: argument, common knowledge, and improvisation in teamwork', in Engeström, Y. and Middleton, D. (eds) *Cognition and communication at work*. Cambridge: Cambridge University Press.

Ottesen, E. (2007) 'Teachers "in the making": building accounts of teaching', *Teaching and Teacher Education* 23(5), 612–623.

Rasmussen, I. (2005) 'Project work and ICT: studying learning as participation trajectories', PhD thesis no. 46, Faculty of Education, University of Oslo, Oslo: unipublished.

Roth, W.-M., Hwang, S.W., Goulart, M.I. and Lee, Y.J. (2005) *Participation, learning and identity dialectical perspectives*. Berlin: Lehmanns Media.

Roth, W.-M., McGinn, M.K., Woszczyna, C. and Boutonne, S. (1999) 'Differential participation during science conversations: the interaction of focal artefacts, social configurations and physical arrangements', *Journal of the Learning Sciences* 8, 293–347.

Scribner, S. and Cole, M. (1981) *The psychology of literacy*. New York: toExcel.

Shotter, J. (1984) *Social accountability and selfhood*. Oxford: Basil Blackwell.

Chapter 10

Breaking out of a professional abstraction

The pupil as materialized object for trainee teachers

Annalisa Sannino

Introduction

The transition from abstract notions of pupils to specific understandings of concrete individual pupils and differences among them is often seen as a natural consequence of novice teachers' exposure to interactions with pupils. Teacher training programmes can take this transition for granted. Trainee teachers (hereafter called 'trainees') are expected to move from abstract notions of pupils taught at the university to real teaching experiences in schools which materialize the abstract notions. In this chapter I argue that this transition instead represents a critical phase and a learning challenge in the professional development of teachers.

The chapter discusses the materialization of the pupil as a professional object for Italian elementary school trainee teachers who were involved in a project of developmental intervention (Engeström 2007). Davydov's (1990) theory of learning as ascending from the abstract to the concrete and Leont'ev's (1978) notion of object are used as theoretical lenses to conceptualize this process. The project aimed at introducing in the school a computer-mediated learning practice internationally known as the 'Fifth Dimension' or the '5D' (Cole 1996; Nilsson and Nocon 2005). The 5D was used as an interventionist methodology of teacher education for university students who would become teachers (for an analysis of this 5D as a school-based innovation, see Sannino 2008).

The 5D was designed to be a response to the critique by the trainees of the traditional university internship programme in the school which did not allow them to interact directly with the pupils. During the phase of preliminary ethnographic fieldwork, interviews were conducted in which these trainees repeatedly pointed out their need to directly interact with pupils in order to prepare themselves for the teaching profession.

The chapter analyses the intervention as a process of progressive discovery of pupils as the concrete object of the trainees' activity of teaching. More specifically, the chapter aims to answer the following research questions: what are the dynamics that characterize the materialization of pupils as professional object for trainee teachers? And what is the relevance of these dynamics in terms of improvement of learning in teacher education and the 5D type of research interventions?

The 5D intervention project and two conceptions of pupils

The 5D is a model of learning and teaching activity, stemming from cultural-historical psychological theories of learning and development (Cole *et al.* 2006). In partnerships between universities and local communities, the 5D promotes collaborative research efforts that emphasize children's potential and initiatives through individualized learning. The 5D activities are characterized by the participation of undergraduate students in dyads or in small groups with children, and by the use of a rich variety of ICT-based and other artefacts (Cole 1996). One of these artefacts is a maze through which children move according to rules, but also independently choosing learning tasks of their interest. Learning tasks are illustrated to children in task cards in which one can select among progressive levels of difficulty. Children are encouraged to communicate by writing with a mysterious figure generally called the Wizard (named 'Giò' in the case analysed in this chapter).

Cole (2005) summarises the theoretical underpinnings and the purpose of the 5D intervention as follows:

> Children's educational activity is not confined to standard classroom environments, with strict teacher control and one-to-many forms of discourse associated with transmission forms of education. Rather, the modes of participation are more 'horizontally' organized to encourage active student participation.... The basic idea [is] that while computer and modern communications technologies are important tools, it is the *social use of the technology* that is essential in determining its effectiveness. In particular, the ways in which such technologies are deployed is crucial for creating horizontal social learning environments where children, teachers, community members, members of ethnic minorities, college students, and researchers can collaborate in design and re-design and where each has a voice and is involved in that ongoing co-design.
>
> (Cole 2005: 10–11; emphasis in the original)

The 5D was promoted as a research intervention within a project of collaboration between an Italian university and a local elementary school. The project was designed to be a response to two pressing demands coming from Italian authorities and the local university. First, the Italian Ministry of Education wanted to introduce ICT in instruction starting from the first grade. Second, future elementary school teachers who studied at the university went regularly to the school for internships; they preferred to spend their time during internship more actively than sitting in the classrooms mostly observing what the teacher did and interacting only occasionally with children. The attempt of the researchers was to offer the 5D as an opportunity to meet the new requirement from the Ministry and to offer an alternative to complement the traditional internship in the school.

A total of 13 third-year university students were involved in the project as trainees. The 5D took place in the computer room of the school during the regular teaching hours. The 5D physical arrangement was characterized by 13 computers and a three-dimensional board game which reproduced a labyrinth. Each room in the labyrinth contained two-to-three computer-mediated learning tasks. Each task could be accomplished on three different levels of competence and was explained in a brief guide called a 'task card'. One or two first- and fourth-grade pupils were assigned to each trainee during weekly sessions of three hours for a period of three months. The trainees assisted the pupils in accomplishing the computer-mediated learning tasks. The pupils themselves chose the tasks while navigating through the labyrinth. Four researchers and three teachers of the school were present to supervise and support the trainees. The trainees were asked to write ethnographic field notes after each session.

Meetings between researchers and trainees were held in the school after each 5D session. During these meetings participants discussed salient moments or difficulties as experienced by the trainees and as reported in their field notes. Researchers who participated in the meetings were also the instructors at the university who organized a course based on Vygotsky's works. All the trainees took part in the course before the beginning of the project.

The project made visible two conceptions of pupils. Teaching in this school and the trainees' teacher education programme were primarily based on a conception that requires going through age-appropriate curriculum units according to the teacher's plan. This conception was captive of a tradition which does not allow the pupils to act independently, and restricts manifestations of their individual potential. The 5D intervention, on the other hand, was based on a conception that assigns a more active role to the pupils in the school. The characteristics of these two conceptions will be elaborated in more detail in the next sections of the chapter.

The extraordinary act as ascending from the abstract to the concrete

From a theoretical point of view, the analysis draws on Leont'ev's (1978) notions of need and object, and on Davydov's (1990) notions of empirical and theoretical generalization. According to Leont'ev:

need is in itself not capable of evoking any kind of positively directed activity.... Only as a result of its 'meeting' with an object that answers it does it first become capable of directing and regulating activity. The meeting of need with object is an extraordinary act.

(Leont'ev 1978: 54)

Paraphrasing Leont'ev, the need to teach is in itself not capable of evoking positively directed activity of teaching. Only as a result of its 'meeting' with the pupils as an object that answers this need does it first become capable of directing and regulating teaching activity. The meeting of the need to teach with the pupil as an object is an extraordinary act. Leont'ev's notion of object is not reducible to the everyday meaning of the term object, which would imply unidirectional teaching processes dominated by teachers who objectify pupils. Neither does the everyday notion of object apply to the idea of trainees' need to discover the pupils as the object of their activity of teaching. For Leont'ev (1978), the object is the driving force to which the activity is directed. It has a dynamic life of its own and it resists attempts at control. When the trainee teachers are brought to discover pupils' peculiarities and potentials, the encounter between the need to teach and the pupils to be taught (the object of teaching) is made possible. The dynamic nature of the pupil gives the need a direction.

In the extraordinary act, there is an aspect of breaking out that Leont'ev does not take up. The extraordinary act does not consist merely in the meeting of one's need with an object, like in the case of a hungry person who finds food and fills their need with it. For trainee teachers, the need to teach was fed with a pseudo-object, corresponding to the abstract notion of pupils acquired through reading and university lectures. In other words, the need to teach was nourished with a professional abstraction. In dialectical epistemology this kind of abstraction is an instantiation of empirical thinking. The empirical thinking into which the trainees were socialized was overwhelmingly present in the field notes written by the trainees after the first encounter with the pupils. One of the students wrote the following:

TRAINEE 5: The first grader with whom I worked today can be defined as hyperactive, he was not interested in the task, he wanted to play by doing tricks to his buddies, was disturbing with impertinent comments, despite my attempts to encourage and stimulate him. He did not manage to accomplish the task, became nervous and refused to continue. Has difficulties in grasping situations in their globality, in reading and writing, and to find logical connections. He is still in the sensorimotor phase.

The field note operates with abstract categories and classification schemes such as 'hyperactive' and 'sensorimotor phase'. The pupil's observable behaviour is described and categorized in a way that leaves little space for the emergence and nourishment of potentials and possibilities.

The extraordinary act requires breaking out from the pseudo-object. This process is conflictual by nature (Vasilyuk 1988). As my analysis will demonstrate, the puzzlement of the trainees while encountering problematic situations was an indication that they were facing conflicting conceptions of the pupils.

The pseudo-object may be conceptualized using Davydov's notion of abstraction. In dialectical terms an abstraction is an aspect separated from its functional relations in the overall systemic totality to which it originally belongs (Falmagne 1995). Davydov argues that there are two types of abstractions: empirical and theoretical. Empirical abstraction, also called formal abstraction, is a classification of superficial features of phenomena. Theoretical abstraction refers to the identification of the genetic origins of phenomena that may externally be not alike at all. A theoretical abstraction is based on a functional relationship, also called germ cell. While observation and categorization are actions at the root of empirical abstraction, concrete transformation, change and experimentation are actions at the root of theoretical abstraction. One not familiar with Davydov's theory might spontaneously associate empirical with concrete, and theoretical with abstract, based on the ordinary use of these terms. Instead, in dialectical terms the process of ascending from the abstract to the concrete is a movement from empirical to theoretical abstraction.

An example of theoretical abstraction comes from Engels and concerns the steam engine (Vygotsky 1997: 321). The germ cell of a steam engine as it was designed by its inventor in his drawings looks very different from any particular steam engine. Later, starting from this germ cell, steam engines were built in many different ways and shapes, and for many different purposes – for ships, for locomotives, etc. The system of using steam power is thus based on the discovery of a very simple relation which was then modelled for making different variations of it. Theoretical thinking experiments with problematic situations in order to find the germ cell behind them. Then, starting from this original abstract principle, one can observe its different material manifestations and even conceive further new variations as the abstraction is applied to the understanding and construction of the concrete – in this case, concrete pupils in the school.

The teacher education programme of these trainees conveyed a formal abstraction of pupils. The pseudo-object trainees met when they went through their internship was this formal abstraction based on superficial features. The conception of the pupil as a pseudo-object corresponds to the ideas that age determines pupils' capabilities to learn and that the teacher needs to control pupils in order to avoid distraction in learning. The 5D was an attempt to make the trainees overcome this empirical abstraction and move towards a theoretical abstraction. The theoretical abstraction from which the trainee could ascend to the concrete pupil corresponds to Vygotsky' ideas that pupils' capability to learn is expanded by means of social and artefactual mediation by tools and signs, and that pupils' agentive initiatives are crucial for learning.

The trainees were already familiar with these ideas of Vygotsky, having participated in a class and a seminar in which they read his works. This was, however, not sufficient for them to overcome the empirical abstraction. According to Davydov (1988), the starting point for the formation of theoretical abstraction is transformation. Transformation is the first of six learning actions that characterize the process of ascending from the abstract to the concrete. This action, also referred to as 'the main action', consists in experimenting with a task 'in order to reveal the universal relationship of the object under study' (Davydov 1988: 30).

Davydov's description of this first action does not include the individuals' experiential and conflictual encounters with their previously acquired empirical conceptions, which are likely to play a role when they start experimenting. A similar critique was previously formulated by Engeström:

> Davydov's theory is ... oriented to learning processes within the confines of a classroom where the curricular contents are determined ahead of time by more knowledgeable adults.... This probably explains why it does not contain the first action of critical questioning and rejection.
>
> (1999: 384)

In this chapter I will demonstrate that the extraordinary act in which the need meets an object is a process of ascending from the abstract to the concrete, which requires the subject to break out of previously acquired conceptions in conflict with new emerging ones. In this perspective the experimentation appears as a composite learning action that can be realized in four different steps, presented in the next section.

Breaking out from a pseudo-object

The main data collected during the project consist of 113 ethnographic field notes written by the trainees and video-recordings of ten meetings between researchers and trainees. These data serve here an exploratory analysis based on careful reading of the entire corpus. I have tentatively identified a pattern of successive steps that may be further explored as a potential expansion of the first learning action suggested by Davydov (1988). Salient excerpts from these data are used here as examples that elucidate a four-step pattern.[1] The four steps are thus a hypothesis to be tested in further research. Not every trainee went through all these four steps, but in the corpus as a whole they appear distinctively enough to suggest a pattern.

The field notes through the period of the 5D intervention show that the trainees were initially captive of abstract features of the stereotypical pupils. The 5D intervention and the efforts of researchers in the meetings to solicit detailed and self-critical field notes provided an opportunity for the trainees to open up and to start transcending this abstraction. In particular, the field notes written towards the end of the project document this turn towards a different type of abstraction.

Step 1: contrasting different views

While experimenting with teaching in the 5D, the trainees began to describe teaching experiences with pupils which were in contrast with the practices of teacher's control and age-appropriate tasks. The trainees came upon characteristics of the pupil that were unknown to them and discovered individual potentials of each pupil. In this step, which coincided with the beginning of the 5D, they mainly emphasized that children can do things on their own.

TRAINEE 4: Giulia had never worked with a computer before. I had my hand on her hand on the mouse and half way through I realized that my hand was not guiding her any more. She was moving autonomously on the desktop.

TRAINEE 8: We were working on a task on the food chain. Lorenzo and I established a relation of collaboration. He asked for help when he needed help, otherwise he continued on his own. The teacher came to point out that the task we were working on was based on the programme of the third grade and that there were therefore notions involved that the pupils did not have yet. Lorenzo, however, understood immediately these notions. After the first reading he summarized: 'Sheep eat grass and the wolf eats the sheep. The grass is a producer, the sheep a primary consumer, and the wolf a secondary consumer.'

The process of breaking out of a pseudo-object or an empirical abstraction is a conflictual process. The conflict here is between the realization of the pupils' potentials (as displayed in these excerpts) and the contrasting conception of the pupil to be given age-appropriate tasks. This contrasting conception often materialized in comments like the one of the teacher mentioned by trainee 8. As the excerpt illustrates, concrete evidence of the pupil's performance in the given task disconfirmed the teacher's comment on the task's inappropriateness for a first-grade pupil. This conflict led the trainees to a second step.

Step 2: experiencing conflicting views

As the 5D sessions continued, the trainees started to point out that they were encountering difficulties. These difficulties were reported by referring to superficial features of the pupil or of the task, which, they thought, made the pupil no longer work well on the tasks. For instance, in the following field note excerpts the pupils are described as distracted or bored, and the task too difficult as such. These problems encountered by the trainees were also taken up during the meetings with the researchers who suggested that the trainees should experiment with mediating artefacts.

TRAINEE 6: Today he [the pupil] was particularly distracted.... He did not show interest in what we were doing. The task card required the reading of the clock taking into account the position of the sun or the moon through a window. 'But I do not know how to do it,' he said. I reassured him, telling that we would accomplish the task together. I started by explaining the procedure several times, and he followed counting the hours and the minutes. During the accomplishment of the task he continually asked for help from me. He tried to complete the task during the time we had available, but he did not succeed. I hope that next time he will be less distracted because I am sure that he can make it.

While the trainees were allowed to perform teaching in the 5D, their need to teach did not take an immediate effect as they were puzzled by two types of problematic situations for the pupil and for themselves.

The first type of problematic situation concerned interferences and attempts of control by the school teachers, exemplified in the next two excerpts.

TRAINEE 4: I had difficulties with a pupil who wanted to write to Giò, and was thinking about a sentence. Then the teacher came and told her what to write. The teacher often interferes that way.
RESEARCHER: She replaced the pupil's voice with her own.
TRAINEE 4: And she replaces also our own voice.
TRAINEE 5: The pupil was associating alphabetical letters with pictures. For instance she associated the letter 'A' with the picture of an apple. And the pupil was very capable to accomplish this task. The teacher came to sit by and said, 'Let's see what you are doing', and took over accomplishing the task herself. When the task was completed she said to the pupil, 'Very good, you have finished.' I was tempted to tell the teacher, 'That is not so. You have completed the task, not the pupil'.... The pupil thought she had actually finished, but I told her, 'Look, the task should be done by yourself, not by the teacher', and she started over again.

The second type of problematic situation concerned difficulties encountered by the pupils in the course of the accomplishment of demanding tasks. In the meetings they reported on these situations as problems that were difficult or impossible to solve. These considerations led to suggestions to withdraw the pupil from the demanding task and to give him or her an easier one instead, as in the next two excerpts.

Excerpt 1

TRAINEE 6: He refused to work. I tried to explain the task in every possible way, using the simplest possible words. Nothing, he refused.

RESEARCHER 1: Did you notice differences between this task and the others which he accomplished participatively?

TRAINEE 6: It's just the clock that he does not manage to understand.

RESEARCHER 1: He does not manage to understand the system of the clock.

RESEARCHER 2: Also my pupil refused to accomplish a task, because it was difficult, it was really difficult, and he could not make it. During the week I built an instrument which could help him. You could think about something practical ...

TRAINEE 7: My pupil did the task of the clock last time. The difficulty consisted in distinguishing between day and night.... I had to convey to her the difference between day and night, when there is the sun and when there is the moon. With the help of drawings in the notebook I explained that 1 o'clock can be written 13:00 when there is the sun, and 1 when it is night.

RESEARCHER 1: You might want to try with some mediational means which could bring him to gradually accomplish this task which is clearly too hard for him.

Excerpt 2

TRAINEE 8: Today he was working on a task of geography. It was very complicated because he had to find on the atlas a lot of towns which were indicated. The teacher told me, 'You see, in this situation, for instance, the difficulty does not encourage him to go on.' Yes, but the fact is that this task is very complicated.

RESEARCHER 1: And then what happened, did the pupil make progress, has he finished the task, is he about to finish it?

TRAINEE 8: He should finish it, but I suggested him to ask for permission from Giò to change the degree of difficulty [in the computer program] ...

RESEARCHER 1: The lower degree of difficulty is merely a puzzle to put together. Also there is the fact that the pupil has chosen himself this level of difficulty, clearly expecting that this would be more

complicated than the easier level. You do not want him to think that
he is not good enough to accomplish more complicated tasks. This
should not happen ...

TRAINEE 8: The point is that I see him almost bored because he has to look
for so many towns.... I saw that he was a little bored, that's why.

RESEARCHER 1: We might want to wait a little.

RESEARCHER 2: Perhaps the atlas is in itself too complicated. What if you
would look for some other support?

RESEARCHER 1: Like which kind of instrument?

RESEARCHER 2: Perhaps something you could make by yourself. Study the
task card – when you know it, you know its characteristics.

TRAINEE 8: Perhaps I could make an atlas with capitals only.

RESEARCHER 2: Good.

RESEARCHER 1: That is useful. If you want you can bring the task card home
and create your own mediating artefact to use in this context and with
this child.

Discussions in meetings with the researchers on the difficulties the
trainees were encountering led to a third step.

Step 3: experimenting with mediating artefacts

The trainees started building and experimenting with mediating artefacts,
by following the suggestions given during the meetings and by looking at
what other trainees were doing. For learning how to read the clock they
created a cardboard clock. For learning how to list words in alphabetical
order they created a surface with movable letters of the alphabet. Simpli-
fied maps of Italy were also built. The data provide evidence that these
artefacts had indeed impacted on the pupils' learning, as indicated in the
following examples.

TRAINEE 8: Today while we were working Lorenzo told me, 'I asked my
sister the question: "Where is Milan?" and she answered "In Sicily."
And I said, "What are you talking about? It is in Lombardy" to her who
is a third-grader!'

TRAINEE 8: At the beginning of the 5D Lorenzo could not find even three
districts, and did not know to which regions they belonged. Now he
associates the districts he already knows to the regions without looking
for them on the map.

In spite of the evidence of the impact of the artefacts on the pupils'
learning, in the field notes this third step is still reported with reference to
the pupil in terms of the empirical abstraction. In this sense, as Davydov
(1990: 301) also has pointed out, the trainee's method of constructing and

using the artefactual mediation went ahead of her own words. As the following field note excerpt shows, despite the evidence that the artefact had an impact on the learning of the pupil, the trainee referred only to the visual aspects of the artefact as the solution to the pupil's difficulty with the clock (see Davydov 1990: 32 for a critique of superficial visualization).

TRAINEE 6: The instrument I prepared has made the task easier and this time Luca has accomplished it without caprices. The clock full of colours and with cartoons which represented animals made the task fun.

At the same time, however, a new step became visible.

Step 4: establishing dialectical connections

In the 5D, trainees started to establish dialectical connections between the pupil, the task and the mediating artefact. These connections evolved towards a theoretical abstraction and were expressed in the field notes in the form of concrete episodes. They discovered connecting features of the learning child that initially remained unnoticed because the trainees focused only on external features of the pupil and the task. By explaining to themselves the systemic constellation of the pupil's difficulties in accomplishing the task and the mediating artefact as an instrumental support, the trainees began to see the pupil in a new light, as in the following field note excerpts.

TRAINEE 6: The teacher passed by and asked Luca what he was doing. Luca explained to her that the cardboard clock allowed him to accomplish the task and to learn how a clock functions.... He said, 'Teacher, now I explain to you how the clock works. The smaller hand is the hand of the hours, the bigger one is the hand of the minutes.' And he continued that way, answering correctly all the questions that the teachers asked. The teacher looked surprised. I think she did not expect to get such detailed answers.

TRAINEE 8: This morning I was working with Lorenzo and another pupil came by.... This pupil noticed that Lorenzo was using the geographical map I made for accomplishing the task and asked, 'How come he got that and I didn't?' I told him that perhaps he did not need it.

The two trainees, by writing these field notes, showed that they had developed a keen eye and appreciation for the social and artefactual mediation as wells as for pupils' agentive initiatives of learning. With the end of the 5D project coinciding with the end of the school year, this did not allow further observations of the development of this fourth step. The two examples from trainee 6 and trainee 8, however, illustrate that the trainees were developing sensitivity for the potentials and needs of each child, met through individualized interactions and with the use of mediating arte-facts. This new feature in their perception of teaching and learning is especially noticeable if we compare the two examples provided for step 4 and the first excerpt by trainee 5 given at the beginning of this chapter. The description of the pupil, classified as hyperactive in the excerpt by trainee 5, was based on an empirical abstraction. Descriptions such as those in the excerpts by trainees 6 and 8 imply a clear movement from initial empirical abstraction towards theoretical abstraction.

Conclusion

As in many other countries, in Italy, teacher education involves practice periods in schools. However, in Italy, elementary school teacher education was only recently brought into the university with a Master's degree requirement. Within the practice periods, a particular tension arises between trainees who study at the university and the school teachers who supervise them but often do not have a university degree. This tension often translates into keeping trainees mainly in the position of passive observers and giving them minimal access to real teaching.

Trainees' need to interact with pupils on learning tasks is not likely to meet the object of teaching – the pupil in his or her full life and learning potential – if the practice in their educational programme is based exclu-sively on traditional classroom situations. Future teachers need extra-ordinary situations such as the 5D where children can break out of the predetermined pupil role and express their potential. Trainee teachers who are exposed to these extraordinary situations have a chance to start fulfilling their need with the true object of teaching.

This process of discovery of the object is, however, not just a con-sequence of the creation of a stimulating context such as the 5D. In addi-tion to that, the trainees take steps of ascending from the abstract to the concrete. The four steps identified above are only part of this process. The analysis points out that experimentation and transformation as the first phase in the process is fed by conflictual encounters both within the indi-viduals who carry with them a previously acquired empirical abstraction and in the interaction with authorities who represent and reproduce the empirical abstraction.

The analysis presented in this chapter leads to the conclusion that active exposure and increased interaction with pupils individually, in a developmental context such as the 5D research intervention, can provide a chance for the trainees to dwell in the materiality of the object of their future profession. In my analysis I expand on Davydov's (1988) first learn-ing action of transformation. I suggest that we may distinguish four steps

within this action: (1) contrasting different views; (2) experiencing conflicting views; (3) experimenting with mediating artefacts; and (4) establishing dialectical connections. The first two steps are not included in
Davydov's definition of the first learning action. These four steps may be
used as tools for facilitating and empowering the process of overcoming
empirical abstraction among trainee teachers involved in 5D type
interventions.

My motive as a researcher in initiating this project was the conviction
that in order to change the school we need to nourish the mentality of
future teachers. One might object that in this experiment we were training 5D teachers and that the school, differently from the 5D, is a place
where the teacher must face 20 or 30 pupils at a time. Although it is legitimate to point out the number of pupils in a classroom, a more crucial
issue is the *type* of interaction with the pupil in traditional classroom settings. The main formative aspect of the 5D experiment for these trainees
consisted in the realization that pupils are different from one another
and that, as teachers, they need to learn to interact differently with each
pupil. In the long run, this can also have an impact on a classroom as a
whole. Schools receive trainee teachers who are taught to reproduce the
'normal school experience'. Possibilities of change in this sense lay in
proposing and implementing new experiences for trainees and pupils.
This is where, in my view, the 5D has its place. The 5D is a space that
opens up the true object of teaching, even though it cannot be directly
transplanted in traditional teaching. The 5D should find a place in
school, without wanting to replace school. The 5D can function as a
developmental laboratory and as a transitional space in which trainees
can experience the object in its full potential. This would be a way to
meaningfully train future teachers, and to make use of the knowledge
they bring to school from the university.

Acknowledgement

I warmly thank Viv Ellis and Yrjö Engeström for their invaluable comments on an
earlier version of this chapter. The statements are, however, solely my
responsibility.

Note

1 These data are excerpts from field notes and conversations that were produced
   to carry on the practical work of the 5D rather than to explicate the trainees'
   cognitive learning processes. Similarly to previous studies of dialectical thinking
   in everyday contexts (Basseches 1984), the excerpts are suggestive and incom-
   plete by their very nature.

References

Basseches, M. (1984) *Dialectical thinking and adult development*, Norwood, NJ: Ablex.

Cole, M. (1996) *Cultural psychology: a once and future discipline*, Cambridge: Harvard University Press.

Cole, M. (2005) 'Foreword: Why a fifth dimension?', in M. Nilsson and H. Nocon (eds) *School of tomorrow: teaching and technology in local and global communities*, Bern: Peter Lang.

Cole, M. and The Distributed Literacy Consortium (eds) (2006) *The fifth dimension: an after-school program built on diversity*, New York: Russell Sage.

Davydov, V.V. (1988) 'Problems of developmental teaching', *Soviet Education*, XXX (9): 3–83.

Davydov, V.V. (1990) *Types of generalization in instruction: logical and psychological problems in the structuring of school curricula*, Reston: National Council of Teachers of Mathematics.

Engeström, Y. (1999) 'Innovative learning in work teams: analyzing cycles of knowledge creation in practice', in Y. Engeström, R. Miettinen and R.L. Punamäki (eds) *Perspectives on activity theory*, Cambridge: Cambridge University Press.

Engeström, Y. (2007) 'Putting activity theory to work: the change laboratory as an application of double stimulation', in H. Daniels, M. Cole and J.V. Wertsch (eds) *The Cambridge companion to Vygotsky*, Cambridge: Cambridge University Press.

Falmagne, R.J. (1995) 'The abstract and the concrete', in L.M.W. Martin, K. Nelson and E. Tobach (eds) *Sociocultural psychology: theory and practice of doing and knowing*, Cambridge: Cambridge University Press.

Leont'ev, A.N. (1978) *Activity, consciousness, and personality*, Hillsdale: Prentice-Hall.

Nilsson, M. and Nocon, H. (eds) (2005) *School of tomorrow: teaching and technology in local and global communities*, Oxford: Peter Lang.

Sannino, A. (2008) 'Sustaining a non-dominant activity in school: only a utopia?', *Journal of Educational Change*, 9(4): 329–338.

Vasilyuk, F. (1988) *The psychology of experiencing*, Moscow: Progress.

Vygotsky, L.S. (1997) 'The historical meaning of the crisis in psychology: a methodological investigation', in R.W. Rieber and J. Wollock (eds) *The collected works of L.S. Vygotsky: Vol. 3. Problems of the theory and history of psychology*, New York: Plenum Press.

Part III

Cultural-historical designs for teacher education

Chapter 11

Deviations from the conventional

Contradictions as sources of change in teacher education

Thurídur Jóhannsdóttir

The theory of expansive learning put forward by Engeström (1987, 1999a, 2001a, 2007a) offers a systematic way of analysing disturbances caused by inner contradictions within activity systems, considered as the driving force for development of the systems. Contradiction analysis is used in this Icelandic case study to analyse the development of student teachers, the schools where they work and an online teacher education programme. The analysis reveals how student teachers and teacher educators develop their practices by dealing with contradictions. The method opens up an understanding of possibilities and constraints for development at individual and collective levels and uncovers motives that may direct possible future development of interacting activity systems like schools and teacher education.

Activity theorists argue that a qualitatively better form of an activity always begins as an exception from the rule (Engeström 1999b; Ilyenkov 1982). The distance programme under study deviates from the conventional form of teacher education in Iceland. The inception of the programme in 1993 is analysed before turning to the situation in 2003–2006 in order elicit possibilities for school development and the development of teacher education. The affordances for both student teachers and schools of having simultaneous access to the activity of the teacher education programme and the development of practice in the schools are explained. This Icelandic interplay between schools and teacher education sheds light on the issue of partnerships between schools and higher education, a concern in developing teacher education (Darling-Hammond 2005; Edwards and Mutton 2007; Furlong *et al.* 2000; Hallinan and Khmelkov 2001).

Context in Iceland

Iceland is a small nation of 320,000 people in a big country, where more than two-thirds of the inhabitants live in the urban southwest. Following the introduction of stricter legislation about the professional responsibilities of

those holding teaching positions in 1978, shortages became evident as up
to 25 per cent of teachers in compulsory schools (pupil age 6–15) did not
have the qualifications required (Jóhannsdóttir and Skjelmo 2004)
Responding to pressure from school districts and from uncertified teachers, in 1993 the University College of Education in Reykjavík launched a
full distance learning programme for the Bachelor of Education degree
for teaching in compulsory schools.

At the time a grassroots movement of small schools in sparsely populated areas had started to build up Internet connections with the aim of
connecting all schools in Iceland to the World Wide Web (Jónasson 2001).
It grew into a nationwide network, The Iceland Educational Network, in
which the contribution of the teacher profession to the project of developing the programme was crucial. Emerging ideas on life-long learning and
social justice regarding access to education for marginalised groups
together with affordances opening up with the Internet facilitated the
realisation of the distance BEd programme. Further, professionals in
schools and the state district educational services played an important
role. The interaction of new technology and new ideas made it possible to
initiate the programme in response to the need for teachers with appropriate education in the schools (Mýrdal 1994).

Early on in the programme, student teachers generally worked as teachers in districts where there had been a shortage of certified teachers. In a
1996 survey conducted as part of an evaluation study on the first cohort
(Jónasson 1996, 2001), about 90 per cent lived in rural areas and nearly 90
per cent were teaching alongside their studies. With the development of
information technology, increasing emphasis has been put on the compat-
ibility of online and on-campus programmes and special rules for admission as a distance student have been abolished. Student teachers may now
apply for either programme, distance or conventional, irrespective of resi-
dence. In 2004, the percentage of distance students living in rural districts
had decreased to 57 per cent (Kennaraháskóli Íslands 2006), yet 42 per
cent of distance student teachers were teaching in schools (Björnsdóttir
2009). Thus, despite the changed rules for admission, the programme still
serves rural communities and meets the need for professional qualifications of non-certified teachers.

Field of study and data

In the distance programme, the conventional three-year BEd course of
study has been lengthened to three-and-a-half or four years, or longer if
needed. A blended approach is used where face-to-face sessions at regular
intervals play an important role. Initially the course schedule was adapted
to students who were teaching while being enrolled in the programme.
Face-to-face sessions were usually held during school holidays, and off-

campus sessions were more or less independent study, although students could phone or email teachers for support. The development of online tools has made the distance sessions more tangible as students and lecturers are expected to actively participate online. However, face-to-face sessions are still looked upon as important (Jakobsdóttir 2008), although their duration has diminished and the sessions held on ordinary working days.

The research being reported on here and the argument being developed in this chapter have their origins in a doctoral study of a distance learning programme for initial teacher education in Iceland.[1] It is based on ethnographic fieldwork where cultural-historical activity theory has guided the collection, analysis and interpretation of rich data collected over three years (2003–2006). The main research questions explore the significance for school development of being linked to the teacher education system over time. At the same time I explore the significance of student teachers working as teachers during their university studies, on the one hand for student teachers' learning and for the possibilities it brings to the potential development of teacher education on the other.

The study began in 2003 when a group of researchers, including myself, examining the use of information and communication technology, were visiting schools in a sparsely populated coastal district. During the visit, I came to realise that in some of the schools several of the teaching staff were enrolled in initial teacher education through the distance programme and that in some schools distance student teachers had been regularly employed since 1993. In one small school, all the teachers had got their teacher qualification in the distance programme while a principal in another was regretting that teachers without certification in his school had not gained access yet. This beginning developed into ongoing fieldwork and regular visits to five schools in this district for the next three years.

In three of the schools, I interviewed teachers who had been enrolled as pioneers when the programme started in 1993, in order to gain insight into the experience of the first cohort and explore the history of the distance programme from their perspective. In this chapter I refer to one of them, Elisabeth, who at that time was and still is employed in Waterside School, situated in the biggest town with about 3,000 inhabitants and a service centre for the region. At the time of fieldwork I interviewed several teachers in Waterside who were then enrolled in the distance programme. The main participant representing student teachers enrolled in 2003–2006 however was Lilith, a woman in her thirties, who had just started in the programme at the time of my first visit and was willing to let me follow her for the next three years. In Coastline School, situated in a fishing town of about 1,000 inhabitants, the situation was similar to Waterside: distance student teachers had been employed since 1993 and among those enrolled in 2003–2006 was Sarah, in her thirties, in the second year of the programme when I first met her and who agreed to participate. On the other hand, Creek School, situated in a small village with around 300 inhabitants, was having its first experience of distance students during the time of fieldwork and Samuel, a student teacher in his forties, chose to participate in the study.

During spring term 2005, I obtained access to several online courses in which these three students were enrolled. I had an opportunity to trace their inputs on the course web-boards and explore student and teacher online interactions. I also observed the face-to-face sessions in the beginning and middle of the term. Transcripts of interactions in three courses were analysed using Engeström's triangular model (Engeström 1987, 1990, 1999a) to capture individual actions in the context of the collective activity. By conceptualising two interacting activity systems as the unit of analysis in analysing the distance student teachers' actions in their schools and in the programme, as suggested by Engeström in third-generation activity theory (Engeström 2001a), it has been possible to explore the development of individuals in the context of systemic development. Such analyses have been conducted with data concerning all three main participants, Lilith, Sarah and Samuel, both as teachers in their schools and students in the programme, where their individual development have been explored in the context of the relevant activity, providing detailed descriptions on which the contradiction analysis used here is based.

Theoretical background

Cultural-historical activity theory is based on the dialectical perspective on development requiring that all phenomena are studied as processes in motion driven forward by contradictions inherent in the unit being investigated (Blunden 1997; Ilyenkov 1977). Based on Hegel's dialectical philosophy, development is explained in terms of how people overcome the constraints of a situation by *breaking away* and transforming it (Skirbekk and Gilje 1999: 486). In such circumstances, people find themselves in a double bind situation meaning that they receive contradictory messages on which they are unable to react (Engeström 1987).

Second stimulation for mediating development

Vygotsky developed the method of double stimulation where a mediating tool is made available to the subject for mastering such situations (Vygotsky 1978: 74; Ellis, this volume) with the aim of enhancing agency and self-regulation of subjects. Engeström suggests that the method can be applied for enhancing agency in collective activities such as workplaces. He explains that we can think of 'the potential second stimulus as something that has culturally appropriate general affordances but also sufficient ambiguity and malleability so that the subject will have to transform it into a situationally effective mediating device by "filling" it with specific content' (Engeström 2007b: 374).

Engeström (2007a) has also addressed the importance of understanding the interplay between conceptual and material tools. New material tools bring about the need for new concepts, visions and ideas just as new ideas and visions call for new material tools. This challenges typical approaches in studying technology-mediated learning and work by regarding concepts and visions as an essential part of the technology (Engeström 2007a: 36). The interplay of material and conceptual tools form integrated toolkits to be used for mediating learning and developing practice. Engeström suggests the notion of instrumentality (or a tool constellation) to represent this kind of composite of mediating tools, and argues that this kind of toolkit is needed for developing an activity. Access to integrated toolkits can serve as a powerful second stimulation for subjects in breaking away from double bind situations and transforming work and learning. Online programmes with interplay of new ideas and new tools may function as such toolkits.

Contradiction analysis

Activity systems are constantly dealing with outside influences that have to be appropriated and modified to internal factors in the relevant systems (Engeström 1990, 2001a). This process of appropriation causes disturbances in the systems as contradictions arise in the wake of intruding elements. Contradictions in activity theoretical terms are historically accumulating structural tensions that become noticeable in disturbances and innovative solutions (Engeström 2005a: 314). The imbalance has to be dealt with by the systems, keeping them going and in constant development. In this way, historically new forms of social activity emerge when internal contradictions are resolved (Engeström 2007a).

Engeström's theory of expansive learning (Engeström 1987, 1999a, 2001a, 2007a) suggests that contradictions can be identified at four levels. The method is based on ascending from the theories of inner contradictions inherent in all human activity to concrete disturbances in practice within activities (Engeström 1999a). The resolution of first-level contradictions leads to an emergence of contradictions on the second level, and so on. Conflicts, disturbances or tensions in the systems are my analytic focus and are explored to identify contradictions and their resolution. The latter process is an important source for development of both individuals and activities and is a driving force for change, whereas a lack of resolution limits development, leaving people in a double bind situation.

The method of contradiction analysis is embedded in an expansive learning cycle that presupposes that four levels of contradictions may be detected. The cycle depicted in Figure 11.1 is used as a framework for understanding development in activity systems.

The cycle begins with individuals questioning or criticising the practice of the activity of which they are a part. The need state of an activity system arises from primary contradictions that may be identified within each element of the activity system. The questioning reflects a need for change in the practice because of tensions or disturbances caused by primary contradictions, the most important being in the object of activity. *Primary contradictions* are recognised as inner conflicts between use value and exchange value, and are reflected in conflicts between an ideal type of work and reality in practice (Pasanen *et al.* 2005).

The second step is initiated when people experience a double bind situation when tensions caused by secondary contradictions disturb the practice. The double bind situation puts a pressure on people to search for solutions. Changes from outside constantly change the object of an activity initiating new contradictions. *Secondary contradictions* arise between the components of activity systems, and Engeström (1990) claims that they are the driving force behind disturbances and innovations. For example, changed objects or new tools with an unchanged division of labour or rules cause disturbances and prevent development of the activity.

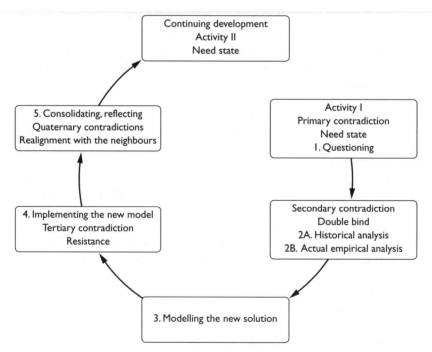

Figure 11.1 The expansive learning cycle (source: adapted from Engeström, 2001).

Individuals learn and develop as they face and resolve such contradictions (Toiviainen 2003: 36).

The third step includes forming new models for enhanced practice by re-conceptualising the object and motive of the activity or forming new ones in search of future oriented innovative solutions to the problematic situation. The fourth step is the implementation of the new model which, in turn, may cause *tertiary contradictions* to arise between new and old forms of practice when some practitioners resist reforms or there is a resistance in the system where the conventional activity continues to be the general practice. The process of appropriation of novelties into an activity system causes imbalances and disturbances which have to be dealt with on a collective basis so that all elements and their interplay are reconsidered because: 'every new mode of man's action in production, before becoming generally accepted and recognised, first emerges as a certain deviation from previously accepted and codified norms' (Ilyenkov 1982: 83–84).

The last step in the expansive learning process is evaluation and consolidation of the new form of practice. However a new way of functioning of one activity system may initiate disturbances in its neighbouring activity systems. *Quaternary contradictions* thus arise on a systemic inter-organisational level where interacting systems need to collaborate on co-configuring their activities for developing a qualitatively better way of functioning (Engeström 2001a, 2005b).

Using contradiction analysis within the framework of the expansive learning cycle opens up an opportunity to study the development of individuals in the context of their activities as well as the development of collective activities, i.e. the schools and the distance programme. Analysing quaternary contradictions between two interacting systems enhances understanding of the zone of proximal development for teacher education and school development.

Individuals and collective activities: developing practice

The expansive learning cycle serves as a framework for presenting and interpreting how student teachers develop their practices in the schools and the teacher education programme between which they move. First, the historical phase of the programme is examined to sharpen understanding of the interplay of the two activities. Second, an example is given of one student teacher enrolled some ten years later (2002–2006) developing his or her practice as a teacher while studying. Third, contradictions in the activity system of the distance programme, based on the online course web-boards and interviews with the three main participating student teachers, are analysed. Last, contradictions arising between the two interacting systems and emerging shared motives are identified. In the contradiction analysis, motives of the activities emerge and may be used to direct future development (Toiviainen 2003).

The theory of double stimulation (Engeström 2007b; Vygotsky 1978) is used to explain how participation in two different activity systems might open up possibilities for using experience gained in one system to break away from a double bind situation in the other. Engeström's notion of instrumentality (Engeström 2007a) can help to explain the interplay of material and conceptual tools and how they may serve as a second stimulation for individuals in breaking away from challenging situations at the same time as initiating new contradictions.

The distance programme as stimulation for school development: the example of Elisabeth

Elisabeth was one of the pioneers in the first cohort of distance student teachers. She explained how problems that the schools in the district had been encountering increased pressure on authorities to establish an unconventional programme to meet the need for qualified teachers. At the time she taught in Waterside which is rather a big school (400–500 pupils) in the main town of the district. She recalls that the school had a poor reputation in the community and results from national examinations confirmed that pupil attainment was not satisfactory. Elisabeth describes how a group of women teachers, without formal certification, started to question aspects of the school and wanted to enhance professional practice. In terms of activity theory they were in the first phase of the expansive learning cycle dealing with *primary contradictions* in the activity of the school. They were experiencing a double bind situation when dealing with conflict between ideal type of work and reality in practice.

These women had undertaken other kinds of further education but felt that in order to be able to make an impact on school development they needed teacher education. They and others in the same situation put pressure on district authorities to explore alternatives to on-campus education. Concerted pressure from such sparsely populated districts around Iceland led to the establishment of the distance education programme. Six women who were teaching in Waterside school were among the first distance learning students. Elisabeth explained how their education made them more secure and enhanced their position as teachers, allowing them to stand up and make arguments for change, using newly acquired knowledge from courses in the programme. Their mission was to change the image of the school in the community. They wanted to change how they talked about pupils and how they interpreted the role of the school and of teachers. Elisabeth recalls that they had an ideal type of work for school practice in mind that guided their development of reality in practice: 'We wanted to ... become a sort of good school ... the pupils happier so that we could look at the group leaving the 10th grade standing here outside the school and look proudly into the future' (interview, May 2004).

They were expanding the object of activity of the school by rethinking what a good school should do for pupils. For them, education was not only about knowledge and attainment in exams but also about happiness and well-being and caring about their future. In dealing with the primary contradictions between what they found to be the ideal school practice and the reality in daily practice, they started by trying to change the ways in which teachers talked about the pupils:

> We stopped talking about how tedious Jacob could be and difficult, 'just like his grandmother used to be'. Instead we began talk about what we could do to make Jacob feel better, and how we could organize our teaching so that the slower pupils could manage their learning tasks somehow.
>
> (Interview, May 2004)

They were dealing with *secondary contradictions* between new understandings of the pupils and old ways of talking about them. They also had to change old mediating tools such as ideas and methods for teaching and learning that caused disturbances, and for that they intended to use the study programme as stimulation. When looking back, they felt they had succeeded in developing professional talk and that participation in the programme gave them self-confidence to make their case in support of their ideal form for practice. In this case the distance education programme may be seen as a second stimulus for the teachers to break away from the double bind situation and develop school practice.

Dealing with contradictions in school development: the example of Sarah

Coastline School is (in Iceland) a medium-size school (100–150 pupils) situated in a typical fishing industry town. As in other compulsory schools in Iceland, the object of activity has been changing in accordance with demands from society, where ideas on the role of schools have been changing. School authorities have tried to enhance learner autonomy by promoting changed teaching methods and the breaking up of the traditional schedule. This has worked for short periods but then teachers have returned to the original set-up. The teachers seem to be in a double bind situation since they admit they would like to work according to a more ideal type of work while being unable to change their practices in reality.

Sarah was teaching in Coastline and studying in the distance programme during 2002–2006. Monitoring her for three years provided an opportunity to analyse and understand how she overcame the double bind situation and developed her teaching practice. The experience of working as a support teacher in another school before she started to teach in Coast-line made her question the practices there:

> I think like at home you see, there are many good ideas for doing some kind of developmental work but somehow it stops, we do not arrive at working them out all the way. Yes I think that there is a bit of stagnation you see.
>
> (Interview, January 2006)

The earlier experience supported her in generating her ideal form for school practice and, after entering the teacher education programme, the ideal form was supported both in individual courses and in practice teaching.

Sarah feels that for teachers the most important thing is to reconsider how they think of pupils, and how they look at each of them as individuals, with their personal characteristics and needs. She regards personal communication and mutual respect between teacher and pupils, and among pupils, as the foundation for good teaching. Sarah dealt with the *primary contradictions* by reinterpretation of the object of school activity, the pupils' education, more or less without discussing it with her colleagues. What supported her were perspectives and ideas from outside, from another school and from the teacher education programme.

Secondary contradictions arise between old tools and the re-conceptualised object when it comes to the use of teaching methods and learning material to fit the changed object of activity. In this case the tools, textbooks and workbooks in interplay with teaching methods include *primary contradictions* as their ideal function is to be instructive as a resource for pupils' learning but in reality teachers use them to control pupils' behaviour. Sarah explains how she had to use workbooks as an instrument of control while she was getting to know the children and developing acceptable way to communicate. That took several months and she admits that after four months she was about to give up, but then her methods started to work: 'I remember the first lesson when everybody was working. They were all working and no disturbance. I remember it was an enormous triumph, in January I was really about to give in' (Interview, April 2005).

After that she could start to use the learning material in an ideal way as a resource for pupil learning, choosing according to individual needs and giving pupils agency to select material to work on and progress at different rates. The tool that she used for support was exact documentation of each pupil's progress using a spreadsheet. This material tool, in interaction with conceptual tools (in the form of theories of teaching and learning she had come to know in the teacher education programme), seems to have served as the second stimulation she needed to break away from a double bind situation and develop her practice. This is in accordance with Engeström's claim about the importance of interaction of material and conceptual tools for mediating actions in an activity.

At the time of data gathering, *tertiary contradictions* had not arisen between Sarah's advanced practice and the school practice in general as her mode was still in the form of innovation from below and had not been worked with collectively on a systemic basis. However, other incidents in the school suggest that it would have to react collectively to changes from outside. A problematic situation had come up when the older pupils complained about how teachers addressed them and didn't take their perspectives into account. Having re-conceptualised their role and status according to contemporary discourse on individualised teaching, where the school is supposed to meet their personal needs, pupils did not accept the old form of authority where school authorities control without listening to their views. These are identified as *secondary contradictions* between a changed object of activity and old rules for communication in the school as a collective activity system.

Sarah is an example of an individual change agent working on implementing a qualitatively better model of practice in Coastline. She dealt with the contradictions in the old form for activity and worked out new solutions and tried them out. The next step in the development would be that the new form is then taken over by others (Ilyenkov 1982) and Sarah related how her colleagues were starting to come to her in order to learn from her approaches.

Students and lecturers dealing with contradictions in the programme

Now we turn to how contradictions cause disturbances in the activity system of the programme and how both students and lecturers need to break away from double bind situations brought about by the contradictions for developing the practice.

The most important *primary contradiction* is found in the object of each activity. In teacher education this is between its use value, where a student's motive for learning is its usefulness for developing one's practice as a teacher, and the exchange value, i.e. the grades achieved and the professional licence necessary for a teaching career. The situation of the student teachers in this study makes the ideal form more attainable since having responsibility as teachers is likely to support them in acting as responsible students and working as teachers makes them likely to appreciate the use value of their studies.

The Internet played an important role in launching the programme in 1993 and has since, in interplay with new ideas about teaching and learning, become a powerful tool, initiating tensions that call for resolutions. Learning management systems have become part of general practice in the programme, affording tools such as threaded discussion and possibilities for sharing documents which have opened up space for students' online collaboration. This has developed in interplay with educational theories that stress the sociocultural side of learning. Lecturers have in turn developed instructional approaches enhancing student agency to participate and contribute to the online activity.

Analysis of the development of the programme reflected how teacher educators dealt with *primary contradictions* between supporting and controlling student learning. The theories of Vygotsky (1978) remind us of the importance of enhancing agency in learning situations which calls for teachers to weaken their control. That affects the traditional division of labour between teachers and students, and analysis of interviews with students and transcripts of courses reveal how students and lecturers are dealing with transformations in their roles.

When student teachers are given agency in their learning tasks they struggle with contradictions that arise between the conventional old rule of students who were supposed to take directives from the teacher and the transformed new role where they are supposed to take responsibility for their studies. Sarah recalls:

> I thought it was really difficult because I did not know what she wanted us to do. But at the same time I thought: Why is it bothering me? I should be doing this for me and not for her.
>
> (Interview, January 2006)

Sarah experiences tensions when the teacher educator weakens control but at the same time her reactions reveal how she is reinterpreting her role as a student and learning to take responsibility. However, lecturers might go too far in weakening the control thereby depriving students of guidance. Lilith gives an example:

> Yes, sometimes he needs to control better what is going on in WebCT. He definitely should be more active but he says that he is afraid of controlling too much and directing our discussions so that we would try to do what we think the teacher would like us to do. So we dig through it on our own.
>
> (Interview, January 2006)

This reflects how both students and lecturers were dealing with contradictions in the process of transforming their ideas, although not necessarily being in tune with each other. *Secondary contradictions* are found between the new transformed understanding of the student teacher (the object) and old teaching methods and modes of communication. Teaching methods that imply more student control demand a reconsideration of communication built on hierarchical status where the lecturer has power and students take orders. In addition, both teachers and students have to learn to communicate online where the traditional social cues of the school environments are absent. Lilith describes how student teachers deal with this:

> It takes the first year to learn how to communicate on the WebCT. ... Someone says something that turns everything upside down. ... We are putting forward our opinions but we need to mind how we say things. ... Because, communicating online is so new to most of us.
> (Interview, January 2006)

The problem, however, has been that only some of the teacher educators participate in this process, while others are absent or hesitant, not knowing their role in the new situation (online communication and changed roles). Conventional teacher–student communication lags behind the advanced form which is being developed online. The contradiction analysis showed tensions when teachers' communication was perceived as authoritative by students who don't accept the traditional power relations between teachers and students once they have transformed their understanding of their roles respectively. In such cases teacher educators act as if the object of activity is still the old one, while students feel that they are participating in a more advanced programme. That leads to *tertiary contradiction* arising between the object/motive of the older form of the activity and the object/motive of a developed form of the activity. Samuel's experience of this is shown in the following.

Normally, online learning management systems are platforms for teaching and learning, and students experience them as an important replacement of classrooms. Online discussion has become a common form for communications and students are accustomed to using the Web for collaboration. Therefore it causes tensions when lecturers use old approaches based on one-way delivery of material where no online activity is assumed. Describing one course, Samuel recalls that: 'They sent a letter every ten days ... we were only supposed to read" (interview, January 2005). The teachers didn't use the WebCT and that became problematic since the students felt that they were deprived of support both from the teachers and each other, and also of the right to respond, to write back to what they had been reading. Because there were no obligations to participate online (or hand in assignments), the students neglected the course. They had developed their practices as online learners in accordance with what they had interpreted as the accepted model for distance learning. Their reaction was to interpret the teachers as remnants from the old days – 'still living in the turf cottages' as they put it – and bit by bit their activity decreased and about one-third did not complete the course.

Interaction of the schools and the programme

The last phase in the expansive learning cycle is to identify *quaternary contradictions* that emerge between the activity system of the programme and the activity systems of the schools. Despite causing disturbances, principals appreciate the positive effect on school development when teachers are enrolled in the distance programme. Face-to-face sessions and practice teaching, however, are problematic since in both cases the students have to be away from their classes. On-campus sessions collide with the school start in the fall, an important time for planning and preparing internal work and procedures as well as receiving new pupils; all especially valuable for professional development of student teachers and of themselves as learners. Pupils are vulnerable if their teachers are absent when schools start in the autumn and, like Lilith says, 'it is ridiculous that this is not shown regard for when the face-to-face sessions are planned. ... It is a precious cargo we have onboard' (referring to the pupils in the classroom) (interview, April 2005).

Two contradictions are identified here. First, a programme for student teachers to develop professional competence plans its schedule in a way that deprives them of a valuable opportunity to do so. Second, teacher education, the ideal form of which builds on notions of children's education and well-being, operates without regard to the situation of those students working as teachers in schools, planning for them to be away at a time when pupils are vulnerable. The *quaternary contradiction* analysis reveals emerging common motives and objects of activity of two interacting systems. Here the original motive of the distance programme of serving the schools and the pupils emerges. In order to further develop, both the schools and the teacher programme need to focus on their shared objects and negotiate co-configuration of their activities on a systemic level.

Summary and conclusion

Using the expansive learning cycle in analysing student teachers encountering school development by dealing with contradictions in schools opens up an understanding of the interaction of individual and systemic development. Their example shows how teacher education can serve as a second stimulus for school teachers, supporting them in breaking away from their double bind situations when dealing with primary and secondary contradictions and developing their practices. However, it also shows the constraints of individual development since, when it comes to tertiary contradictions, they have to be dealt with at an institutional level, which in turn may initiate quaternary contradictions between interacting systems.

In the teacher education model focused on here, the student teachers work as teachers while enrolled in initial teacher education. Contradiction analysis reveals disturbances arising in the programme when the objects of activity as well as tools are changing; that is, student teachers working as teachers instead of pre-service students and online tools instead of class-rooms. The interplay of new online tools and new theories on learning and teaching, along with policies to meet social as well as individual needs, have initiated new approaches in the programme. Students and teacher educators, although not all of them, have reacted by redefining their roles. In dealing with tensions arising in this situation, student teachers can use their experience as teachers in the schools as a second stimulation sup-porting them in taking responsibility in the student role. Acting as a responsible student includes adopting the ideal form where the use value of learning has higher priority than the exchange value. The distance stu-dents are in this respect different from conventional student teachers and their case can be interpreted as a deviation that points towards future development where the object of teacher education could be expanded.

Historically, the object of teacher education programmes has been to educate teachers. The object of the schools is to educate children but at the same time to be a workplace where teachers participate in professional development. In the schools where the student teachers work, the object of the activity has been expanded and the schools have in effect shared the responsibility for educating teachers and the teacher education institu-tion, by implication, shared the responsibility of professional develop-ment. This new object has affected the schools and thus caused disturbances. To develop the systems by resolving disturbing contradic-tions, negotiation on a systemic level is needed with shared objects as a point of departure.

Contradiction analysis and the expansive learning cycle reveals how fruitful it is to consider schools and teacher education as interacting activ-ity systems and the need to co-configure their activities (Engeström 2004). Analysing the contradictions arising between the schools and teacher edu-cation has shown the original motives that are supposed to direct these activities towards their ideal form. Taking the historical phase into account in the analysis has also been of crucial importance. It is remarkable to notice that the distance programme was initially launched as a 'deviant' form of teacher education in response to a need state in the schools. Real-ising how the district schools took the initiative, supported by a grassroots movement of teachers interested in using new technology to serve educa-tional needs, seems to be a good example of how interplay of new tools and new ideas (instrumentalities) initiates change in activity systems. Ten years later (2003–2006) my claim is that student teachers teaching in schools use their access to the distance programme as a means of second stimulation. Within the activity system of the programme, student teachers experience interplay of new tools and new ideas which supports them in breaking away from double bind situations in developing their practices.

Analysing the distance programme from an activity theoretical perspective offers a powerful way of understanding its significance for school development. Enhanced understanding of schools and teacher education as interacting systems reveal the need for co-configuring their activities and to direct their future development by building shared motives.

Acknowledgement

Professor Jón Torfi Jónasson and Professor Allyson Macdonald at the University of Iceland are thanked for their support in writing this chapter.

References

Björnsdóttir, A. (2009) *Fjarnemar* [*Distance student*]. Unpublished research report. Háskóli Íslands: University of Iceland.

Blunden, A. (1997) 'Vygotsky and the dialectical method', *Lev Vygotsky Archive*. Online, available at: www.marxists.org/archive/vygotsky/index.htm (accessed 28 August 2006).

Center for Activity Theory and Developmental Work Research (2003–2004) *The activity system*. Online, available at: www.edu.helsinki.fi/activity/pages/chatand-dwr/activitysystem/ (accessed 26 May 2009).

Darling-Hammond, L. (ed.) (2005) *Professional development schools: schools for developing a profession* (2nd edition). New York: Teachers College Press.

Edwards, A. and Mutton, T. (2007) 'Looking forward: rethinking professional learning through partnership arrangements in initial teacher education', *Oxford Review of Education*, 33(4), 503–519.

Engeström, Y. (1987) *Learning by expanding: an activity-theoretical approach to developmental research*. Helsinki: Orienta-Konsultit.

Engeström, Y. (1990) 'Developmental work research as activity theory in practice: analyzing the work of general practitioners', in Y. Engeström (ed.) *Learning, working and imagining*. Helsinki: Orienta-Konsultit OY, pp. 69–106.

Engeström, Y. (1999a) 'Innovative learning in work teams: analyzing cycles of knowledge creation in practice', in Y. Engeström, R. Miettinen and R.-L. Punamäki (eds) *Perspectives on activity theory*. Cambridge: Cambridge University Press, pp. 377–404.

Engeström, Y. (1999b) 'Activity theory and individual and social transformations', in Y. Engeström, R. Miettinen and R.-L. Punamäki (eds) *Perspectives on activity theory*. Cambridge: Cambridge University Press, pp. 19–38.

Engeström, Y. (2001) 'Expansive learning at work: toward an activity theoretical reconceptualisation', *Journal of Education and Work*, 14(1), 133–156.

Engeström, Y. (2004) 'New forms of learning in co-configuration work', *Journal of Workplace Learning*, 16(2), 11–21.

Engeström, Y. (2005a) 'Knotworking to create collaborative intentionality capital in fluid organizational fields', in M.M. Beyerlein, S.T. Beyerlein and F.A. Kennedy (eds) *Collaborative capital: creating intangible value*. Amsterdam: Elsevier, Vol. 11, pp. 307–336.

Engeström, Y. (2005b) 'Object-oriented interagency', in G. Rückriem (ed.) *Developmental work research: expanding activity theory in practice*. Berlin: Lehmanns Media, Vol. 12, pp. 89–117.

Engeström, Y. (2007a) 'Enriching the theory of expansive learning: lessons from journeys toward co-configuration', *Mind, Culture and Activity*, 14(1/2), 23–39.

Engeström, Y. (2007b) 'Putting Vygotsky to work: the change laboratory as an application of double stimulation', in H. Daniels, M. Cole and J.V. Wertsch (eds) *The Cambridge companion to Vygotsky*. Cambridge: Cambridge University Press, pp. 363–382.

Furlong, J., Barton, L., Miles, S., Whiting, C. and Whitty, G. (2000) *Teacher education in transition: reforming professionalism*. Buckingham: Open University Press.

Hallinan, M.T. and Khmelkov, V.T. (2001) 'Recent developments in teacher education in the United States of America', *Journal of Education for Teaching*, 27(2), 175–185.

Ilyenkov, E. (1977) *Dialectical logic, essays on its history and theory* (H.C. Creighton, trans.). Moscow: Progress.

Ilyenkov, E. (1982) *The dialectics of the abstract and the concrete in Marx's Capital* (S. Kuzyakov, trans.). Moscow: Progress.

Jakobsdóttir, S. (2008) 'The role of campus sessions and face-to-face meetings in distance education', *European Journal of Open, Distance and E-Learning*, 11.

Jóhannsdóttir, T. and Skjelmo, R. (2004) 'Flexibility and responsibility in teacher education: experiences and possibilities in Iceland and North Norway', in L. Pekkala, W. Greller, A. Krylov, L. Kullerud, S. Mýrdal, O. Snellman and J. Spence (eds) *On top of it: overcoming the challenges of ICT and distance education in the Arctic*. Rovaniemi: University of the Arctic Press and University of Lapland, Faculty of Education, pp. 85–98.

Jónasson, J. (1996) *Spurningalisti nemenda 1996* [*Questionnaire for students 1996*]. Iceland University of Education.

Jónasson, J. (2001) *On-line distance education: a feasible choice in teacher education in Iceland?* Unpublished Master of Philosophy thesis, University of Strathclyde.

Kennaraháskóli Íslands (2006) *Kennaraháskóli Íslands, ársskýrsla 2005* [*Iceland University of Education, Yearly Report 2005*]. Reykjavík: Kennaraháskóli Íslands.

Mýrdal, S. (1994) 'Teacher education on-line: what gets lost in electronic communication?', *Education Media International*, 31(1), 46–52.

Pasanen, A., Toiviainen, H., Niemelä, A.-L. and Engeström, Y. (2005) 'Exploring contradictions for collective learning.' Paper presented at the First International ISCAR (International Society for Cultural and Activity Research) Conference – *Acting in changing worlds: learning, communication, and minds in intercultural activities*.

Skirbekk, G. and Gilje, N. (1999) *Heimspekisaga* [*Philosophy History*] (Stefán Hjörleifsson, trans.). Reykjavík: Háskólaútgáfan.

Toiviainen, H. (2003) *Learning across levels: challenges of collaboration in a small-firm network*. Helsinki: University of Helsinki Department of Education.

Vygotsky, L.S. (1978) *Mind in society: the development of higher psychological processes*. Cambridge, MA: Harvard University Press.

Chapter 12

'What have we learnt after we had fun?'

An activity theory perspective on cultures of learning in pedagogical reforms

Yongcan Liu and Linda Fisher

Introduction

The new century has witnessed rapid political, economic and social global change. To keep up with this change, wide-ranging reforms have been introduced in different countries. In the developing world in particular, to meet the challenges of a new global economy and of social transformation, various imported reforms have been initiated in different areas and at different levels. Yet, these reforms have encountered the same difficulty, namely, meeting both domestic needs and international standards. A typical reification of the interaction of the local and the global is the co-existence of two systems at the same time.

In Chinese education, similar change has been taking place. To 'align with the world', many educational reforms reflecting 'a world culture of schooling' (Anderson-Levitt 2003) have been initiated. Liberal pedagogy has been imported and adopted, with experts from the West invited to act as advisers. In actual implementation, however, many reforms are met with resistance from the local community. As a consequence, it is common to see two pedagogical systems operating at the same time within one institution, with the traditional pedagogy featuring the textbook-governed and teacher-led way of teaching on the one hand and the liberal pedagogy emphasizing student-centredness and a communicative way of teaching on the other.

The present research is situated within such a context of 'one community, two systems' (Liu 2009). It was conducted in a university department in China, offering a BEd degree programme in English education[1] for pre-service teachers. Within the department, liberal pedagogy was strongly promoted and the student teachers enrolled on the programme were expected to transform into liberal practitioners whose use of new teaching methods would affect their own students after graduation. In the course of development of the programme, however, this liberal pedagogy was met with strong resistance from some student teachers, who still identified very well with the traditional pedagogy. Using the third generation of activity theory as a conceptual framework, this chapter aims to uncover how different voices, of traditionalism and liberalism, reveal the incongruities of different cultures of learning that underpin the co-existing pedagogies in the community. The analysis is guided by the following two questions:

1   How do the foreign experts and student teachers in the community view the liberal pedagogy featuring communicative teaching and student-centred learning?
2   How do their views of traditionalism and liberalism reveal the incongruities between the cultures of learning that underpin the co-existing pedagogies in the community?

Critical thinking and creative learning

The university department discussed here (Department of English Education) is located in a university in the south of China. In its brief 14-year history (1995–2009), the university's development has been marked by three waves of reform, featuring institutional restructuring and pedagogical innovation. The latest wave of reform was based on an inspection report of the Chinese Ministry of Education in 2005 on the quality of teaching. One way to reform the current teaching system, according to the report, is to introduce a liberal pedagogical system characterized by interaction and student-centredness. As an initial initiative of a wider range of pedagogical reforms across disciplines in the university, therefore, a new department focusing on English teacher education was established to experiment with a liberal pedagogy.

In the first year of its operation, the Department of English Education consisted of one foreign expert called Richard from North America, three Chinese teacher educators and 161 student teachers enrolled in the programme. The foreign expert, with 44 years of experience of teaching and teacher education, was invited to act as an advisor of liberal pedagogy. The three Chinese teacher educators, each having different experience and backgrounds, were mainly responsible for the day-to-day teaching and administration. The 161 student teachers were the first enrolment of the BEd programme in English Education and were expected to become English teachers after graduation. The 'co-configuration work' (Victor and Boynton 1998) among them aimed to 'produce a new generation of English teachers equipped with liberal thinking' (translated from self-evaluation report 2005). To this end, a core course called 'Critical Thinking and Creative Learning' was developed, and its purpose was to liberate the student teachers from the traditional way of teaching and learning. Various liberal ideas and concepts, such as student-centredness, interactive teaching and formative assessment, were introduced by the foreign expert through lectures. Opportunities were provided for the student teachers to experience 'liberalism' through micro-teaching, presentations and extra-curricular activities. These pedagogical changes, covering different aspects of teaching and learning, were summarized by 'Five Differences' in the faculty's self-evaluation report produced for the inspection by the Ministry of Education:

1   A different concept of teaching: from 'teacher-centred education' to 'student-centred education'.
2   A different curriculum: from simplicity to multiplicity.
3   A different teaching method: from one-way transmission to multi-way interaction.
4   A different testing method: from mechanical to flexible and varied.
5   A different learning environment: reaching beyond the classroom to the Internet, and into society.

(Translated from the self-evaluation report 2005)

In the course of implementation of the programme, however, different voices emerged, reflecting what may be called 'one community, two systems'. An analysis of the contrasting voices, therefore, can provide a better understanding of the incongruities between the traditional and the liberal cultures of learning.

Culture of learning

Culture of learning, as Cortazzi (2000: 83) indicates,

> draws attention to what is usually taken for granted about learning, about teachers' and students' roles and relations, appropriate methods, about the use of textbooks and materials, and about the use of language for learning. All of these aspects of learning can receive very different emphasis in different cultures.

Researchers have noted the importance of culture in learning and communication since the late 1980s (Buttjes and Byram 1991; Byram 1989, 1997; Cortazzi and Jin 1996a, 1999, 2002; Hinkel 1999; Scollon and Scollon 2001; Watkins and Biggs 1996, 2001). Since the mid-1990s, there has been strong interest in the Chinese culture of learning, and this line of research is largely based on two phenomena in a global context. The first is the great academic success of Confucian-heritage-culture (CHC) students in foreign countries, and the other is the failure of many imported educational reforms in CHC countries (Watkins and Biggs 1996, 2001). The two phenomena form a strong contrast, and researchers started to wonder about the underlying cultural reasons for these findings.

Watkins and Biggs' (1996, 2001) influential works on Chinese learners represent one of the first attempts to look at the Chinese culture of learning from both psychological and sociocultural perspectives. A common theme that arises from these edited collections is that the Confucian culture of learning has a different interpretation of 'the role of repetition', 'intrinsic and extrinsic motivation', 'collective versus individual orientations' and 'internal contributions' from that of the Western tradition (Biggs 1996; Biggs and Watkins 1996). They further argue that CHC students' learning strategies, which are underpinned by the cultural tradition, enable CHC students to excel at academic study (see also Hu 2002; Jin and Cortazzi 2006).

The research on the Chinese culture of learning has advanced greatly in the past decade, largely due to Cortazzi and Jin's continual endeavour in this area. Since their state-of-the-art review of English-language teaching and learning in China (Cortazzi and Jin 1996b), they have published numerous research studies on the Chinese culture of learning and its relationship to language teaching and learning. For example, in their comparative research on British, Chinese and Malay students, Cortazzi (2000) and Cortazzi and Jin (2002) confirmed their earlier claim that people from different cultures have different assumptions, beliefs and expectations about 'good teachers', 'good students' and 'questioning in the classrooms'. They also indicate that since a 'global classroom' reflects a multicultural society, the cultural elements should be incorporated into the teaching and learning process, as well as into textbook and material design (Cortazzi and Jin 1999). A cultural synergy model (Cortazzi and Jin 1996a) has been suggested by them in order to develop 'such attitudes and abilities as tolerance for ambiguity, open-mindedness, flexibility, respectfulness, adaptability, sensitivity and creativity' (Cortazzi 2000: 98). Jin and Cortazzi (2006) further propose a participation-based language learning model, aligning it with the changing practices of English-language teaching in China. One of the central elements in this multi-dimensional model is the curiosity and willingness to learn about other cultures of learning.

Other researchers have explored the Chinese culture of learning from a comparative perspective. For example, Scollon (1999) explored the concept of culture of learning from the perspective of Socratic and Confucian discourses. She argues that as Socratic and Confucian discourses have different interpretations of 'the goal of education', 'the roles of teacher' and 'participant frameworks', people who are socialized into a different 'discourse' community would fall back on the beliefs, assumptions and expectations that are culturally situated in the community. Along the same lines, Lee (1996) (see also Biggs 1996; Biggs and Watkins 1996) has analysed the learning context for Chinese learners from a cultural perspective and finally concludes that the Confucian tradition has greatly influenced people's teaching and learning values. In a comprehensive review, Hu

(2002) discusses the potential cultural resistance to communicative language teaching in China. He further summarizes the Chinese culture of learning as represented by four Rs (reception, repetition, review, repro duction) and four Ms (meticulousness, memorization, mental activeness, mastery), which are at odds with some of the principles that are derived from the liberal culture of learning. He finally concludes that whether a methodology can be effectively implemented is 'largely determined by the sets of values and beliefs that these teachers and students have been socialized into' (Hu 2002: 102).

The research literature on the Chinese culture of learning seems to indicate that Chinese learners have been socialized into a culture of learning characterized by a set of values, beliefs and expectations derived from the Confucian tradition. Liberal pedagogical reforms, which have been taking place in China, therefore greatly challenge the deep-rooted cultural values with which the members of the local communities identify. This chapter uses the third generation of activity theory as a conceptual lens to consider this issue.

Activity theory as a conceptual lens for understanding the differences between cultures of learning

Engeström (2001) notes that cultural-historical activity theory (CHAT) is marked by three generations of development. The first generation is based on Vygotsky's (1978) idea of double stimulation effect of object-oriented mediation and the focus is on individual persons. The second generation contextualizes learning in an activity system (Leont'ev 1978) and expands the subject–mediation–object triad with three added elements: rules, community and division of labour (Engeström 1987). The third generation addresses the issue of cultural diversity, which views the conflicts arising in the interaction between multiple systems with different histories and cultures as essential in development and learning (Engeström 2005, 2007).

The third generation of CHAT highlights the concept of 'boundary-crossing', which gauges the nature of a process whereby multiple agencies work together and form new meanings through interaction and negotiation. This new development, as Engeström (2001: 136) points out, indicates that 'the door is open for formation of the third generation of activity theory'. Echoing Engeström's claim, this research explores the possibility of using the third generation of activity theory as a conceptual lens for understanding the possible conflicts and the boundary-crossing process between the 'global' and the 'local' from an educational perspective. Figure 12.1 provides an activity theory perspective on the interaction of different cultures of learning in the context of 'one community, two systems'.

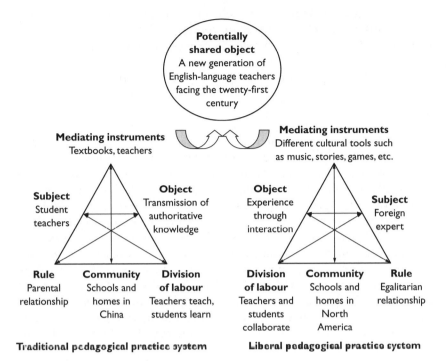

Figure 12.1 An activity theory perspective on cultures of learning.

Within the department under investigation, the traditional system, which derives from the local Chinese tradition, embodies Confucian values, while the liberal system, which is imported from the West, reflects a liberal ideology in Western society. As these systems do not share the same cultural and historical development, problems will arise when they interact with each other. In the context of 'one community, two systems', as in the present case, these problems are reified in multiple voices in the community. An analysis of these voices, therefore, can offer insights into the incongruence between different cultures of learning that underlie different systems. The department as the 'workplace' where the BEd programme was operated, therefore, constitutes 'the third space' for expansive learning (Gutierrez *et al.* 1999). Engeström defines expansive learning as involving 'learning what is not yet there. It is creation of new knowledge and new practices for a newly emerging activity, that is, learning embedded in and constitutive transformation of qualitative transformation of the entire activity system' (2004: 4).

Moreover, from a research perspective, by contrasting the voices of the local students and the foreign expert, this chapter also contributes to the process of intercultural learning for language teacher education that the BEd programme aimed to achieve, since it facilitates the externalization of conflicts for reflection and appropriation. To summarize, the third generation of activity theory provides a conceptual lens for understanding mutually linked activity systems between which contradictions exist, and a potentially shared space for expansive learning is created.

Method

Deriving from a larger research project, this chapter explores three particular data sets. The first is a lengthy interview with the foreign expert. The analysis of this set of data mainly focused on how liberal pedagogy was represented and interpreted by the foreign expert. The second set of data is based on three focus group interviews with six volunteer students each. All interviews were conducted in an office, they lasted for about 60 to 90 minutes and were audio-recorded simultaneously on both a professional tape-recorder and a digital pen. In view of the student teachers' language preference, the focus-group interviews with them were conducted in Chinese and later translated into English. The third set of data comprises the email exchanges between the foreign expert and the student teachers over the year. These email exchanges were usually instigated by student teachers raising a particular pedagogical issue that they were complaining about. This inquiry was followed by the foreign expert's email response and some more exchanges between them for clarification. The email corpus was provided by the foreign expert with the student teachers' identity removed. To analyse the data, we employed codes matching different aspects of the activity theory conceptual model, the most salient of which (object, mediating instrument, rule and division of labour) we present in detail here.

A point worth noting is that, in order to change the traditional pedagogy, a strong version of liberalism, which is based on Freire's (Freire and Shor 1985) philosophy of reconstructivism, was introduced. The foreign expert reiterated, on many occasions, that he was well aware that the extreme practices might cause strong resistance in the community. Nevertheless, he believed that since the programme was in its first year of operation, it was necessary to communicate a strong message at the beginning. Another reason for doing this, he claimed, was the Chinese students' reluctance to express their preferences, thereby necessitating extreme practices to provide opportunities to better understand the students' reactions to liberalism, as they might show stronger resistance. We were also aware of the multi-voiced nature of the responses to the reforms, and that some student teachers were happy with the changes.

For the purpose of this study, however, we only focus on the resistant voices of some of the student teachers with the aim of contrasting their conception with Richard's 'strong' version of a liberal pedagogy. Through this analysis, we aim to reveal the incongruities between different cultures of learning without necessarily implying that there are no overlaps between 'cultures'; nor do we claim that resistant voices do not exist in the pedagogical reforms in the West. In the following sections we examine the historically accumulated structural tensions, or contradictions, in both activity systems. The disturbances and conflicts that arise as a result of the two systems coming together are considered thematically via an activity theory lens.

Object: transmission of knowledge or experience through interaction

One of the key conflicts that arose concerned the very nature of the objective of the course, and fundamental conceptions about teaching and learning. The traditional model conceives of teaching and learning as a one-way process, with knowledge transmitted from teachers to students, whereas the liberal model views it as an interactive process, which is collaboratively accomplished.

Richard explained why a communicative way of teaching was needed in China in the interview:

> The high school classes need to place much greater emphasis on inferential as opposed to literal reading comprehension. The deeper understanding (or higher level thinking) required to both read and write English at the inferential level will need teachers who can help students to see the meaning 'behind' the words. This means the students must be able to read, write and think critically. In other words, I am preparing the students for the teaching of English as it will be, not as it is. Education is not a static field. Even in China it continues to evolve and develop, and communicative ability in English requires students who cannot only pass examinations in English, but also present their thoughts with good communicative and argumentative skills.

Nevertheless, many student teachers following Richard's course found it difficult to get at 'solid knowledge' through a communicative way of teaching, because 'correct answers' were not provided by teachers and many felt that they were not learning anything after interaction with their colleagues. For example, a student complained:

> The teachers never give you an accurate answer and tell you the knowledge points. They would say that this will do and that will do. I am just very confused. I am all right with the communicative activities, but we need an accurate answer. Without an answer, how do we know whether we are right or wrong? A good teacher should share what

she/he thinks is right, rather just say, 'You can decide on your own.' I feel that is irresponsible.

Scollon (1999) notes that in the Confucian cultural tradition the purpose of education is to transmit the authoritative knowledge accumulated over thousands of years. Since knowledge embodies the collective wisdoms of the ancient sages, it must not be misrepresented and miscommunicated, and both teachers and students have joint responsibility for the accuracy of the transmission process. In the liberal tradition, however, the objective, as the critical thinking and creative learning course in this chapter aimed to achieve, is to experience the learning process through interaction and communication. It seems that the different purposes of education in different traditions have culturally scripted subjects' expectations of how teaching and learning should be conducted. Naturally when 'new elements' were introduced into the activity system, some individual participants became very uncomfortable and needed to express their unease as they began their deliberate effort to deliver collective change.

Mediating tool: textbook-governed or mediated by artefacts

Another disturbance was visible over the mediating tools used in teaching. The traditional way of teaching is mainly governed by textbooks, while the liberal way of teaching is livelier, featuring group activities and drawing on a wide range of cultural artefacts. For example, narrative as a mediating tool of teaching has been well acknowledged in the liberal tradition.

In the interview, Richard further explained the benefits of using stories and narratives as the mediating tool for teaching:

> Story is probably one of the most useful methods we have in teaching a foreign language like English. The problem with many of the courses used in Chinese to teach English is that they use textbooks which contain material which is not very interesting to students or does not relate significantly to their lives. This makes the student become bored with the language learning. Story can help to make your classroom lively and very relevant. It is also an excellent way to relate the learning of the L2 to the need for vocabulary that can be used every day – not just found in examinations or in a dictionary. Everyone likes to listen to and tell stories – especially if they are important to us or relate to the lives of others. As Jerome Bruner (1990) has reminded us, 'Our mind strives constantly to construct meaning from its environment. Story is one of the best ways we have to make sense out of our world, and it is that sense-making ability of stories that make them so important to us.'

Nevertheless, many students perceived these new teaching instruments as bringing about mere fun. For example, one student ridiculed them, saying in an email:

> What have we learnt after we had fun? The whole classroom is possessed with laughter! For passers-by, we may have a good time! Do we? I have no idea! We talk; we laugh; we shout; we have jokes; we tell stories. We have great fun, actually. That's what we have done for the two semesters. We are not afraid of standing in public and speaking. We can speak English whenever we want! Obviously enormous progress has been made without doubt! Nevertheless, I have a king-sized headache! The problems are even worse! The terrible pronunciation pushes me into despair. I hate to be a nitpicker. Even some teachers still have great problems. However, we still have fun. The grammar mistakes make me feel hopeless. Sorry for being so demanding, but that's the thing being neglected. A teacher came over and said, 'Do pay attention to your grammar, I do not understand.' However, we still have fun. The Chinglish! I couldn't help laughing. I am not complaining! That's the biggest mistake we can make! However, that makes us laugh. We still have fun!

In the Confucian cultural tradition, the textbook-governed and teacher-fronted teaching style has been considered as the best way to achieve the purpose of knowledge transmission. This method has been considered effective because knowledge is made visible in textbooks for reference, and teachers, by standing and speaking loudly in front of the class, can make the process of transmission transparent. 'Dui Da'an' ('checking answers'), for example, a common practice in Chinese classes, is the best illustration of this cultural value. Teachers will provide the correct answers in the front of the class and explain why the answers are correct by relating them to a particular knowledge point in the textbook. Students on the other hand will copy down the answers and learn by heart.

In the liberal culture of learning, however, answers may not be provided by teachers but negotiated among students in 'fresh talk' (Goffman 1981). Knowledge is not merely stored in textbooks but co-constructed between people. Students who do not rely on written text but can convince other people with spoken arguments will be praised (Scollon 1999: 21). Compared with the textbook-governed and teacher-fronted teaching, which is transparent and easy to follow, knowledge that evolves in an interactive way is more fluid and difficult to identify. As the data above show, many students were not satisfied with the lack of correction provided by their teachers, which could further pose a great challenge for teachers. If teachers did not tell their students what they thought was right, their students might think that they had not prepared the lessons well, and as a result they might be considered 'irresponsible'.

Moreover, the traditional culture of learning maintains that learning should be achieved by painful and punitive measures. This value is evidenced in many Chinese stories of self-punishment for laziness. In comparison, the liberal tradition encourages having fun in learning and maintains that learning should not be 'punitive' (Ho 2001: 99). As the data above indicate, what the student teacher referred to as 'we talk; we laugh; we shout; we have jokes; we tell stories' was meant to 'take the drudgery out of the learning process and to inject elements of entertainment' (Hu 2002: 96). However, the student's taken-for-granted belief that learning should be painful had scripted her conception of the light-hearted measures such as using stories in teaching as merely creating a lot of fun and leading to no learning. Hence her scepticism: 'what have we learnt after we had fun?'

Moreover, the examination culture also comes into play. Students have often been reminded that if they have fun in learning, it implies that they do not work hard enough and are very likely to fail in exams. Since learning is 'socially constructed as a serious and tough task' (Ouyang 2004: 62), they feel that they at least are doing something if they are punished by teachers and required to recite, read aloud and copy repetitively. In contrast, the light-hearted methods, which do not seem to require much hard work, make them feel guilty for having fun and 'doing nothing'. The students' comments draw attention to the disturbance caused by the need to reconceptualize learning tools.

Rule and division of labour: teacher-centred or student-centred?

The new BEd programme aimed to shift the teacher-centred model of teaching towards a more student-focused model. The underlying assumption of this change is that Chinese students are reluctant to take responsibility for their own learning. They passively follow their teachers and painstakingly keep up with the level of instruction. The new programme aimed to empower the students by giving them the freedom to make decisions on their own and involve them in the process of course development. The student teachers, therefore, were expected to decide what and how they wanted to learn and make contributions to the teaching plans.

Richard talked about his observation of local resistance to this change in the interview:

> A lot of teachers don't like to give up the stage. A lot of our teachers are not comfortable with sharing the stage. And certainly there are enough students around who are also uncomfortable with that. They

don't want to stand up in class. They don't want to raise their hands. They don't want to take their chance and turns. They just sit back as they did in middle school, and are spoon-fed. So when you have reluctance of a number of students to change, it is difficult to produce change.

Yet, many student teachers had a different view about this change and explained their resistance from a cultural perspective. For example, in an interview a student teacher explained:

Most of the time, our parents believe that if we want to have a meteoric rise in our careers overnight, we just have to do what our teachers ask us to do. China's education system has been brought together over many years, all the way from ancient times to the present. That type of education is the sort where the students absolutely must obey the teacher, where the teacher is a very knowledgeable person; he knows a lot of things, and if you follow him there's no way you'll go wrong. If you have something a bit new to say, you never dare to say it. If you speak up, then you're afraid of being told off. To do things in that way isn't realistic at all. It makes you feel uncomfortable, with no sense of security. I think that when the Chinese do things, they like to keep their feet on firm ground, and so feel safe.... I don't mind being independent, but a teacher's advice is very important, because they are more experienced than we are. Authority is authority! I feel safer when I follow the authority's advice and you are more likely to succeed.

Student-centredness in the liberal tradition reflects an equal division of labour between teachers and students. This egalitarian relationship, however, greatly challenges the deeply-rooted parental relationship between masters and apprentices (see Salili 2001) and a hierarchical division of labour in the traditional culture of learning. Hierarchy symbolizes the authority and power of possessing knowledge. People at the top of the hierarchy were considered the most learned and would have been qualified to become teachers (Biggs and Watkins 2001; Lee 1996). With the ownership of knowledge, teachers could decide to whom they would 'transfer' their knowledge. Those who were able to 'respect, obey, listen, and follow their instruction, and [did] not challenge them' would receive the authoritative knowledge (Salili 2001: 79). For many students in the present study, the curriculum and teaching plans symbolized the knowledge owned by teachers. When they were invited to make contributions to the decision-making process, they questioned their legitimacy to change the old division of labour. In many student teachers' minds, 'teachers teach, students learn' still remained an accepted division of labour, while teachers' roles such as collaborators, facilitators and knowledge co-constructors had not been widely accepted as the 'normal' labour that teachers perform.

Authoritarian moralism in the Confucian culture of learning, however, is also based on the rule of 'mutually obliging responsibilities' (Ho 2001: 99). Students should not complain about their teachers' strict training, while teachers have the responsibility for their students' ultimate success. As a consequence, teachers have an expectation that students will not challenge them, while students expect that their success is guaranteed under the teacher's leadership. Student-centredness in the liberal culture of learning, however, inadvertently breaks this rule. In the present case, from the teachers' perspective, a student's autonomy and independence implied that students no longer needed 'parental guidance'. This emphasis on independence greatly challenged teachers' authority and self-image as role models in the parental relationship. Teachers might feel that they were losing face and credibility, since their students might no longer have trust in them. From the students' perspective, since teachers were not to take responsibility for their learning, they were very worried about how their independent decisions would impact on their success or, more worryingly, failure. It seems that the mutually agreed rule of leading and being led was broken, which led to a situation of uncertainty.

Schools and families constitute a wider community, which can perpetuate different cultures of learning. Most Chinese learners have been socialized into a traditional culture of learning from a very young age. The view that teachers are the authority of knowledge and paragons of morality has been reproduced in both school and family. If students challenge their teachers' expertise and make independent decisions, they will be considered to be breaking the rules and 'told off'. Such an experience is not uncommon among Chinese students. Before going to school, the last sentence that children hear from their parents is usually, 'You must listen to the teachers.' At the end of the school day, upon their return home, the first question they are asked is, 'Did you listen to the teachers today?' In a parent–teacher meeting, a typical compliment given by teachers is, 'This child is very submissive in the school.' As the student's comment above suggests, it is a common belief among parents that if their children want to have a 'meteoric rise', they have to do what their teachers tell them to do. After a long time of being socialized in this way, many students have got used to following teachers' instructions and do not want, or are unable, to make their own decisions, even when they are given the opportunity to do so.

Conclusion

This chapter has centred on the conflicts arising when two activity systems, here 'traditional' and 'liberal' pedagogical practice systems, come into contact in an educational initiative in a Chinese university setting. Due to different cultural and historical development, the traditional and the liberal pedagogies are underpinned by different cultures of learning respectively: one derived from the Confucian cultural tradition while the other from the liberal tradition in the West. The two systems each have different distinctive learning objects. To achieve their respective objects, different mediating instruments are employed, different rules followed and different divisions of labour created. Moreover, since the subjects are socialized into different communities, different cultures of learning are therefore reproduced by these communities. Engeström (2007) notes that interaction of different systems that do not share the same cultural and historical development will inevitably cause conflicts. He notes, though, that 'a critical triggering action in the expansive learning process ... is the conflictual questioning of the existing standard practice' (Engeström 2001: 151). From a research perspective, this chapter helps the examination of the 'conflictural questioning' process by externalizing the possible conflicts in cultures of learning that underlie different pedagogical systems. With this exposure of conflict in view, the third generation of activity theory provides a lens to conceptualize the incongruence reflected in teachers' voices, with a vision to reforming the existing pedagogy and creating a new culture of learning.

Yet, a culture of learning is not easy to change. It takes time and will happen only after considerable explicit re-examination of the existing culture of learning and the taken-for-granted beliefs and values underpinning it, as well as the development and use of new mediating tools and new division of labour. If 'expansive learning activity produces culturally new patterns of activity' (Engeström 2001: 139), then, albeit in a non-linear fashion, this process has begun in this university department. In this chapter, our focus is to explore the possibilities of using the third generation of activity theory to conceptualize the learning context of 'one community, two systems'. For future analysis, we will continue this line of research and look closely at the development of 'cultural synergy' (Cortazzi and Jin 1999) as one form of expansive learning. It seems to us that using the third-generation activity theory as a conceptual tool for the examination of how differing cultures of learning arrive at some form of synergy holds considerable promise for the development of teachers' intercultural awareness in teacher education programmes in a global context.

Note

1 BEd in English Education in this chapter refers to an undergraduate programme in a university department that prepares undergraduate students to teach English as a Foreign Language in China.

References

Anderson-Levitt, K.M. (2003) 'A world culture of schooling?', in K.M. Anderson-Levitt (ed.) *Local meanings, global schooling: anthropology and world culture theory*, New York: Palgrave Macmillan.

Biggs, J.B. (1996) 'Western misperceptions of the Confucian-heritage learning culture', in D.A. Watkins and J.B. Biggs (eds) *The Chinese learner: cultural, psychological and contextual influences*, Hong Kong: CERC and ACER.

Biggs, J.B. and Watkins, D.A. (1996) 'The Chinese learner in retrospect', in D.A. Watkins and J.B. Biggs (eds) *The Chinese learner: cultural, psychological and contextual influences*, Hong Kong: CERC and ACER.

Biggs, J.B. and Watkins, D.A. (2001) 'Insights into teaching the Chinese learner', in D.A. Watkins and J.B. Biggs (eds) *Teaching the Chinese learner: psychological and pedagogical perspectives*, Hong Kong: CERC and ACER.

Buttjes, D. and Byram, M. (eds) (1991) *Mediating languages and cultures: towards an intercultural theory of foreign language education*, Clevedon: Multilingual Matters.

Byram, M. (1989) *Cultural studies in foreign language education*, Clevedon: Multilingual Matters.

Byram, M. (1997) *Teaching and assessing intercultural communicative competence*, Clevedon: Multilingual Matters.

Cortazzi, M. (2000) 'Languages, cultures, and cultures of learning in the global classroom', in W.K. Ho and C. Wards (eds) *Language in the global context: implications for the language classroom*, Singapore: SEAMEO, RELC.

Cortazzi, M. and Jin, L. (1996a) 'Cultures of learning: language classrooms in China', in H. Coleman (ed.) *Society and the learning classroom*, Cambridge: Cambridge University Press.

Cortazzi, M. and Jin, L. (1996b) 'English teaching and learning in China', *Language Teaching*, 29, 61–80.

Cortazzi, M. and Jin, L. (1999) 'Cultural mirrors: materials and methods in the EFL classroom', in E. Hinkel (ed.) *Cultures in second language teaching and learning*, New York: Cambridge University Press.

Cortazzi, M. and Jin, L. (2002) 'Cultures of learning: the social construction of educational identities', in D.C.S. Li (ed.) *Discourses in search of members: in honour of Ron Scollon*, New York: American University Press.

Engeström, Y. (1987) *Learning by expanding*, Helsinki: Orienta-Konsultit Oy.

Engeström, Y. (2001) 'Expansive learning at work: toward an activity theoretical reconceptualization', *Journal of Education and Work*, 14, 133–156.

Engeström, Y. (2004) 'New forms of learning in co-configuration work.' Paper presented to the LSE Department of Information System's ICTs in the contemporary world: work management and culture seminar, Helsinki. Online, available at: www.lse.ac.uk/collections/informationSystems/pdf/events/2004/engestrom.pdf (accessed 23 May 2009).

Engeström, Y. (2005) *Developmental work research: expanding activity theory in practice*, Berlin: Lehmanns Media.

Engeström, Y. (2007) 'Putting Vygotsky to work: the change laboratory as an application of double stimulation', in H. Daniels, M. Cole and J.V. Wertsch (eds) *The Cambridge companion to Vygotsky*, New York: Cambridge University Press.

Freire, P. and Shor, I. (1985) *A pedagogy for liberation: dialogues on transforming education*, Basingstoke: Macmillan.

Goffman, E. (1981) *Forms of talk*, Philadelphia: University of Pennsylvania Press.

Gutierrez, K.D., Baquedano-Lopez, P. and Tejeda, C. (1999) 'Rethinking diversity: hybridity and hybrid language practices in the third space', *Mind, Culture, and Activity*, 6, 286–303.

Hinkel, E. (ed.) (1999) *Culture in second language teaching and learning*, Cambridge: Cambridge University Press.

Ho, I.T. (2001) 'Are Chinese teachers authoritarian?', in D.A. Watkins, and J.B. Biggs (eds) *Teaching the Chinese learner: psychological and pedagogical perspectives*, Hong Kong: CERC and ACER.

Hu, G.W. (2002) 'Potential cultural resistance to pedagogical imports: the case of communicative language teaching in China', *Language, Culture and Curriculum*, 15, 93–105.

Jin, L. and Cortazzi, M. (2006) 'Changing practices in Chinese cultures of learning', *Language, Culture and Curriculum*, 19, 5–20.

Lee, W.O. (1996) 'The cultural context for Chinese learners: conceptions of learning in the Confucian tradition', in D.A. Watkins and J.B. Biggs (eds) *The Chinese learner: cultural, psychological and contextual influences*, Hong Kong: CERC and ACER.

Leont'ev, A.N. (1978) *Activity, consciousness, and personality*, Englewood Cliffs: Prentice Hall.

Liu, Y. (2009) 'Learning as negotiation in communities of practice: an ethnographic study of teachers' learning in the workplace in a university department of English education in China', unpublished dissertation, University of Cambridge.

Ouyang, H. (2004) *Remaking of face and community of practices: an ethnography of local and expatriate English teachers' reform stories in today's China*, Beijing: Peking University Press.

Salili, F. (2001) 'Teacher–student interaction: attributional implications and effectiveness of teachers' evaluative feedback', in D.A. Watkins and J.B. Biggs (eds) *Teaching the Chinese learner: psychological and pedagogical perspectives*, Hong Kong: CERC and ACER.

Scollon, R. and Scollon, S. (2001) *Intercultural communication*, Oxford: Blackwell.

Scollon, S. (1999) 'Not to waste words or students: Confucian and Socratic discourse in the tertiary classroom', in E. Hinkel (ed.) *Culture in second language teaching and learning*, Cambridge: Cambridge University Press.

Victor, B. and Boynton, A. (1998) *Invented here: maximizing your organization's internal growth and profitability*, Boston: Harvard Business School Press.

Vygotsky, L.S. (1978) *Mind in society*, Cambridge, MA: Harvard University Press.

Watkins, D.A. and Biggs, J.B. (eds) (1996) *The Chinese learner: cultural, psychological and contextual influences*, Hong Kong: CERC and ACER.

Watkins, D.A. and Biggs, J.B. (eds) (2001) *Teaching the Chinese learner: psychological and pedagogical perspectives*, Hong Kong: CERC and ACER.

Chapter 13

When third space is more than the library

The complexities of theorising and learning to use family and community resources to teach elementary literacy and mathematics

Lori A. Norton-Meier and Corey Drake

Introduction

> Family night was amazing. I learned so much about the children that I have been working with [as part of my practicum] ... it is just a shame that the very classroom I work in doesn't pay attention to kids' funds of knowledge like we discussed in class. It seems like it would be so easy and smart to help kids make these connections between home and school. It just seems like there is a big gap between home and school. How do we help that? I guess my biggest fear right now is that as a student, I see what I need to do to help bridge that gap, but when I am a real teacher, will I forget? All I know is that something happens because I don't see any teachers at the school using kids' outside-of-school experiences or those opportunities to teach kids during the school day.
>
> (Elaine, a junior in teacher education)

This quote from Elaine (all names used are pseudonyms) illuminates the complexity that pre-service teachers face as they attempt to navigate the world of being a student of education, a teacher of children and a community member or guest. Elaine was a university student in a teacher education programme in the United States. As part of her teacher education experience, she participated in a research study and partnership project during her methods semester, where the focus was on learning to examine student learning through the lens of 'funds of knowledge' and through recognising the rich resources that are present in the lives of students and the communities where they live. 'Funds of knowledge' refers to the intellectual and social knowledge that exists in families and communities (Gonzalez *et al.* 2005). In her quote, Elaine reveals the complexity of the roles she is taking up and illuminates how she is becoming a critical assessor of classroom practice.

In this chapter, we present a documentary account of findings and stories from this partnership, as well as student quotes that provide evidence of the successes, challenges and learning that resulted from the partnership. Four cohorts of elementary pre-service teachers participated in the partnership between a university teacher education programme and a local elementary school. This partnership was designed to help pre-service teachers learn about incorporating family and community resources into literacy and mathematics instruction.

Recently, we attempted to describe this work with pre-service teachers. We theorised our work by drawing on cultural-historical activity theory (CHAT) and building on the conceptualisation of 'third space' provided by Gutierrez, who described third space as 'a place where two *scripts* or two normative patterns of interaction intersect, creating the potential for authentic interaction and learning to occur' (Gutierrez *et al.* 1997: 372; emphasis in the original). At the end of our presentation, one listener suggested that third space is what happens in the library at the elementary school when we co-teach our methods courses there.

It was at that moment that we began to understand the complexities of theorising our work.

A surface analysis using cultural-historical activity theory (CHAT) and the conceptualisation of third space might conclude that the third space created through our work was a physical space – perhaps the school library where we co-taught our methods courses. However, looking more deeply, it is clear to us that, while we have in fact created a physical third space, the spaces we are most interested in are both more complex and more abstract than the library. They are spaces of learning, teaching, pushing against boundaries and exchanging resources. It is our goal with this chapter to use CHAT (informed by the work of Vygotsky 1978) to better understand these spaces and, in particular, to explore the resources, roles and tools that have been created and taken up (or not) within these spaces and, more generally, in our work in teacher education.

Particularly in this chapter, we analyse our work with pre-service teachers using the CHAT principle related to the centrality of context and activity (Brown and Cole 2002). For the purposes of our discussion, we 'interpret context as "that which weaves together," emphasising the co-constitution of the phenomena of interest ... [such as] the ways that ideologies, artefacts, institutions, and individuals coordinate such that a particular pattern ... emerges' (Brown and Cole 2002: 228). In studying the dimensions of context and activity, we are given a means of identifying crucial elements of the phenomenon and how they relate to each other, including the interplay of subjects, their competing or complementary objectives, meditational artefacts, communities and the division of labour. In the following discussion, we will share our original thinking in organising this project and the research, and then examine the notions of context as they emerged in this study of pre-service teacher learning.

About this project

Across the profession, there are growing calls for teacher candidates to be better prepared to meet the demands of working with students and families from all backgrounds (Cochran-Smith and Zeichner 2005). One approach to preparing pre-service teachers to work productively with diverse students is to support them in learning how to use the varied funds of knowledge of students, families, and communities as instructional resources for elementary teaching. Despite a growing body of research on the existence and instructional value of these funds of knowledge, relatively little work has explored how pre-service teachers might learn to access or leverage these funds as resources in their own instructional practices (though recent examples of important work in this area are presented by Gonzalez *et al.* 2005; Rodriguez and Kitchen 2005).

Theorising our work with pre-service teachers

Our framework for understanding pre-service teacher learning related to families and communities as resources for mathematics and literacy instruction locates this learning as happening concurrently in an elementary school, in the community in which the elementary school is located, and in university classrooms (see Figure 13.1 for a visual representation of our model for this work). In considering how to document and understand pre-service teacher learning within this framework, we turned to prior work that has theorised and operationalised teacher learning in a variety of ways. Most relevant to our project, we anticipated seeing pre-service teacher learning in terms of changes in:

- personal narratives of self as a learner and teacher (e.g. Drake 2006; Norton-Meier 2005);
- professional identities and practices as elementary teachers (e.g. Graue 2005; Wohlwend 2008);
- understandings of the mathematics and literacy practices and resources of children, families and communities (e.g. Drake 2005; Gonzalez *et al.* 2005).

The design of the partnership project is based on a common commitment to funds of knowledge as a pedagogical resource (Gonzalez *et al.* 2005; Moll and Greenberg 1990). At the same time, the research being done in and on the partnership builds primarily on the theoretical construct of third space (Moje *et al.* 2004). Together, these two theoretical

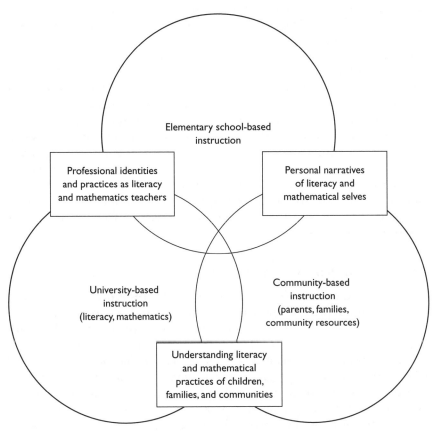

Figure 13.1 Model of the theoretical framework that guides our work.

constructs can help teacher educators and researchers to understand the multiple third spaces that are potentially created through this university–school collaboration. Through this partnership, pre-service teachers participate in various roles within academic mathematics and literacy practices, across university-based and school/community-based worlds and by means of family/community-based and school-based funds of knowledge. In particular, we are focusing on the third spaces created through pre-service teachers' participation in and exploration of the literacy and mathematics practices and resources of children, families and communities in three intersecting spaces: elementary school, community and university.

Within our framework, we seek to understand how the interactions of various participants and knowledge resources in these overlapping spaces help everyone involved in the project to 'change our perspective of our students' homes and communities from, at best, being irrelevant to the educational process ... to being rich resources for teaching and learning' (Gonzalez *et al.* 2005: 14). In particular, we are interested in how the third spaces are created and sustained, what the boundaries and activities that define each of these third spaces are and how funds of knowledge from different, and previously isolated, spaces (school, university, families, communities) are taken up (or not) in interactions within the newly created third spaces. It is important to note that we recognise that not all of these overlapping spaces become 'third spaces'. Instead, the overlap is a precondition for becoming a third space, but despite our attempts, some never become third spaces because the necessary condition – an exchange of resources – does not occur. This absence of reciprocation continues to be a persisting concern for us and, in the sections that follow, we describe and explore the nature of the overlapping spaces in an effort to understand the supports and barriers to transforming overlaps across settings into true third spaces.

Description of partnership and activities

The data for this study were collected at a Mid-Western university in the United States. Approximately 500 students are enrolled in the Department of Curriculum and Instruction, and literacy and mathematics methods are two of the first methods courses students take in the elementary teacher education programme. The literacy and mathematics methods courses follow admission to the programme, a general practicum, an introductory curriculum and instruction methods course, social foundations of education and educational psychology. As a part of the expectations for the methods courses, the students participate in a practicum for a minimum of 40 hours in an elementary classroom setting. The students must be classified as juniors to enrol and most are first-semester juniors or in their third year of a four-year college experience. Further information about the participants in this study can be found in Table 13.1. The data in Table 13.1 are of particular significance because most of our students have not, as learners, experienced the level or kinds of diversity found at the local elementary school, either in their own K-12 experiences or in their teacher education courses.

As part of this study, pre-service teachers began in Week 3 of the 15-week semester spending time at a local elementary school that serves a significant number of English Language Learners. Initially, they spent two hours per week at the school, with the time gradually increasing until they were spending two full days per week at the school towards the end of the semester. Pre-service teachers participated in a number of activities designed to support them in learning about family and community as instructional resources, including community literacy and mathematics ethnographies and community resource projects. At the same time, the

Table 13.1 Overview of the participants in this study

	Total number of students	Female	Male	Non-traditional students	Diversity
Session 1 – Fall 2006	24	21	3	2	1 Hispanic, 23 White
Session 2 – Spring 2007	26	21	5	3	3 Asian, 23 White
Session 3 – Spring 2008	23	21	2	2	23 White
Session 4 – Spring 2009	24	21	3	0	1 African American, 23 White

pre-service teachers worked with small groups of students on literacy and mathematics interviews, assessments and tutoring, paying particular attention to accessing and understanding family and community resources and using them to plan instruction for their students.

The local elementary school provided an interesting context for this work because its student body was in the process of significant demographic transition due to school closures, redrawn district boundaries and increasing rates of immigration and poverty in the local community. At the beginning of the 2005–2006 school year, nearly 200 out of 256 students in the school were new to the school. During the first year of this project, the student mobility rate at the elementary school was approximately 41 per cent, more than twice that of any other school in the district.

Data sources and methodology

In this study, we sought to understand pre-service teachers' own perspectives on their experiences in the multiple and overlapping spaces of learning. Specifically, our research question was as follows: what were the mediating artefacts (such as activities, roles, ideas and identities) that pre-service teachers found particularly relevant or important to their learning, especially as it related to family and community funds of knowledge? We were also interested in aspects of their experiences that pre-service teachers identified as constraining their learning and aspects that introduced tension or provided occasions for critical assessment. In order to address these questions, we drew on interpretive research methodologies as described by Erickson:

Interpretive fieldwork research involves being unusually thorough and reflective in noticing and describing everyday events in the field setting, and in attempting to identify the significance of actions in the events from the various points of view of the actors themselves.

(1996: 121)

Our data sources included interviews (with both pre-service and in-service teachers), reflective blogs, pre-service teacher written work (including community literacy and mathematics ethnographies, community resource projects, lesson plans and reflections), field notes and artefacts. In this chapter, we focus in particular on the pre-service teachers' reflections and blogs, with supporting evidence from the interview data and other artefacts. The data were analysed using emergent coding. We identified initial themes during a first read through the data and then used those themes to code the full set of data.

We focus our findings on 'defining the overlaps' that developed through our partnership with the local elementary school. In doing so, we focus both on those overlaps that were productive for teacher learning, as well as those that were not. In order to define the overlaps, we identify the key roles, identities and tensions that characterised pre-service teachers' participation in the overlapping spaces. Particularly, we focus our discussion around the key theoretical constructs described above related to the centrality of context and activity: (1) understanding the interplay of subjects; (2) competing and complementary objectives; (3) the role of mediational artefacts; and (4) the division of labour in a constrained system.

Understanding the interplay of subjects: negotiating roles as students and teachers

> Critical sociocultural theory demands that we reflexively examine our positioning as researchers and its effects on learning and the production of knowledge. Viewing research this way also means that we must understand the role of our own autobiographies, or histories of participation, as well as the histories of our research participants.
>
> (Lewis *et al.* 2007: xi)

The interplay of subjects is at the heart of activity theory and, in this study, pre-service teachers, cooperating teachers, parents, elementary students and teacher educators engaged in a variety of contexts to create learning challenges for all involved but, in particular, for pre-service teachers to wrestle with their developing notions of family and community resources. In the above quote, Lewis *et al.* encourage us to understand who we are as researchers and teacher educators, as well as who our students are as learners and research participants. The two authors of this chapter have identified a common interest in funds of knowledge as the foundation for our teaching and research collaboration. We are interested first in understanding the funds of knowledge our pre-service teachers bring to the methods experience by virtue of their prior and on-going participation in activities involving teaching, learning, literacy and mathematics. We are also interested in supporting pre-service teachers in understanding the importance of identifying and building on the funds of knowledge that children bring to the elementary classroom as a result of their participation in the diverse literacy and mathematics practices of their families and communities. In this project, we were interested in the ways in which funds of knowledge related to literacy and mathematics learning and teaching travelled within and across three key overlapping spaces – the university classrooms, the elementary school and the local community. We explored this question through a focus on the *roles* pre-service teachers were positioned into and took on within each of these spaces.

In fact, pre-service teachers took on a variety of roles within these overlapping spaces. Within the university classrooms, their roles were fairly clearly defined as students. However, within the elementary classrooms, their roles ranged from guests to observers to helpers to teachers. Often, these roles shifted over the course of the semester as pre-service teachers became more comfortable in the elementary classrooms, and as cooperating and pre-service teachers worked together to create spaces for pre-service teacher participation as reflected in the following pre-service teacher blog entries (from three separate pre-service teachers; note that all quotes from participants in this study are italicised throughout the chapter):

> *Once the [cooperating] teacher began to have me work with the students one-on-one, I soon learned that the majority of my portion of the semester in this classroom will be spent with two students in particular.*

> *So I figured I would just be observing. This was not the case. I was totally immersed in everything they did.*

> *I'm starting to get more and more excited to be there all day and to become a teacher.*

Within the family and community spaces, pre-service teachers were typically positioned as guests or newcomers, despite the fact they typically lived in or near the community (though generally not in the immediate neighbourhood of the elementary school). Negotiating this range and variety of roles within the individual spaces, and then in the overlaps, often presented a challenge to pre-service teachers.

One example of attempting to negotiate the various roles for the pre-service teachers appeared in Dean's end-of-year digital story. The digital story assignment was the culminating experience for the pre-service teachers in these methods courses. The assignment was to create a digital story using various media (pictures, words, video, audio and movement) to tell us the story of their learning during the semester. Dean chose to create an iMovie using Comic Life where he created two images of himself: (1) Dean as the character 'Assimilate' and (2) Dean as the character 'Accommodate'. As the movie progresses, he is attacked by his arch nemesis, 'Procrastination'. How does Dean move beyond his student identity and his desire to procrastinate? According to Dean, he does this through his desire to learn to be the best teacher he can be and with the realisation that a classroom full of students is counting on him each day. Within this digital story, Dean illuminated the various roles he had to play in this experience of learning to be a teacher.

In addition, a pre-service teacher named Angie mentioned in her written reflection about her first teaching lesson in a third-grade classroom:

> It was difficult for me to just do the basal lesson the teacher gave me to do [out of the scripted teacher's manual]. I have so many ideas going on in my head about things I want to try and how I want to challenge the kids with real books but I also know my place, right now I am the student, I am a guest in the [teacher's] classroom but that doesn't mean I am not dying to try out my own ideas!

Here, Angie struggled with the constraints of her role within this classroom and her perceived inability to put into practice the knowledge about teaching and learning reading that she has gained through her participation both within and outside of this classroom space.

Competing and complementary objectives: the development of teachers in figured worlds

One challenge of teacher education programmes is to understand how to help university students integrate their histories of personal *figured worlds* of schooling and past *relational identities* (Holland *et al.* 1998) as students and adolescents with emerging identities as teachers and adults (Graue 2005). Figured worlds are sociohistoric 'as if' worlds (Holland *et al.* 1998), collectively imagined into being and sustained by groups of people, that create contexts for interpreting and mediating cultural meanings and activity. A classroom indexes figured worlds that range from a one-room schoolhouse to a high-school biology lab, from a first-grade writers' workshop to a university lecture hall. As people participate in figured worlds, they take up relational identities that position themselves and others in complementary and/or opposing identities. Pre-service teachers in the process of becoming (Bakhtin 1981; Ball and Freedman 2004; Britzman

1991) navigate between identities; they are not yet teachers but are more than students. In these positions, they participate in the figured world of teacher education by taking up multiple identities; for example, as students in relation to instructors in a university methods course. In this project, we focus on emerging teacher identities as they engage with children, families and practising teachers in this partnership project. We explore the pivotal nature of this experience for shifting identities and roles for pre-service teachers as well as supporting them in their development as critical assessors of classroom practice.

Despite the challenges created by the need to negotiate among multiple roles, we found that this tension, particularly in the overlapping spaces, was often what prompted pre-service teachers to begin to shift in their perceptions of themselves from students to teachers and, in some cases, from classroom-based teachers to classroom- and community-based teachers (for instance, see Figure 13.2 for pre-service teacher Andrea's depiction of her shifting identity over time). Over time, many pre-service teachers shifted from observing events in classrooms as learners completing university assignments to using what they observed to draw connections to what they were planning to do as teachers.

My Motor Mouth
By Andrea

Past
'Andrea, shut up,' demands dad.
'Andrea, not now, I am trying to watch *ER*,' mentions mom.
'Andrea, you need to raise your hand,' tells the teacher.
'Andrea, do you ever stop talking?' asks my aunt.
'Andrea, tell me later,' groans grandma.
'Andrea, you're annoying,' says my sister.

Present
'Tell me what happened, Andrea,' directs dad.
'You use your social skills well, Andrea,' mentions mom.
'Nice answer, Andrea,' tells the teacher.
'How did you get to be so funny, Andrea?' asks the aunt.
'I'm so proud of you and your hard work, Andrea,' says my sister.

Future
'We are so proud of you,' praise the parents.
'Mommy, tell me a story,' chant my children.
'Teacher, read us a book,' sing the students.
'Darling, can you repeat that?' hums my husband.
'You don't call enough,' mentions mom.
'Look forward to hearing from you soon,' says the sister.

Figure 13.2 Andrea's reflection on her shifting identities over time.

However, there was a tension in many of these statements in that the pre-service teachers' participation in the community and family space was limited relative to their participation in the university and elementary classrooms. Therefore, even as pre-service teachers began to identify themselves as soon-to-be teachers, they sometimes continued to voice deficit views of parents:

When I am teaching I will work hard to be in close contact with the parents so the parents know how their students are progressing in school.

I think that I, as a teacher, will attempt to expose parents to these opportunities through simple homework assignment[s] that expose the student to mathematics in the real world contexts.

On the other hand, pre-service teachers who engaged more directly with families – or who participated in elementary classrooms that included more opportunities for parent engagement – tended to voice different identities in relation to parents, families and community resources:

When I become a teacher I think I will make it a great habit to involve the students' parents as much as possible in my classroom. My 1st grade [cooperating] teacher made it a habit to involve parents to come to the classroom for Royal Readers, and I found that both the students and the parents were very excited about the experience.

I have come to the realization that when students are given the opportunity to create unique experiences to tie to their learning, they are more open to the ideas and are better able to recall the information. Therefore, as a future teacher, I want to utilize all of the possible resources that are available to my students and me.

It was inspiring to me as a future teacher to know that you can create 'field trips' that cost no money, have academic significance, and also pay tribute to learning that takes place in the community.

Given that identity is often defined as and through participation in particular communities of practice (e.g. Wenger 1998), it makes sense that pre-service teachers' identities shifted as they participated in multiple and overlapping spaces. Through these data, the pre-service teachers' figured worlds were revealed. We also gained insight into pre-service teachers' emerging teacher identities as they engaged with children, families and practising teachers in this partnership project. The pivotal aspect of this experience was that it provided spaces for pre-service teachers to shift among and try on various identities and roles.

Amber (another pre-service teacher) created a digital story that illuminated this shift from her personal worlds as a college student to the responsibilities and thinking of a professional. Her digital story opens with her sleeping with a smile on her face with the words: 'Gone are the days of sleeping in, 10:00 classes, and textbook reading.' It proceeds to days of 'the alarm clock going off very early, putting on my teacher costume, and off to face a group of children who love to read, and remind me why I liked to read – before textbooks'.

Maria shared a similar transformation in her digital story. She takes the observer on her journey from an elementary student who loved to read and engage in mathematical investigations, to a high-school student who found her love of the novel, to the college student who studies her craft, to the developing teacher who has the opportunity to daily pull her chair up alongside a child and say, 'Tell me about your work.' She revealed in her journey her figured worlds and her emerging identity as a teacher. This experience created a space for her to wonder about what she will learn from her students and how to begin with what they know, their funds of knowledge, and to create a curriculum that will challenge and stretch each one of her students. Inevitably, as Maria stated, 'This is no easy task, when in so many situations, teachers and schools miss the chance to even see what children have for funds of knowledge.' Thus, the tension emerges.

Mediational artefacts in the third space: pre-service teachers as critical assessors of practices

In the third space, we watched the pre-service teachers transform, and a key mediating activity became the opportunity to engage as critical assessors of classroom practice. As pre-service teachers worked to develop their identities as teachers, tensions across the overlapping spaces became more apparent. The pre-service teachers became 'critical assessors of practices' as they sorted through differences and conflicts in the practices and ideas they were experiencing in each of these spaces. Often, this critical assessment took the form of identifying classroom practices that did not seem to be in the best interests of children:

> *Apparently, math learning for these students seems to take place in the form of worksheets.*

> *The idea of so many children hating math really bothers me and with all the worksheets and monotonous work that they are asked to do, who can blame them?*

On other occasions, the critical assessments focused on differences between the practices discussed and exemplified in the university classrooms and those experienced in the elementary classroom or, in some cases, between one elementary classroom and another. The pre-service teachers did not necessarily evaluate whether one set of ideas or practices was in some way better than the others. Instead, they simply focused on identifying and trying to make sense of the contrasts:

> *Although I understand the significance of teaching math and literacy together, I didn't see overwhelming evidence of this in the two classrooms where I was placed.*

> *While one cooperating teacher really enjoyed giving students worksheets, my other cooperating teacher really focused on interacting with the students and having them complete projects to understand a certain topic.*

> *The kids and the teacher were very welcoming. I found the teacher's teaching style to be very traditional, but effective.*

One set of tensions that arose for us as teacher educators in regards to the overlapping spaces was how to make practices and ideas related to literacy and mathematics in each of the spaces more visible to all of the participants. For instance, in many cases we believed that there were literacy and mathematics practices ongoing in the community and elementary classroom spaces that we did not have access to and therefore could not make visible to the pre-service teachers. In another case, the pre-service teachers in one cooperating teacher's classroom did not see or recognise significant family engagement practices occurring in the classroom even though we, as teacher educators (and parents), were able to notice and appreciate these practices. An ongoing question for us, then, focused on how to gain meaningful access to all of the spaces (and their overlaps) and how to support pre-service teachers in developing lenses for seeing more of what happens in elementary and community spaces.

In Bettina's digital story, which became a key meditational artefact in her learning, she told the story of a child she observed who was marginalised by the system. She titled her digital story, 'Just a bunch of scribbles', and she tells the story of first meeting a second-grade child who sat in the back of the classroom. While others wrote stories, this child simply made scribbles across the page. The child, who received special education services, sat on the edges of the classroom, so Bettina recognised that the teacher was giving him a message just by his location in the classroom. One day, Bettina decided to sit down next to him and asked him to tell her a story. He did, and then they began to write it together. The classroom teacher came by and said, 'Oh, he doesn't write, why don't you find someone else to work with today?' The child turned his paper back over and returned to creating his scribbles across the page. Bettina concluded her digital story with a promise to never marginalise a child with her words or actions, or fail to see the potential in 'just a bunch of scribbles'.

Finally, Gabby, in her lesson plan reflection with fifth-grade students, struggled with the narrow definitions of literacy and teacher knowledge that are presented in scripted programmes. She struggled with the disconnect between what is known about learning and how the scripted programme works against learning and against teaching:

> *I must say, this basal is very anti-intellectual. The script implies that I cannot think or make decisions about what children can learn and should learn. There is no place for me to build on children's prior knowledge and tap into their funds of knowledge. It is apparent why children are becoming unmotivated to read and to learn with such mundane texts and why teachers are leaving the profession – where is the trust and the intellectual engagement for teachers?*

The division of labour in a constrained system: confronting double binds when third space is more than the library

> The research ... compels us to give greater emphasis than usual to the institutional, historical, and cultural contexts within which individuals are constituted and which include as well as exclude particular relationships and meanings.
>
> (Lewis *et al.* 2007: xi)

The use of sociocultural theory allows us to account for larger systems of power as they both shape and are shaped by individuals in particular contexts. As described above in the theoretical overview (pp. 198–200), our primary interest as designers of this new programme was in the multiple overlaps created through integrating (1) mathematics and literacy; (2) university-based, school-based and community-based instruction; and (3) family/community knowledge and school-based knowledge. A persisting challenge for us as teacher educators is how to continue to expand and sustain these overlaps so that pre-service teachers can put ideas about funds of knowledge into practice. At the same time, we must ourselves be critical assessors of our own practices as we work to understand the overlap (or lack thereof) between our ideas about classroom and community literacy and mathematics and the ideas and practices of the elementary classroom teachers, families, community members and, of course, children.

As we reviewed and analysed our multiple sources of data, we became aware of the 'double binds' that emerged for our pre-service teachers as they learned to negotiate the various roles and identities of their figured worlds while simultaneously developing as critical assessors of classroom practice. The term 'double binds' has been used by several researchers to refer to large-scale societal dilemmas that are insolvable by individual action (Engeström 1990; Lundell and Beach 2002; Wohlwend 2008). The pre-service teachers wanted to succeed and meet the expectations of the professors, teachers, supervisors and certifying body. At the same time, they were confronted by, and critical of, the very ways that schools are structured to work against exploring the funds of knowledge and resources present in families, homes and communities. In many cases, the pre-service teachers came up against a deficit view of the relationships among families, literacy and mathematics. Yet, the experiences they had when examining the research, working with children, exploring the community and talking with parents showed them the strengths that are present in both the lives of the people they met and the spaces they investigated. For us, as the teachers of these methods courses, we are reminded that 'teaching and learning are a complex mix of intentional choices and unexamined compliance' (Wohlwend 2008). The reality is that the double binds themselves become the spaces of mediation and provide the opportunity to examine teacher choice and agency that can lead to 'strategic shifts from one identity position to the next, opening opportunities for resistance and critique' (Wohlwend 2008).

In conclusion, we are compelled to go back to the question posed by our administrator: 'So, you are telling us that third space is what happens in the library at the elementary school when you co-teach your methods courses together?' We believe there is a simple answer to that question: 'Yes, and so much more.' Third space is not only a physical location, but a space where our students are allowed to explore their figured worlds, to engage in the act of becoming while simultaneously engaging and struggling with ideas and practices related to learning, teaching and funds of knowledge and to begin to understand how those ideas and practices play out within and across the multiple and overlapping spaces of university, elementary school and community.

References

Bakhtin, M.M. (1981) *The dialogic imagination: four essays* (M. Holquist, ed., C. Emerson and M. Holquist, trans.). Austin: University of Texas Press.

Ball, A.F. and Freedman, S.W. (eds) (2004) *Bakhtinian perspectives on language, literacy, and learning.* Cambridge: Cambridge University Press.

Britzman, D.P. (1991) *Practice makes practice: a critical study of learning to teach.* Albany: State University of New York Press.

Brown, K. and Cole, M. (2002) 'Cultural activity theory and the expansion of opportunities for learning after school', in G. Wells and G. Claxton (eds) *Learning for life in the 21st century.* Oxford: Blackwell Press, pp. 225–238.

Cochran-Smith, M. and Zeichner, K.M. (2005) *Studying teacher education: the report of the AERA panel on research and teacher education.* Mahwah: Lawrence Erlbaum.

Drake, C. (2005) 'Community mathematics education: a framework for teaching elementary mathematics methods', in G. Lloyd, M. Wilson, J. Wilkins and S. Behm (eds) *Proceedings of the 27th Annual Meeting of the North American Chapter of the International Group for the Psychology of Mathematics Education*. Roanoke: Virginia Polytechnic Institute and State University.

Drake, C. (2006) 'Turning points: using mathematics life stories to understand the implementation of mathematics education reform', *Journal of Mathematics Teacher Education*, 9(6): 579–608.

Engeström, Y. (1990) *Learning, working, and imagining: twelve studies of activity theory*. Helsinki: Orienta-Konsultit Oy.

Erickson, F. (1986) 'Qualitative methods in research on teaching', in M.C. Wittrock (ed.) *Handbook of research on teaching*, Vol. 3. New York: Macmillan, pp. 119–161.

Gonzalez, N., Moll, L.C. and Amanti, C. (eds) (2005) *Funds of knowledge: theorising practices in households, communities, and classrooms*. Mahwah: Lawrence Erlbaum.

Graue, E. (2005) 'Theorizing and describing pre-service teachers' images of families and schooling', *Teachers College Record*, 107(1): 157–185.

Gutierrez, K., Baquedano-Lopez, P. and Turner, M.G. (1997) 'Putting language back into language arts: when the radical middle meets the third space', *Language Arts*, 74(5): 368–378.

Holland, D., Lachicotte, W., Skinner, D. and Cain, C. (1998) *Identity and agency in cultural worlds*. Cambridge, MA: Harvard University Press.

Lewis, C., Enciso, P. and Moje, E.B. (2007) *Reframing sociocultural research on literacy: identity, agency, and power*. Mahwah: Lawrence Erlbaum Associates.

Lundell, D.B. and Beach, R. (2002) 'Dissertation writers' negotiations with competing activity systems', in C. Bazerman and D.R. Russell (eds) *Writing selves/writing societies: research from activity perspectives*. Fort Collins: The WAC Clearinghouse and Mind, Culture, and Activity, pp. 483–514. Online, available at: http://wac.colostate.edu/books/selves_societies/lundell_beach/lundell_beach.pdf (accessed 21 May 2009).

Moje, E.B., Ciechanowski, K.M., Kramer, K., Ellis, L., Carrillo, R. and Collazo, T. (2004) 'Working toward third space in content area literacy: an examination of everyday funds of knowledge and discourse', *Reading Research Quarterly*, 39(1): 38–70.

Moll, L.C. and Greenberg, J.B. (1990) 'Creating zones of possibilities: combining social contexts for instruction', in L.C. Moll (ed.) *Vygotsky and education: instructional implications and applications of sociohistorical psychology*. Cambridge: Cambridge University Press, pp. 319–348.

Norton-Meier, L. (2005) 'A thrice-learned lesson from the literate life of a five-year-old', *Language Arts*, 82(5): 286–295.

Rodriguez, A.J. and Kitchen, R.S. (eds) (2005) *Preparing mathematics and science teachers for diverse classrooms: promising strategies for transformative pedagogy*. Mahwah: Lawrence Erlbaum.

Vygotsky, L. (1978) *Mind in Society*. Cambridge, MA: Harvard University Press.

Wenger, E. (1998) *Communities of practice: learning, meaning and identity*. Cambridge, MA: Cambridge University Press.

Wohlwend, K.E. (2008) 'Double binds and discourses of learning to write: explaining writing development, explaining ourselves.' Paper presented at the National Council of Teacher of English Assembly for Research Conference. Indiana University, Bloomington, IN. 15–17 February 2008.

Chapter 14

Learning-for-teaching across educational boundaries

An activity-theoretical analysis of collaborative internship projects in initial teacher education

Charles Max

Being and becoming a teacher has experienced a considerable shift during the last decades, due to the changing demands of schools and students, rising discussions and new expectations about the work, the role and, first and foremost, the appropriate qualification of teachers in order to meet the challenges of the twenty-first century. Pressure for reconfiguring initial and in-service teacher education is growing considerably as economically developed and developing nations are reforming their educational systems (Jakku-Sihvonen and Niemi 2006). The need for change is multi-faceted.

Historical and contextual changes in work organisations, described as a shift away from industrial-era towards post-industrial-era concepts such as 'co-configuration' (Victor and Boynton 1998) or 'knotworking' (Engeström *et al.* 1999a), propose fundamental revisions of educational outcomes in response to competition, position and power issues in a globalising market. Given that teacher competencies become increasingly emphasised as a key factor affecting learning, school practices and educational outcomes (Max 1999; Perrenoud 1999; European Commission 2005; Schratz 2005), the quality of teacher training is attracting increasing political attention in Europe (see Peck *et al.* 2009: 16). These concerns are further intensified by the ongoing Bologna process (for detailed information, please refer to the official website of the European Commission) transforming the European academic landscape at a general structural level as well as by high-stakes accountability policies which begin entering higher education (Craig and Deretchin 2007).

While the effectiveness of teacher education programmes comes under public discussion, the argument of this chapter is that reform efforts in initial teacher education (ITE) have to reach beyond academic boundaries and meet change endeavours of in-service teachers in order to develop culturally new patterns of classroom activity. Initiatives to develop a novel learning culture in ITE across institutional boundaries have received relatively little theoretical or empirical research (Tsui and Law 2007) that could enhance our understanding of systemic change dynamics in and through ITE reforms and underpin further efforts for programme renewals. In this sense, this chapter is focusing on the complex processes of mutual learning in the innovative ITE programme at the University of Luxembourg and the transformative potential of joint *learning-for-teaching* activities during the semester internship intended for stimulating development across institutional boundaries, both on the organisational and individual level.

Using CHAT for researching development across boundaries

With regard to the growing body of research on organisational development underpinned by cultural-historical approaches (Chaiklin and Lave 1993; Engeström *et al.* 2002; Engeström and Tuomi-Gröhn 2003; Hakkarainen *et al.* 2004), we consider the CHAT framework as highly valuable for co-configuring and re-configuring learning and teaching practices in initial teacher education and for 'creating new systems of human social–practical activities' (Yamazumi 2005: 14). Our purpose is to set up an open, theory-based research framework in order to empirically study ITE-related praxis as a developmental process, both individual and social levels dialectically interlinked, in contrast to purely descriptive accounts of organisational change efforts. In this section we will briefly explain how the core principles of AT allow us to address salient tensions related to reform efforts, organisational change and learning practices in ITE.

Third generation AT as unit of analysis

CHAT, as explained in the introduction chapter of this book, takes the object-oriented, artefact-mediated collective activity system as its unit of analysis, described by Davydov and Radzikhovskii as the 'minimal unit of "evidence" that preserves the properties of the whole' (1985: 50). Especially Engeström's third generation of CHAT seems well suited for our research purpose as it investigates change dynamics at the level of work places (Engeström 2005; Yamazumi *et al.* 2005), institutions (Daniels 2006; Daniels *et al.* 2006) and agencies (Leadbetter *et al.* 2007) where different activity systems interact and where social and cultural diversity grows into a core research issue (see Matusov 2007 for an extended discussion). Furthermore, it allows for modelling the systemic dynamics at and across organisational boundaries at a structural level; that is, between the university and local schools.

Particular attention is directed to emerging tensions and conflicts that are conceptualised as potential areas of rupture, innovation and change, leading to learning and development on both the individual and organisational level. This unit of analysis offers promising possibilities to move beyond linear causation models and depict human social phenomena as 'multiple systematically interacting elements' (Engeström and Miettinen 1999: 9).

Development as general research methodology

ITE programs, like any other activity system, move through cycles of qualitative transformations that are recurrently initiated through external and internal reform efforts. Currently, claims for quality assurance and training effectiveness call for a closer monitoring of training practices and developmental changes of participants, so that an ongoing research practice on learning and teaching has to be implemented at a programme level. Regarding the continual improvement of ITE, the cultural-historical approach has strong arguments to frame this data-driven research work, as development is not only understood as an object of study, but as a general research methodology. Thus, the training practice is conceived as a developmental experiment that includes active participation of researchers, who gather ethnographic data of the current practices and collect the multiple voices, points of view, traditions and interests of the different participants about educating teachers with respect to their specific roles and personal histories. These multiple data allow for acknowledging underlying tensions and contradictions within and across the activity systems that may serve as levers to initiate a deliberate collective change effort. These formative interventions (see Engeström 2001 for a larger discussion) are mediated by researchers acting as 'change-agents' (Tuomi-Gröhn 2005; Yamazumi 2006; Jahreie and Ludvigsen 2007) within the bounded systems and advocating a strong interest in their improvement. However, acting as a change-agent in an ITE programme requires first and foremost the legitimacy to scrutinise the existing practices of the community, a topic that has to be of deliberate concern to the programme and its various members. Thus, the study of a training system becomes 'a multi-voiced construction of its past, present and future zones of proximal development' (Engeström and Miettinen 1999: 10).

The contradictory struggle for constructing the object of training teachers

The object of an activity system is constructed through a collaborative and dialogical process in which different perspectives and multiple voices meet, collide and merge. 'The different perspectives are rooted in different communities and practices that continue to coexist within one and the same collective activity system' (Engeström 1999: 382). A cultural-historical analysis allows for the contradictory struggle of object construction, both upon and within a teacher education programme.

Teacher training as social practice has evolved from different epistemological perspectives and within various political discourses over lengthy periods of time. Furthermore, it carries diverse layers and strands of history, engraved in artefacts, rules and conventions, and conceptualised under the term of 'historicity'. The material and cultural-semiotic tools that people use and historically produce(d) in social activity continue to shape their thinking upon learning and teaching. Subsequently, any attempt to co-configure training practices within ITE programmes – or to expand the general object of ITE – is questioned by academic, professional, political and everyday discourses on teacher training.

At the general historical-political level, the overall object of ITE is constructed according to the societal value of the activity, the political requests and the theoretical underpinnings and tools able to shape the training activity. At the local–contextual level, the motive of a particular training activity emerges in face-to-face interactions between the actors involved, interrelating the overall object of the programme with contextual essentials.

At both levels, the construction of a shared object occurs through processes of dialogical interaction and meaning-making 'in which participants both reproduce and transform, internalize the culturally pre-given and create new hybrid practices, texts and identities' (Kostogriz 2000: 3). Kostogriz brings the struggle of object construction down to two incommensurate systems of knowledge construction that apply for ITE as well.

From an idealist epistemological perspective, educating teachers may be seen as an apolitical activity 'directed at the acquisition and processing of information by the individual mind' (Kostogriz 2000: 9). Teaching expertise is developed through mastering a predefined collection of fundamental knowledge, specific competencies and technical skills.

The materialist perspective, however, defines ITE as a social practice that 'cannot ignore contradictions in social relations and tensions between dominant and subjugates bodies of knowledge and ways of knowing' (Kostogriz 2000: 10). Knowledge is generated through an ongoing process of tension and struggle between controversial positioning and alternative discourses in the area of practice. 'The essence of these contradictions is relations of power in the processes of its cultural-historic production. Hence, knowledge is not a thing in itself, a product but a process-object of human activity' (Kostogriz 2000: 10).

Boundary zones, boundary objects and boundary-crossing tools

An emphasis on dialogue, meaning-making and contradictory struggle among different parties, sharing a common concern about educating teachers, directs our attention towards methods to enhance exchange and negotiation across common boundaries. Wenger *et al.* mention that 'While the core of a practice is a locus of expertise, radically new insights and developments often arise at the boundaries between communities' (2002: 153). Entering new ground compels practitioners to review their well-established practices and assumptions. As journeys across contextual boundaries may be seen as 'a source of deep learning' (Tsui and Law 2007: 1290), we draw on complementary analytic concepts such as boundary zones (Tuomi-Gröhn 2005), boundary objects (Tuomi-Gröhn and Engeström 2003) and boundary-crossing tools in order to understand interactions and mutual learning across boundaries more thoroughly.

The term 'boundary zone' (Konkola 2001, cited in Tuomi-Gröhn 2005: 58) designates a space where elements from two activity systems enter into contact. In regard to the similar concept of 'third spaces' (Gutiérrez *et al.* 1999), we characterise boundary zones as being polycontextual, multi-voiced, multi-scripted and shaped by alternative and often oppositional discourses, positionings and practices. These in-between spaces might be seen as extended opportunities of a community to transform conflicts and tensions about a shared concern into rich zones of innovation and expanded learning. However, and with particular attention to our focus of analysis, some communities 'resist the transformations whereas others opportunistically view these emergent activities as potentially fruitful contexts for development' (Gutiérrez *et al.* 1999).

The notion of a 'boundary object' commonly outlines how a 'concrete artefact or shared mental model' (Tuomi-Gröhn 2003: 203) facilitates interaction and collaboration among partners, communities or networks. The core feature of a boundary object may be its potential for facilitating and promoting collaboration between partners (Tuomi-Gröhn 2003: 203). Boundary objects are

> both plastic enough to adapt to local needs and the constraints of several parties employing them, yet robust enough to maintain a common identity across sites. Like the blackboard, a boundary object 'sits in the middle' of a group of actors with divergent viewpoints.
>
> (Star 1989: 46)

Various communities may attribute different meanings to a particular boundary object, but it has constituents in common that make sense across boundaries. Ludvigsen *et al.* speak of 'co-objects to which members of different communities attribute common meaning' (2003: 293). The process of creating and managing a boundary object is emphasised by Star and Griesemer as 'a key process in developing and maintaining coherence across intersecting social worlds' (1989: 393).

However, the concept of 'boundary object' remains rather vague to date, being understood either as a mediating tool or an object (of an activity). Using the term 'object' as a synonym for 'mediational tool' seems to be at odds with the common CHAT framework that conceives 'object' as being the driving force that gives durable direction and purpose to the activity. In this respect, we use the term 'boundary object' as a negotiated and jointly developed object of an emerging (boundary zone) activity with a heterogeneous team of boundary crossers as its subject.

A boundary-crossing tool, however, is a material or semiotic artefact (Wartofsky 1979) that is introduced from one context into another by boundary-crossers or specific 'change agents' (see above, pp. 214–215). It may give rise to a new boundary object with a specific boundary zone activity that might also generate alternative practices mediated through new tools, rules or roles. These innovations may lead to sustainable systemic change within and across the bounded activity systems. In that regard, Edwards and Mutton (2007: 508) inform that a boundary object's potential to reshape practices may decrease as soon as 'it enters each system as a tool to be used within the system rather than a joint object to be worked on.... The category systems of the school may begin to shape how the tool is used.' The authors stress the need for working continually on the joint object in order to maintain its potential for reconfiguring practices across boundaries and to keep the collaboration between the systems alive. But, even when an increased interaction takes place in the boundary zone, not all exchanges will promote mutual development. I presume that these changes are related to cases where a shared boundary object is created (see inquiry considerations below, pp. 218–220).

Referring to the aforementioned conceptual work on boundaries, we now briefly elucidate the use of boundary object and boundary-crossing tool within the specific *learning-for-teaching* activity of the novel BA programme at the University of Luxembourg.

Internship as boundary zone

The ITE programme strives to create innovative spaces for learning and development across taken-for-granted boundaries, i.e. learning in transdisciplinary modules across academic disciplines, interacting through multimodal media across semiotic domains and *learning-for-teaching* activities across different educational contexts. For students of the programme, the overall object is to become 'experts on learning' through a research-oriented study approach that stresses a thorough understanding of the children's learning processes within classroom activity. Referring to the dialectics of enacting theory and theorising practice, participative internships and practical studies are at the very heart of the semester work as this concern governs how students will organise their *learning-for-teaching* process as well as their *teaching-for-learning* work.

In order to facilitate meaningful interactions across contextual boundaries, student pairs and the classroom teacher(s) co-develop – with the support of their university tutor – a Collaborative Classroom Inquiry (CCI) project for the internship time. According to the study theme of the semester, e.g. 'promoting auto-regulated learning', the team jointly conceives, conducts and documents learning activities related to a co-developed internship topic. The students collect multimodal data, evidencing the enacted pedagogical intent, in order to analyse and understand the learning processes that took place.

Furthermore, relevant excerpts of the data and the final inquiry reports are uploaded on a Web-based learning platform for critical analysis and collaborative interpretation in the academic context. The enacted learning culture around shared documents and processes aims at generating meaningful resources for planning and realising further study work with special emphasis on reconsidering, detailing and diversifying practices.

The systemic view (see Figure 14.1) displays the internship as boundary zone in between the activity systems of school and university with their related object and tools. Potential areas of conflict are the differing objects of training teachers, i.e. developing expertise in learning vs. expertise in teaching, and the specific focus of attention during internship such as analysing learning processes vs. teaching lessons. In this sense, the boundary zone may be understood as an 'in-between arena of polycontextual practices' (Edwards 2005: 4) where elements of both activity systems are woven together according to Cole's dynamic conception of context as 'that which weaves together' (1996: 135). It creates a specific boundary practice that is productive of and partly produced by a new activity system according to a co-developed boundary object.

A specific boundary-crossing tool, i.e. the Collaborative Classroom Inquiry (CCI) assignment, mediates joint questioning and the construction of a shared pedagogical concern as regards the particular classroom context as well as the joint work of the students–teacher team before, during and after the internship period. In this sense, it generates a joint boundary object that gives durable direction and purpose to the local–contextual training activity.

Considerations driving inquiry

A cultural-historical research framework 'calls for complementarity of the system view and the subject's view' (Engeström and Miettinen 1999: 10). Following this tenet, we have to model the boundary zone activity placed within the broader network of other activity systems as looking at it from above, but focus also on the views of the participants 'through whose eyes and interpretations the activity is constructed' (Engeström and Miettinen 1999: 10).

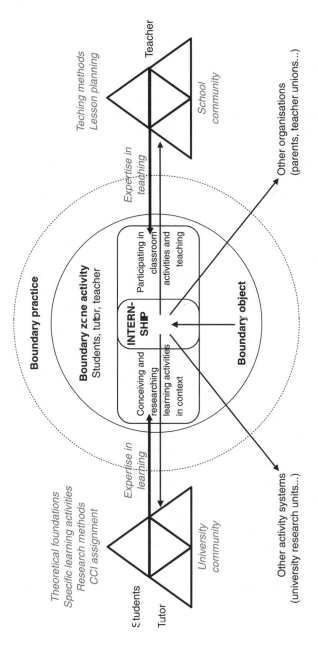

Figure 14.1 Bridging academic and professional contexts through boundary zone activity in ITE (according to Tuomi-Gröhn 2005: 34).

In AT, modelling is a method for arranging the interacting elements of activity systems on the structural level and for systematically planning the inquiry on the process level. Referring to our unit of analysis, the AT trian gles help us to (re-)construct the general structure of the boundary zone activity (see Figure 14.1) and explore the interactional dynamics within and among the activity systems involved. Furthermore, this model facilitates the process of reconstructing and instantiating the object of the specific boundary activity that 'often takes the form of problem finding and problem definition' (Engeström 1999: 381). As a visual representation of the activity under scrutiny the model mediates, as a material and ideal-semiotic artefact, types of epistemic work according to different practical research purposes. 'Certain artefacts are particularly useful for asking and answering "what?" questions, while others are better suited for "how?" and "why?" questions' (Engeström 2006: 1790). For our analysis, the heuristic qualities of the triangles are useful for scrutinising the developmental potential of the collaborative inquiry work through questions emphasising learning among the actors involved, i.e. Who is learning? What is learned? Why and how does learning occur?

We will cross these precise questions and the four principles of the activity-theoretical framework, i.e. unit of analysis, multivoicedness, historicity and contradictory struggle, in an analytic AT-learning grid similar to Engeström's expansive learning matrix (2001: 138). This tool helps us to analyse the occurring talk during the four tutorial sessions (subject view) with respect to the specific activity-theoretical concepts (vertical lines) and to the relevant learning issues (horizontal lines). Critical fragments of the conversational data are placed into the corresponding cells of the grid while the related structural dynamics and emerging tensions are accentuated in the systemic model as well.

This analysis allows us to get insight into the interrelation between the use of CCI as a 'boundary-crossing tool' and the emergence of a 'boundary object' in this joint learning zone. More precisely, by narrowing the focus to student dyad–teacher–academic tutor interactions, we will be able to address (a) how a shared object is generated/negotiated, (b) how the research approach is sustained or adjusted during internships, joint tutorials and CCI projects, (c) to what extent and which kind of developmental improvements are generated through this boundary object.

Views on boundaries: insights from joint tutorial sessions

The following four excerpts from audio-taped tutorial sessions (selected from a corpus of over 30 hours of recordings during the years 2006–2008) illustrate negotiation processes during the internship period between the internship students and the classroom teacher (excerpt 3) and final comments in the joint evaluation session after the internship with the academic tutor as well (excerpts 1, 2 and 4). The recordings are transcribed according to conversational analysis conventions in order to emphasise also the interactional dynamics within the talk. The original languages (mostly Luxembourgish) are used in the transcript with an interlinear English translation. Lines indicate Te1–4 (four teachers), Tu1–2 (two different university tutors), Pat, Liv etc. (eight different students).

As you can see from the transcript, teacher 1 does not really appreciate the joint work on learning issues (L 01) when compared to experiences during former teaching-centred internships (L 04). The teacher's personal interest for accepting students within the class (L 06) has been so far

```
01   Te1:   also mir hätte secherlech kéinnte bësse méi op dat schoulescht
            agoe
            so we could have focused of course a bit more on the schoolish
            thing
02          e besse méi didaktik kucken oder esou
            look a bit more at didactics or so
03   Tu1:   mmhh
04   Te1:   mir hätten och kéinte denken ech vill méi nach vunenee leieren
            we could also have I think learned much more from each other
05          well dat as ee vun den haptursache gewecht
            because that has been one of the main reasons
06          firwat ech emmer stagiäre geholl hun=
            why I always accepted student teachers (in my classroom)=
07          =well sie och eppes matbruecht hun=
            =because they also brought something along
08          =duerch déi diskussiounen an déi iddien
            =through these discussions and these ideas
09          déi sie dann och matbruecht hun
            which at that moment they also brought along
10   Tu1:   mmhh
11   Te1:   wou mir als klass och nees eppes bäigeléiert hun
            through which we as a class again learned something new
12   Tu1:   mmhh
13   Te1:   an dat ass eigentlech hei komplett (.) flach gefall=
            and this is in fact here completely (.) missing=
14   Tu1:   mmhh
15   Te1:   =t ass guer net méi (.) t huet guer net méi stattfonnt
            =it is not anymore (.) it did not happen anymore
```

Excerpt 14.1 Teacher highlighting differing views of the internship assignment (joint evaluation tutorial).

to challenge the current didactical repertoire (L 02) by alternative methodological approaches, that students of the former teacher training
approach used to apply during internship time (L 07, 00). Learning
usually takes place through discussions (L 08), but as this time the internship topic differs (inquiring learning processes vs teaching lessons), not
any learning or potential improvement of the class practices (L 11) could
be evidenced (L 13, 15). For this teacher, developing expertise takes place
through applying appropriate models according to an ideal-rational
account. As the internship experience is not really inspiring for the
teacher, any further collaboration with the programme is – at this point –
not even certain.

As regards our focus on the use of the CCI assignment as a boundary-
crossing tool and the emergence of a boundary object, short extracts and
own reflections are placed into the 'AT-learning' grid for a synoptic
overview.

From a systemic point of view, we might infer that a jointly negotiated
'boundary object' does not really develop within the 'boundary zone' as
the teacher does not move into sharing the students' inquiry work on
learning activities within the classroom. The teacher's point of reference
for training students is a broad methodological repertoire to teach lessons.
This conventional view refers to the historicity dimension of the training
activity, highlighting how the diverse layers and strands of history,
engraved in artefacts of the bounded activity systems, continue to mediate
people's thinking within joined training activities. Both objects co-exist
within the boundary zone according to an arrangement between the
teacher and the students. Accordingly, any improvement of the school
practices could not be evidenced (L 13–15). The conflicting objects on
teacher training generate tensions in the boundary zone that are displayed
as flashes in the model below. These underlying tensions are of major
interest for planning upcoming developmental work to do with internship
teachers in order to facilitate the development of a joint boundary
practice.

The present excerpt provides interesting evidence for the dialectics
between the individual and organisational level of development. Teacher
2 sounds very enthusiastic about the learning experiences in the shared
boundary zone and appreciates the new approach (L 04) that is in strong
contrast to the former teacher training practice (L 10). The teacher mentions the necessary rupture in the educating practice (L 10) triggered by
the new assignment and points also to the emotional dimensions of the
change process (L 03, 04, 14). Furthermore, teacher 2 emphasises the shift
from being the confirmed expert and model teacher (L 12) with the related
mentoring duties (L 13) to the novel joint-learning experience (L 14). In
the broader interview (data beyond the excerpt range), teacher 2 expressly
appreciates that more flexibility is given, no fixed patterns and models are

Table 14.1 Relating conversational data to learning and CHAT principles in internship team I

	Activity systems as unit of analysis	Multi-voicedness	Historicity	Contradictory struggle and expansive work
Who is learning?		Class and teacher did not improve (L 11)		
Why do they learn?			Teaching practices improved through student inputs (L 06–07)	
What do they learn?		Didactical issues of school practice were missing (L 02) Improvement of didactical and methodological knowledge did not happen (L 13–15)	Methodological repertoire to teach lessons is the teacher's point of reference (according to former TT approach)	Former teacher training approach and teaching centred internship work are in conflict with new approach (tension)
How do they learn?	Learning from each other (L 04)	Teacher is the teaching expert (professional background)	Applying models that students brought to the class in former TT approach (L 09) Joint discussions about methodological repertoire to teach lessons (L 08)	Ideal-rational account of constructing knowledge and developing expertise (tension)

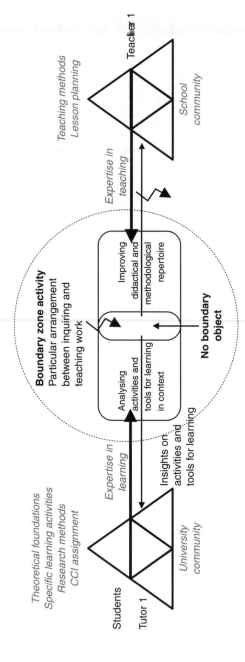

Figure 14.2 Modelling the boundary zone activity of internship team 1 (excerpt 1).

```
01    Te2:    an ech hun dat elo immens flott fonnt als iddi
              and I appreciated this now as a very interesting idea
02            ewéi sie do koume (.) an am unfank hun ech geduecht
              as they were coming along (.) and at the beginning I thought
03            O MAMM (.)
              MY GOD (.)
04            an herno ass dat fir mech awer och eng ganz flott sach gin
              and later on however this became a very amazing thing for me
05            (-) wou ech och elo geduecht hun (.)
              (-) whereas I have been thinking now (.)
06            bon (.) wann dat esou klappt dann
              well (.) when this goes well then
07            <<schmunzelnd> mechst de mol esou virun (.) ne?>(.)
              <<amused> you keep on going this way (.) right?> (.)
08    Tu2:    mmhh
09    Te2:    t war och e (-) t huet mech beräichert
              it was also (-) it was enriching for me
10            well t war mol net (.) t war net sou: wi=wie soss
              because it was not even (.) it was not as: as=as usual
11            et war een emmer sou (.) d virbild fir d studenten (.)
              i always was used to be (.) the model for the students (.)
12            oder virbild <<unverständlich> wor e>
              or the model <<unintelligible> was a>
13            et huet een hinne dann sou (.) .hh sou=esou musst d et machen
              i told them then so (.) .hh you have to do it this way
14            (.) an dës kéier war et fir mech genau sou (.) N::EILAND=
              (.) and this time for me it was absolutely (.) NEW:: TERRITORY=
```

Excerpt 14.2 Teacher talking about the enriching experiences during the internship (joint evaluation tutorial).

prescribed and rich opportunities are provided to negotiate shared pathways for working in the specific environment. From the conversational data, we summarise the relevant excerpts in our analytic grid.

From a systemic point of view, the joint classroom activity is fuelled by a co-developed boundary object on 'designing workshops promoting auto-regulated learning', which reshapes the common classroom practice even beyond the internship time (L 07). The boundary activity also reconfigures the traditional division of labour within the internship team through a shift of the teacher role (L 11–13). This excerpt shows that the CCI assignment as a boundary-crossing tool (L 1) has the potential to create an internship activity that triggers sustainable development across boundaries.

This excerpt from a tutorial session at the beginning of the internship is putting closer stress on the ongoing interaction and meaning-making

Table 14.2 Relating conversational data to learning and CHAT principles in internship team 2

	Activity systems as unit of analysis	Multi-voicedness	Historicity	Contradictory struggle and expansive work
Who is learning?	Teacher, students, children	Teacher (L 09)		
Why do they learn?	'Joint workshop activities' as shared object of the boundary activity (L 04)	Mentoring students as a journey towards new learning territory (L 14)	Critical stance to former role as model teacher (L 11–13)	Teacher shifts role from teaching expert (model) to co-learner (L 11–13)
What do they learn?		Personal enrichment (L 09)	Keep on running the reshaped practice (L 07)	Change of classroom practices through the joint experiences (L 06–09)
How do they learn?				Overcoming uncertainty at the start of internship (L 02–03)

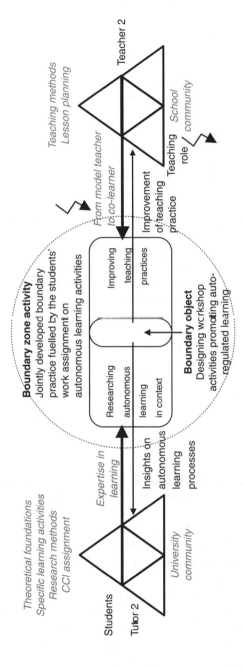

Figure 14.3 Modelling the boundary zone activity of internship team 2 (excerpt 2).

```
01   Te3:    nee (.) et get souvill tse kucke bei    [kanner
             no (.) there is so much to look at with [children

02   Pat:                                            [mmhh

03   Te3:    mee ech wees net genau wéi dir dat e:hh (..) musst e:hh (.)
             but i do not know exactly how you e:hhh (..) have to e:hh (.)

04   Te3:    [opschaffen gell?
             [work it out do you?

05   Pat:    [jo bei eis=bei eis ass dat och
             [yes we=we we also

06           ee:hh [fir eis ass et och net (.) net esou einfach
             ee:hh [for us also it is not (.) not so easy

07   Te3:          [<unintelligible> xxxx>

08   Pat:    well mer och fir d éischt musse kucken:
             because we also have to look first

09           wéi=wéi mer eis mussen uleëen dass och .hh (1,5)
             how=how we have to organise ourselves so that .hh (1,5)

10           bëssen esou eng=eng (..)
             a little bit a=a (..)

11           jo du wees net richteg :wéis de dech solls uleeën
             yes you do not know exactly :how to organise yourself

12           an du wees dass de eppes muss [SCHREIwen
             and you know that you have to [WRITE something

13   Te3:                                  [mmhh

14   Pat:    an dat (.) dat kënnt mengen ech erréischt
             and that (.) i think that this will only happen

15           einfach erréicht [wärend dem temps de terrain
             only happen      [during the internship

16   Te3:                     [jo dat kënnt mat der zäit
                              [yes you get there by-and-by

17           [jo jo jo
             [yes yes yes
```

Excerpt 14.3 Students and the teacher are discussing the shared work before the second internship time (preparation tutorial).

process in the team so that the episode may also be analysed according to conversational analytic features to determine the participants' ways of turn-taking, constructing sequences of utterances across turns, identifying and repairing problems, etc.

Teacher 3 shares the students' research concerns (L 03–06) and is interested in using the boundary-crossing CCI assignment as a tool for expanding knowledge about the children's cultural background. The teacher suggests circumstances to investigate this topic (L 01) by drawing upon experiences with the children. Furthermore, teacher 3 shares the worries of the students about achieving the inquiry project successfully

Table 14.3 Relating conversational data to learning and CHAT principles in internship team 3

	Activity systems as unit of analysis	Multi-voicedness	Historicity	Contradictory struggle and expansive work
Who is learning?	Students Teacher			Teacher as a team member, a co-learner and a co-researcher Teacher expands the object of mentoring students from teaching to research issues (L 01)
Why do they learn?	Constructing shared boundary object about children's cultural resources for learning	Teacher helps to elucidate the given assignment (L 03–04) Tries to better understand the CCI approach and to cooperate (L 03–04)	Teacher's knowledge fund about children works as a resource to see rich opportunities for researching and learning (L 01)	
What do they learn?	How to run an inquiry project (L 11–12) and to analyse empirical data (L 22–23) Insights into children's cultural background (L 19)			
How do they learn?	Joint solving of core problems (L 06) Through negotiating and discussing	Through exchanging views and perspectives (L 20–24)	Learning through experience (L 16)	

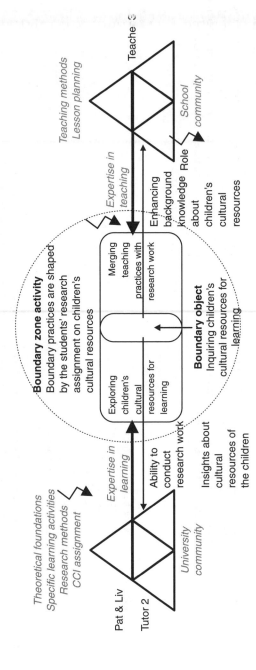

Figure 14.4 Modelling the boundary zone activity of internship team 3 (excerpt 3).

```
01   Te4:   mat engem aneren aa:n (.) jo (.) kucken
            with a different gaze (.) yes (.) looking
02   Te5:   well ech mengen dat (.) wei d Te4 scho sot virdrun (.)
            because i think that (.) as Te4 already mentioned before (.)
03          dat ass amfong e:hh (.) dat vernoléissege mir amfong hei
            that is in fact e:hh (.) we disregard this indeed here
04          e bëssen well mer eben och d zäit net ëmmer hun
            a little bit because we do not always have the time
05          mer kënnen eis net e ganze mueren dohinner setzen an
            we cannot sit down somewhere during an entire morning and
06          de Kanner mol nokucken wann se spillen (.)
            watching the children play (.)
07          .hhh bon natiirlech wann elo emol e problemkand
            .hh well of course when there is a problematic child
08          mär hun el[:o an engem grupp hu mer der puer dé:i
            we have no[:w in a group we have some which
09   Tu2:             [mmhh
10   Te5:   .hhh e bëssen opfälleg sin e:h (.) oder (.)
            .hh are a little bit conspicuous e:h (.) or (.)
11          deen een ass elo am moment zwar nëmmi hei (.)
            one has left the group for the moment (.)
12          mais da kuckt een och (.) mat engem aneren du emol
            but you start looking (.) with a different glance
13          (.) wei se sech dann dee moment behuelen gell? (.)
            (.) how do they behave at that moment or? (.)
14   Te5:   an ech mengen dat ass eis amfong och eréischt e[lo OPgefall
            and i think that we realised this indeed only a[t this moment
15   Te4:                                                   [mmhh

16   Te5:   oder bewosst gin wou sie eben hei am stage waren (.)
            or appreciated it when they were here in internship (.)
17          dass een eben effektiv méi misst oppassen dorobber (.)
            that you indeed have to pay more attention to that (.)
18          .hh mee wéi gesot (.) et huet een net emmer zäit (.)
            .hh but as said (.) we do not always have time (.)
19          a wann och e:h (.) näischt onopfälleg e:hh opfälleges ass
            and when e:h (.) nothing unconspicuous e:hh conspicuous happen
20          da kuckt een o net (.)
            you do not look (.)
```

Excerpt 14.4 Teachers reflecting their joint work with the students (joint evaluation tutorial).

(L 15–16) and helps solving current problems with regard to the inquiry process (L 15–26) and interpreting the data accurately (L 24). This commitment beyond the regular classroom work underlines the ongoing team-building process and the group's efforts to develop joint ways to investigate the topic under inquiry (L 19). A process of expanding the object of the mentoring activity can be observed, as the teacher changes the stance from 'being the expert teacher' to 'being a co-learner and a co-researcher' in boundary practices that merge teaching and research. The 'AT-learning' grid sums up the following fragments of the selected episode.

On the systemic level, this excerpt highlights how the boundary-crossing tool mediates research-related discussions in the boundary zone related to different purposes such as a progressive construction of a shared boundary object for the internship activity, a shared understanding and planning of the inquiry process itself, with issues related to collecting and analysing data, a closer analysis of the assignment itself for possible feedback about the preparatory work at the university. We have visualised these areas of change by flashes in the systemic model.

This last excerpt highlights the dynamics among the individual and organisational learning by stressing the internal and external struggles of teachers when rethinking their practices. Both teachers display a critical stance towards their own teaching practice and question their roles as organisers or observers (L 15–16). On the one hand, they advocate how video-taping and analysing the children's learning activities might generate a more differentiated view on a child's abilities (L 14–17). On the other hand, they continue to legitimate their long-standing practice referring to common teaching duties (L 05–06), problematic learning issues (L 07–13) and official time constraints (L 04, 18). The joint experiences keep on questioning the classroom practices even beyond the boundary activity, but we cannot say whether any change occurred at the long-term level.

On the systemic level, the teachers' critical reflections about their classroom practice evidence the developmental impact of the boundary-crossing tool on the local school level.

Conclusion

The present study focuses on theoretical and practical issues regarding learning activity within joint boundary zones during internship time. Particular attention is paid to the processes that are mediated through the boundary-crossing CCI assignment. The potential of this tool is of major interest for the scientific evaluation of the programme as it was introduced deliberately as a boundary-crossing tool to enhance interaction, collaboration and learning within and between the university and the local schools.

The four excerpts illustrate how *learning-for-teaching* and *teaching-for-learning* activities are negotiated and co-constructed within the shared

Table 14.4 Relating conversational data to learning and CHAT principles in internship team 4

	Activity systems as unit of analysis	Multi-voicedness	Historicity	Contradictory struggle and expansive work
Who is learning?		Teachers		
Why do they learn?	Boundary object has generated new learning experiences during internship (L 14–16)	Critical stance to own teaching practice (L 03)	Teachers legitimate their teaching practice referring to common teaching duties (L 04–07, L 18)	Inner conflict about a teacher's role: organiser (conventional) and/or observer (new) (L 16–20)
What do they learn?		New ways of looking at classroom activities (L 01) Different view on teaching and learning processes (L 17)		Teachers reconsider the way they look at children's learning – until now, they had looked at conspicuous behaviour (L 10–11)
How do they learn?		Teachers learn through students' research practices (L 16)		

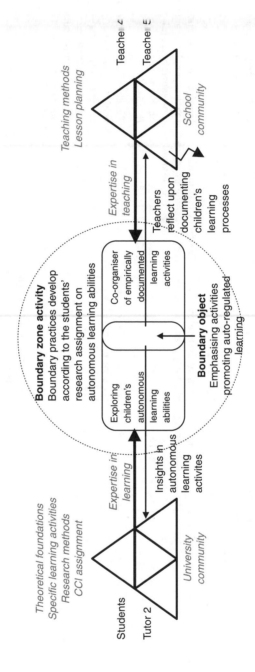

Figure 14.5 Modelling of the boundary zone activity of internship team 4 (excerpt 4).

Table 14.5 Development processes within the four internship teams

	Time	Participants	Boundary object according to semester theme	Development through boundary activity
Excerpt 1	At the end of internship	Students School teacher Academic tutor	No evidence	
Excerpt 2	At the end of internship	Students School teacher Academic tutor	Designing workshop activities promoting auto-regulated learning	Change of classroom practices through the joint experiences Students got insights on autonomous learning processes
Excerpt 3	At the beginning between phase 1 and 2	Students School teacher	Inquiring children's cultural resources for learning	Joint knowing about doing research in classrooms and about the children's culturual background
Excerpt 4	At the end of internship	Students School teacher Academic tutor	Emphasising activities promoting auto-regulated learning	Teachers rethink their monitoring of children's learning processes Students get insights on autonomous learning processes

boundary zones and might enhance the student teachers' expertise on the one hand, and develop the teachers' classroom practice on the other hand. The data emphasise the CCI tool's potential to create boundary practices that relate research concerns on learning and teaching to classroom practices. However, different kinds of scenarios occur with varying results.

A look at the most promising experiences show that a shared boundary object is of crucial importance for the emergence of novel boundary practices which may also enhance sustainable qualitative changes across the contexts (excerpts 2 and 4). Referring to processes of dialogue and mutual feedback, the boundary object has to be considered as a real driving motive of the boundary activity system in settings where the student dyad and the teacher succeed in interweaving their classroom work around a joint object. Excerpt 2 (as well as excerpts 3 and 4) illustrates the potential for sustainable transformation and long-term benefit for the local community.

A closer look at the boundary objects of the four excerpts reveals that the latter are co-developed according to the salient interests of the partners. Whereas the students' interest respects the general learning theme of the semester, the teachers bring different interests into play, e.g. joint change effort (excerpt 2), interest in enhancing the knowledge about the children's cultural background (excerpt 3), organising workshops fostering autonomy (excerpt 4). The co-constructed boundary objects facilitate the collaboration within the teacher–student team and shape the quality of the *learning-for-teaching* activities by merging perspectives of both activity systems. As the shared object is jointly re-conceptualised, it allows for a broader range of *learning-for-teaching* possibilities than within the boundaries of each single activity system.

Moreover, the co-developed boundary practice is sustained by jointly developed tools, e.g. workshop sessions that serve either as conceptual or material mediators for transformations in the school context and as focus of inquiry for the students. They mediate the development of a shared work culture that draws on the resources of its participants to launch a process that none could achieve alone (see excerpt 2). The related discussions (excerpt 3) illustrate that participants seek appropriate support and information and create interactions across contexts. These horizontal movements impinge on the development of all the partners involved and evidence the formation of horizontal transfer and expertise. By achieving this kind of mutual 'horizontal' process, the ITE approach sustains knowledge construction on learning and teaching as a process-object across bounded activity systems.

With regard to the division of labour in activity systems, the co-developed boundary activity often induces a shift in the roles and professional identities of the participating teachers. The latter engage in the joint productive activity by expanding their role to co-learners or even to co-researchers. In excerpt 2, the teacher reconsiders the conventional teaching-expert model during the novel internship activity that was jointly created by the team (classroom activities for autonomous learning). Excerpt 3 highlights how the expert–novice relationship is permanently negotiated within the student–teacher interactions depending on the topic to be discussed, i.e. researching learning or organising teaching.

In the settings where no shared boundary object arose (excerpt 1), advanced boundary practice is hard to be co-developed. Traditional roles and conventional teaching–learning functionalities, as historically produced in the internship activity, remain unchallenged and continue to mediate the thinking and knowing upon learning and teaching. Although students get space and time for their work assignment, no collaborative project is realised. As a result, sustainable benefits for the classroom community were hard to be evidenced.

As excerpt 1 shows, collaboration is not self-evident since historically grown personal attitudes, interests and local practices mainly influence it that do not rely on learning. In this case, the students and the teacher struggle to form a collaborative team so that the teacher-training programme has to offer further mediational support for promoting this purpose, i.e. specific change workshops, training sessions for mentors.

The interplay between theoretical knowledge and classroom practices seems to shape the development of new pedagogical practices. This study evidences that the creation of novel practices is mediated by theoretical discussions focusing on pedagogical change, data analysis and development and learning conceptions. In sharp contrast to the latter, the related discourse within boundary zones, where no co-created practices emerge, is dominated by terms of classroom management, authority and control.

To sum up, the outcomes of our research confirm the transformative potential of the outlined boundary crossing ITE approach (a) to encourage the collaborating partners, i.e. students, teachers and faculty tutors, to continually re-conceptualise their activities and professional practices and (b) to develop a research and learning attitude with regard to the individual, collective and institutional development across institutional boundaries. In this sense, the available body of data from this research reveals that the boundary-crossing approach has the potential to launch sustainable professional development within an educational system and to serve as a promising approach for conceiving reforms in initial teacher education.

Acknowledgement

I want to thank my colleague, Dr Gudrun Ziegler, and my research assistant, Kristina Hoeppner, from the DICA-lab in the Unit for Sociocultural Research on Learning and Development at the University of Luxembourg, for their critical comments on the first draft and their assistance in writing this chapter.

References

Chaiklin, S. and Lave, J. (eds) (1993) *Understanding practice: perspectives on activity and context*, Cambridge, MA: Cambridge University Press.

Cole, M. (1996) *Cultural psychology: a once and future discipline*, Cambridge, MA: Harvard University Press.

Craig, C. and Deretchin, L. (2007) 'International research on the impact of accountability systems', *Teacher Education Yearbook XV*, Lanham, MD: Rowman and Littlefield.

Daniels, H. (2006) 'Analysing institutional effects in activity theory: first steps in the development of a language of description', *Outlines: Critical Social Studies*, 2: 43–58.

Daniels, H., Leadbetter, J., Soares, A. and MacNab, N. (2006) 'Learning in and for cross school working', in K. Yamazumi (ed.) *Building activity theory in practice: toward the next generation*, Osaka: Kansai University Press

Davydov, V. and Radzikhovskii, L. (1985) 'Vygotsky's theory and the activity-oriented approach in psychology', in J. Wertsch (ed.) *Culture, communication, and cognition: Vygotskian perspectives*, Cambridge: Cambridge University Press.

Edwards, A. and Mutton, T. (2007) 'Looking forward: rethinking professional learning through partnership arrangements in Initial Teacher Education', *Oxford Review of Education*, 33(4): 503–519.

Edwards, R. (2005) 'Literacies for learning in further education in the UK: theoretical and methodological challenges.' Paper presented at the Australian Association for Research in Education Annual Conference, University of Western Sydney. Online, available at: www.aare.edu.au/05pap/edw05015.pdf (accessed 14 September 2007).

Engeström, Y. (1999) 'Innovative learning in work teams: analyzing cycles of knowledge creation in practice', in Y. Engeström, R. Miettinen and R.-L. Punamäki (eds) *Perspectives on activity theory*, Cambridge, MA: Cambridge University Press.

Engeström, Y. (2001) 'Expansive learning at work: toward an activity theoretical reconceptualization', *Journal of Education and Work*, 14(1): 133–156.

Engeström, Y. (2005) *Developmental work research: expanding activity theory in practice*, Berlin: Lehmanns Media.

Engeström, Y. (2006) 'From well-bounded ethnographies to intervening in mycorrhizae activities', *Organisation Studies*, 27: 1783–1793.

Engeström, Y. and Miettinen, R. (1999) 'Introduction', in Y. Engeström, R. Miettinen and R.-L. Punamäki (eds) *Perspectives on activity theory*, Cambridge, MA: Cambridge University Press.

Engeström, Y. and Tuomi-Gröhn, T. (eds) (2003) *Between school and work: new perspectives on transfer and boundary-crossing*, Amsterdam: Pergamon.

Engeström, Y., Engeström, R. and Suntio, A. (2002) 'Can a school community learn to master its own future? An activity-theoretical study of expansive learning among middle school teachers', in G. Wells and G. Claxton (eds) *Learning for life in the 21st century*, Oxford: Blackwell.

Engeström, Y., Engeström, R. and Vähäaho, T. (1999a) 'When the center does not hold: the importance of knotworking', in S. Chaiklin, M. Hedegaard and U.J. Jensen (eds) *Activity theory and social practice: cultural-historical approaches*, Aarhus: Aarhus University Press.

European Commission (2005) *Common European principles for teacher competences and qualifications*. Online, available at: www.see-educoop.net/education_in/pdf/01-en_principles_en.pdf (accessed 15 January 2008).

European Commission (Education and Training Website) *The Bologna Process – Towards the European Higher Education Area*. Online, available at: http://ec.europa.eu/education/higher-education/doc1290_en.htm (accessed 15 February 2008).

Gutiérrez, K.D., Baquedano-Lopez, P. and Tejeda, C. (1999) 'Rethinking diversity: hybridity and hybrid language practices in the third space', *Mind, Culture and Activity*, 6(4): 286–303.

Hakkarainen, K., Palonen, T., Paavola, S. and Lehtinen, E. (eds) (2004) *Communities of networked expertise*, Amsterdam: Elsevier.

Jahreie, C.F. and Ludvigsen, S.R. (2007) 'Portfolios as boundary object: learning and change in teacher education', *Research and Practice in Technology Enhanced Learning*, 2(3): 299–318.

Jakku-Sihvonen, R. and Niemi, H. (eds) (2006) 'Research-based teacher education in Finland: reflections by Finnish teacher educators', *Research in Educational Sciences 25*, Turku: Finnish Educational Research Association.

Kostogriz, A. (2000) 'Activity theory and the new literacy studies: modelling the literacy learning activity system.' Paper presented at the meeting of the Australian Association for Research in Education, Sydney, 4–7 December. Online, available at: www.aare.edu.au/00pap/kos00161.htm (accessed 15 February 2008).

Leadbetter, J., Daniels, H., Brown, S., Edwards, A., Middleton, D., Popova, A., Apostolov, A. and Warmington P. (2007) 'Professional learning within multi-agency children's services: researching into practice', *Educational Research*, 49(1): 83–98.

Ludvigsen, S.R., Havnes, A. and Lahn, L.Chr. (2003) 'Workplace learning across activity systems: a case study of sales engineers', in Y. Engeström and T. Tuomi-Gröhn (eds) *Between school and work: new perspectives on transfer and boundary-crossing*, Amsterdam: Pergamon.

Matusov, E. (2007) 'In search of "the appropriate" unit of analysis for sociocultural research', *Culture and Psychology*, 13(3): 307–333.

Max, C. (1999) *Entwicklung von Kompetenz – ein neues Paradigma für das Lernen in Schule und Arbeitswelt*, Frankfurt a.M.: Peter Lang.

Peck, C. A., Gallucci, Chr., Sloan, T. and Lippincott, A. (2009) 'Organisational learning and program renewal in teacher education: a sociocultural theory of learning, innovation and change', *Educational Research Review*, 4(1): 16–25.

Perrenoud, Ph. (1999) *Dix nouvelles compétences pour enseigner: invitation au voyage*, Paris: ESF.

Schratz, M. (2005) 'What is a "European Teacher"?' Online, available at: www.pa-feldkirch.ac.at/entep/ (accessed 10 November 2006).

Star, S.L. (1989) 'The structure of ill-structured solutions: boundary objects and heterogeneous distributed problem solving', in L. Gasser and M.N. Huhns (eds) *Readings in distributed artificial intelligence*, Vol. 3, Menlo Park, CA: Morgans Kaufmann, pp. 37–54.

Star, S.L. and Griesemer, J.R. (1989) 'Institutional ecology, "translational" and boundary objects', *Social Studies of Sciences*, 19(3): 387–420.

Tsui, A.B.M. and Law, D.Y.K. (2007) 'Learning as boundary-crossing in school–university partnership', *Teaching and Teacher Education*, 23: 1289–1301.

Tuomi-Gröhn, T. (2003) 'Developmental transfer as a goal of internship in practical nursing', in T. Tuomi-Gröhn and Y. Engeström (eds) *Between school and work: new perspectives on transfer and boundary crossing*, Amsterdam: Pergamon.

Tuomi-Gröhn, T. (2005) 'Studying learning, transfer and context: a comparison of current approach to learning', in Y. Engestrom, J. Lompscher and G. Rückriem (eds) *Putting activity theory to work: contributions from developmental work research*, Berlin: Lehmanns Media.

Tuomi-Gröhn, T. and Engeström, Y. (eds) (2003) *Between school and work: new perspectives on transfer and boundary crossing*, Amsterdam: Pergamon.

Yamazumi, K. (2005) 'School as collaborative change agents', in K. Yamazumi, Y. Engeström and H. Daniels (eds) *New learning challenges: going beyond the industrial age systems of school and work*, Osaka: Kansai University Press.

Yamazumi, K. (2006) 'Learning for critical and creative agency: an activity-theoretical study of advanced networks of learning in new school project', in K. Yamazumi (ed.) *CHAT Technical Reports No. 1: Building Activity Theory in Practice: Toward the Next Generation*, Center for Human Activity Theory, Kansai University (Japan). Online, available at: www.chat.kansai-u.ac.jp/publications/tr/v1_3.pdf (accessed 17 February 2008).

Yamazumi, K., Engeström, Y. and Daniels, H. (eds) (2005) *New learning challenges: going beyond the industrial age system of school and work*, Osaka: Kansai University Press.

Victor, B. and Boynton, A. (1998) *Invented here: maximizing your organisation's internal growth and profitability. a practical guide to transforming work*, Boston, MA: Harvard Business School Press.

Vygotsky, L.S. (1978) *Mind in society: the development of higher psychological processes*, Cambridge, MA: Harvard University Press.

Wartofsky, M. (1979) *Models: representations and the scientific understanding*, Dordrecht: D. Reidel.

Wenger, E., McDermott, R. and Snyder, W.M. (2002) *Cultivating communities of practice*, Boston, MA: Harvard Business School Press.

Afterword
CHAT and good teacher education

Willem Wardekker

If, as the Introduction and the contribution by Smagorinsky make clear, cultural-historical (and) activity theory is not a unity but consists of different strands of thought, this is not because researchers working within it are at odds with each other or do not communicate. Rather, as is evident from this volume, they are exploring the many possibilities opened up by its central ideas, and indeed their differences may well prove productive. Maybe the term 'theory' as used here is slightly misleading, as for many it means a well-defined and researchable set of statements. CHAT, however, is in my view more a way of thinking than a coherent whole, a paradigm rather than a theory in that sense. It is a paradigm that invites us to think dialectically; that is, in terms of tensions that produce change and development. In a sense, it may itself be interpreted as produced by the tensions between the two other important paradigms in the study of the human condition: on the one hand, the nomothetic one, inspired on the natural sciences and intent on finding unidirectional and hopefully causal relations, and on the other hand, the interpretative paradigm, inspired by the idea of human beings as free agents, acting on their own interpretations of the world. Vygotsky certainly strove to unite these two ways of doing research, seeing them as one more manifestation of a Cartesian divide which in his day had led to two totally different strands of psychology. A Vygotskian methodology, then, focuses on the interactions (or 'transactions' as Dewey called it) between individuals and their (human) environment, on the limitations and affordances inherent in the context and in the individual, on the productive or prohibitive tensions and frictions between these. It considers causality and freedom of action to be the extremes of a continuum within which human actions take place, and asks after the nature of the circumstances that limit or afford possibilities for acting and for development, while keeping in mind that effectuating those possibilities changes these very circumstances. Development takes place when a way is found to use existing tensions in a productive way to reach a new level of functioning. According to Vygotsky and others, the best way to study this process is to introduce an experimental stimulus that might help to produce such development. As Ellis shows in his chapter, exactly the changes this secondary stimulus introduces allow us to understand how 'the inner structure and development' of processes work.

It is, of course, not enough to have such a general principle. We need to construct models and theories of the way individuals (or collectives considered as individual) and their (institutional) contexts interact dialectically, and we need concrete methods to investigate such interactions. As can be seen from a number of the chapters in this volume, Engeström's theory of interactions within and between activity settings is at this moment one of the most productive and generally used. Although his triangle model is often used purely as a classificatory schema, reminding the researcher of the important factors to be taken into consideration (as in Douglas' chapter), its true power is in the consideration of tensions and contradictions that may induce or prohibit development, as explained by Jóhannsdóttir and by Max. And the 'Developmental Work Research' method uses the outcomes of such an analysis to introduce stimuli that are intended to facilitate development, just as in Vygotsky's own use of the secondary stimulus method.

Although sometimes Engeström's model is equated with activity theory, in my view this is unwarranted. Or rather, I think his theory can and should be expanded – as Engeström himself is doing (e.g. Engeström 2008). The theory and model are particularly good at understanding well-defined activity systems such as industrial work places, and individuals as members of such organizations. They do not, however, draw attention to the wider social, economical, historical and cultural force field in which such systems operate, other than (in the third-generation model) in the form of other well-defined systems having an interaction with the system under study. But (and this may be one of the problems Smagorinsky is alluding to in his chapter) individuals are never just members of one activity system, and so their learning cannot be fully explained within the context of the system under study. It is exactly the wider cultural field that has to be taken into consideration. Moreover, Engeström's models do not afford insight in the emotional and intellectual processes related to the learning and development of individuals, processes that Edwards points out. The ideas Edwards proposes in reference to the work of Vasilyuk, or as developed by Meijers and Wardekker (2003) based on similar ideas of Damasio and Gendlin, can fill this gap. In such models, learning is thought to occur as the result of an emotional crisis, provoked by the subject's recognition that he or she lacks a competence necessary to participate in the changing institutional situation. However, this crisis will only be mastered, and a learning process begun, if the subject experiences the possibility of some kind of continuity with which to master the existential discontinuity. Where the subject does not see this possibility, avoidance or withdrawal will occur rather than learning. Miedema and Stam (2008), for instance, have successfully used this model in conjunction with Engeström's theory. There are also examples in Jóhannsdóttir's chapter.

When used to analyse change processes in schools, Engeström's models are not sufficient in yet another respect. They have not been especially developed for the analysis of education, and as a consequence lack an explicit connection to theories about the nature and the aims of education. They do allow for tensions and contradictions in the object of the (school) system under study, and so can (as Liu and Fisher show) demonstrate that different and even opposing ideas about 'good' education are present, but they do not offer principles to think about the nature of 'good' education or to make a choice for one or another aim of education. In other words, users of the model do not automatically understand the specificity of educational situations. This carries the danger that attention in Developmental Work Research, the 'double stimulation' component of the model, will be focused solely on a smooth running of the system. However, I think that CHAT is not an entirely instrumental and value-neutral theory when used in education. Implied in CHAT is, if not a specific aim for education, then at least a preference for certain aims, just as these are in a way (as I will show below, pp. 243–245) implied in the other paradigms I mentioned. And thus, the researcher comes with a more or less specific educational intention. Researchers in education are never neutral as to the aims of education, or to speak in the Marxist terms Jóhannsdóttir employs, they have specific ideas about what constitutes the 'use value' (as against the 'exchange value') of education. And thus, certainly when they apply methods such as DWR or other versions of the double stimulation method, they have a substantive and ethical responsibility (Edwards 2002; Hostetler 2005).

For the nomothetic paradigm, this implied preference for a certain type of aim in education can be seen, for instance, in the present emphasis on 'evidence-based education'. Its proponents speak of what teachers do in terms of 'interventions' that should have a known, assured and effective outcome. In other words, they rely on the certainty that well-researched knowledge is supposed to afford, and thus prefer to think of knowledge as a 'mirror of reality'. A teacher equipped with such knowledge and the skills to apply it will with a high degree of certainty realise the aims of education. But what aims? These are not talked about much in the discourse on evidence-based education, as they are supposed to be in the political realm. But in fact, there is a hidden aim in this way of thinking: that students to be equipped with well-researched knowledge and skills (only, in this case, not researched by educational science but by all disciplines) so that in the future they will be able to solve most problems with a high probability of success. The implied aim is to provide students with certainties for their future acting, because the knowledge they acquire is (at least partially) of general and hopefully timeless laws. Or more generally still:

students are taught an instrumental and technical worldview. This aim still holds in societal conditions that change quickly; that just means that students (and teachers) need to become life-long learners of the 'new' knowledge turned out by researchers. And it also holds when students are not seen as passive recipients of knowledge but as active acquirers, even when their activity takes the form of inquiry, because (certainly in a Piagetian view) their activity is just a condition for learning the 'right' knowledge. The validity of this view of the relationship between knowledge and action is exactly what is doubted in the Introduction to this volume.

In the interpretative paradigm, on the other hand, both teachers and their students live in a world in which all interactions between humans are more or less unpredictable. This view leads to resistance against the aims of education as envisaged by the dominant nomothetic way of thinking. For, because engaging in an interaction implies engaging in uncertainty, an important aim of education is to learn to handle uncertainty in a positive and creative way. Existing knowledge may help, but can never be more than a heuristic to be used with insight and caution. This view is not far away from a relativistic model of knowledge. It leads to a pedagogy, both in teacher education and in general education, where students are taught to trust their own 'inner resources' and find strength in their own persons – what Edwards calls 'reflection on practices for self-improvement'. Progressive pedagogy, in most of its many forms, emphasizes the development of all faculties and possibilities that a given student potentially has, finding certainties in themselves.

A Vygotskian view, in my interpretation at least, acknowledges that we live in a world of uncertainties. No action is totally determined (although we are still subject to things that happen to us where we have no action alternatives), but no action is totally free and unpredictable either. The Deweyan term 'transaction' expresses this: in acting, we change the conditions for our future actions because every act has an impact on our situation (cf. Edwards' chapter). And in this acting, knowledge is produced. Thus, CHAT proposes 'a view of knowledge as something that is accessed and developed in joint work on a potentially shared object of activity' (Ellis). There is an implied aim of education here too. If our actions, as Edwards points out, do change the social situation of the development of present and future human beings including ourselves (in both intended and unintended ways), both teachers and students need to learn not only to monitor the effects of their actions, but also to 'interrogate the "whys" and "where-tos"' (Edwards). They need to become inquisitive learners and teachers, not primarily in terms of scientific methods, but with a view to the improvement of (their participation in) complex societal practices. In a sociocultural view, researchers, teachers and students cannot limit their inquisitiveness to questions of 'how' to act (in an effective way); they need to engage with the aims of their actions and those of the cultural practices within which they act. In other words, education is always education for a citizenship that is engaged as well as critical.

One implication is that teachers need an insight into their own societal position and situation. Thus Kincheloe, for instance, proposes:

> Indeed, educational reform cannot be conceptualized outside of a deep appreciation of the social, cultural, political, economic forces that shape contemporary Western societies and their educational institutions. Critical teacher researchers, therefore, develop a detailed understanding of these social dynamics and their relationship to the role and purposes of schooling. Comprehending these complex relationships, they are better equipped to understand what operating on the grounding of a critical system of meaning might look like in present conditions. In this context their research abilities enable them not simply to be better teachers but to conceptualize the socio-political landscape in relationship to what it means to be an educated person in the first decade of the twenty-first century.
>
> (2003: 205)

Inasmuch as Kincheloe means to say that teachers ought to be intellectuals with an understanding of their own position in a greater whole, I agree – and this could be a real challenge for teacher education. In a Vygotskian view, however, not every single teacher need have all the understandings Kincheloe mentions at their disposal. Instead, they should be able and willing to interact with other people, including educational researchers. Skills in interprofessional co-operation seem indicated more than doing everything alone, which also means entering into 'the interplay between individual sense and public meaning' (Edwards). But more than anything else, a Vygotskian view implies that education, whether of teachers or of children, is in essence identity formation (Norton-Meier and Drake) with a view to functioning as competent and critical participants in society and in a profession.

In educational interactions, students and teachers together construct 'zones of proximal development', and in this process, both parties have a specific input. Seen from this point of view, neither of the 'cultures of learning' Liu and Fisher describe can be considered very Vygotskian: the traditional culture because it leaves little room for student initiative; the 'liberal' because it denies the intellectual role of the teacher.

Of course, teachers need specific skills and knowledge next to being intellectuals. And in several chapters in this volume, attention is on how teacher students acquire these, guided by additional theories based on CHAT. Sannino looks at how they 'ascend' from book knowledge of students to personal knowledge of individuals, an interpretation that rests on another dialectical tension Vygotsky and Leont'ev identified: that between 'scientific' and 'everyday' concepts, a tension that ideally leads to the formation of 'real' concepts. McNicholl and Childs look at how students learn pedagogical content/content knowledge, which may be another instance of the same tension. In both cases, specific theories are used on what teachers need to do their job; in both cases, the choice of these theories is related only implicitly to the aims of education. Others, such as Smagorinsky, Douglas, and Jahreie and Ottesen, inquire into aspects of the 'social situation of development' of teachers – another theoretical idea derived from Vygotsky. When Boag-Munroe compares two methods of Discourse Analysis, she does so on the basis of theoretical considerations about the contextual nature of transactions. The same is true of Jahreie and Ottesen, who introduce the concept of script in the CHAT context. And, of course, all approaches that use a form of double stimulation are based on Vygotskian theory. From nearly all chapters it is clear, then, that there is a strong interplay between theories and methods. Theories are not just the object of research; methods are also theory-laden. That is not by any means a new idea, but it becomes very explicit in CHAT studies.

Analysing the three parts of this book in more detail, it becomes clear that, in the first part, where the emphasis is on analysis rather than on construction, still ideas play an important role about what constitutes 'good' or 'less good' social situations of development for student teachers and, indeed, what is a good or a less good teacher. Smagorinsky presents a Vygotskian perspective on the development of one student, but between the lines one gets the impression that he is not quite happy with the direction her learning process has taken. Douglas, while focusing on the different learning opportunities afforded by two learning situations, ultimately wants teachers 'to be able to respond to changing situations'. To that end, situations of development are necessary where student teachers can 'work in a responsive way by questioning how their relationships are managed'. McNicholl and Childs analyse the social conditions of learning pedagogical content knowledge, and conclude (among other things) that teachers need to learn to communicate and co-operate with colleagues, and that they need to pay attention to 'pupils as learners and their needs and understandings'. Hjörne, Larsson and Säljö explicitly advocate a broader view of children. But only Edwards tries to find an explicit and systematic answer to the central question, 'What kind of teachers for what kind of learners?', a question that is then followed by, 'And what kind of teacher education for such teachers?' These are, as Edwards remarks, questions that do not have any clear answers, but they need to be asked if we want to develop teacher education into a social situation of development that is conducive for the formation of the kind of teachers we prefer.

The chapters in Part III do not give that kind of answer either. Their value lies more in the analysis of learning processes occurring in situations of change. Max focuses on a new course in inquiry-based collaborative learning, but he does not so much discuss the content or outcomes of this course as the processes in the 'boundary zone' or 'third space' between university and internship school. Whereas he and Jóhannsdóttir use the Engeström model, Norton-Meier and Drake use the theory of identity formation based on the work of Holland. In all three chapters, an important message is that student learning can only be understood if considered in the social and institutional context. And perhaps that is actually the central message of the whole book. It is the expression of yet another tension Vygotsky based his work on: between the individual and the social, leading to an interpretation of development as (among other things) a process of individuation (rather than the socialization of a pre-existing individual).

Part II of the volume pays attention to various methods that can be used to analyse the interaction between learner and context. Interestingly, in all of them the notion of tensions is present, either implicitly or explicitly. Taking into account Ilyenkov's argument that 'a qualitatively better form of an activity always begins as an exception from the rule' (as quoted by Jóhannsdóttir), Jahreie and Ottesen's arsenal of concepts like trajectory, positioning and script may be interpreted as means to analyse the productivity of tensions for learning. Boag-Munroe shows how attention to the wider context of activity can show up tensions that would go unnoticed otherwise. And of course, the interventions that Sannino and Ellis describe are examples of the way tensions can be introduced to produce learning.

In conclusion, then, I am confident that this book does show that 'a cultural-historical perspective on teacher education and development offers a powerful theoretical and methodological lens through which ... to analyse the problem of teacher education' as the Introduction suggests. That is true not in spite of, but rather thanks to, the diversity of methods and viewpoints presented here. However, 'to design new curricula and programmes' the ideas about 'good education' present here need to be developed further. Here I agree with Biesta (2009) that 'learning' is a normative concept that can only be used meaningfully in relation to an idea of the educated person – be it a teacher student or one of their (future) students. As is also clear from the Introduction, this may mean that we will have to rethink both the content and the methods of teacher education. It is evident that we would not always make the same choices as the policy-makers. Education, including teacher education, is always also an enterprise of cultural politics.

References

Biesta, G. (2009) 'Good education: what it is and why we need it', inaugural lecture, Stirling University. Online, available at: www.ioe.stir.ac.uk/documents/ (accessed 7 June 2009).

Edwards, A. (2002) 'Responsible research: ways of being a researcher', *British Educational Research Journal* 28: 157–168.

Engeström, Y. (2008) 'From design experiments to formative interventions.' Paper presented at ICL3, Utrecht, 23–28 June.

Hostetler, K. (2005) 'What is "good" education research?', *Educational Researcher* 34, 6: 16–21.

Kincheloe, J. (2003) *Teachers as researchers: qualitative inquiry as a path to empowerment*, 2nd edn, London: Routledge Falmer.

Meijers, F. and Wardekker, W. (2003) 'Career learning in a changing world: the role of emotions', *International Journal for the Advancement of Counselling* 24, 3: 149–167.

Miedema, W. and Stam, M. (2008) *Leren van innoveren* [*Learning from innovating*], Assen: Van Gorcum.

Index